THE STRUGGLE FOR RUSSIA

THE STRUGGLE
FOR RUSSIA

Power and change in the democratic
revolution

Ruslan Khasbulatov

Edited by Richard Sakwa

London and New York

First published 1993
by Routledge
11 New Fetter Lane, London EC4P 4EE

Simultaneously published in the USA and Canada
by Routledge
29 West 35th Street, New York, NY 10001

Introduction and editorial matter © 1993 R. Sakwa
Text © 1993 R.I. Khasbulatov
Translation © 1993 Routledge Ltd

Typeset in Palatino by LaserScript, Mitcham, Surrey

Printed and bound in Great Britain by
T.J. Press (Padstow) Ltd, Padstow, Cornwall

British Library Cataloguing in Publication Data
A catalogue record for this book is available from the British Library

ISBN 0–415–09292–2

Library of Congress Cataloging in Publication Data

Khasbulatov, R. I. (Ruslan Imranovich)
The struggle for Russia : power and change in the democratic revolution /
Ruslan Khasbulatov; edited by Richard Sakwa.
p. cm.
Translated from Russian.
ISBN 0-415-09292-2
1. Soviet Union–History–Attempted coup, 1991–Personal narratives. 2.
Khasbulatov, R.I. (Ruslan Imranovich) 3. Russia (Federation)–Politics and
government–1991- 4. Soviet Union–Politics and government–1985–1991. I.
Sakwa, Richard.
II. Title.
DK292.K47 1993
947.085′4–dc20   93-9490
CIP

CONTENTS

AUTHOR'S PREFACE

Dear friends

I am very happy that readers from abroad will be able to get to know my book. The work covers many different aspects of our life, and indeed has been in the process of writing since late 1990. The events which have taken place in this country have forced me time and again to return to my pen. In compensation, you can more clearly understand what took place in the Union, and then in Russia, over this period.

The Seventh Congress of People's Deputies is over and a new Prime Minister has been chosen. I hope that the course of reform will change fundamentally, and that the economy will turn its face to the people. I am convinced that this will take place, otherwise it would have been pointless to have exerted so much effort.

I am sure that in the not very distant future Russia will take its rightful place in the international community.

Ruslan Khasbulatov

Moscow, 15 December 1992

INTRODUCTION

Ruslan Imranovich Khasbulatov was born on 22 November 1942 in Grozny, the capital of what was then the Chechen–Ingush Autonomous Soviet Socialist Republic in the RSFSR (Russian Soviet Federated Socialist Republic). On 23 February 1944, Red Army Day, he was deported with his mother and thousands of others to Kazakhstan. The Chechens, together with other peoples of the Caucasus, were accused by Stalin of having collaborated with the Germans during their occupation of the region. From 1960 he studied law at the Kazakh State University in the republic's capital, Alma Ata, before transferring to the Law Faculty of Moscow State University in 1962 and completing his degree in 1965. For his postgraduate studies between 1965–70 Khasbulatov turned to economics. Between 1965 and 1967 he was the Secretary of the Komsomol (All-Union Leninist Communist League of Youth) organisation at the university, joining the Communist Party in 1966. He completed his postgraduate work in the Economics Faculty, defending his Candidate's Dissertation (MA) in 1970 and becoming a Doctor of Economic Sciences in 1980, specialising in economic law.

Between 1970 and 1972 he was first an instructor, then responsible organiser, in the Propaganda and Agitation Department of the Central Committee of the All-Union Komsomol. His career then concentrated on academic life, working between 1972 and 1974 as acting head of the Sector for Coordination of Research on Questions of the Scientific–Technical Revolution at the Institute of Scientific Information and Fundamental Library of the USSR Academy of Sciences. Between 1974 and 1979 he was head of the Sector of Scientific Development of Normative Materials of the Department of Higher Economic Studies, Scientific Research Institute for Questions of High Schools. Between 1979 and 1990 he taught economics at the G. V. Plekhanov Institute of the Economy in Moscow, rising to become a full professor and Chair of Economy of Foreign Countries. He published some ten books and numerous articles on the theory of international economic relations, the economies and societies of capitalist countries, as well as studies of socialist and developing economies.

Once again Khasbulatov's life turned to politics, and he was elected a People's Deputy of the RSFSR in Russia's first semi-democratic elections in March 1990, representing a constituency in his native Chechen Republic. He rose quickly in parliamentary life, and in May 1990, when Boris Yeltsin was elected Chair of the Russian Supreme Soviet, Khasbulatov became First Deputy Chair, in which capacity he presided over some of the most turbulent debates in the Russian Congress of People's Deputies as the democrats and conservatives fought over the fate of Russia and the Soviet Union.

To overcome the perceived crisis of power in Russia, the powers of the presidency were strengthened and Yeltsin became the first democratically elected President of the Russian Federation in June 1991. A contest broke out for the now vacant post of Chair of the Russian Supreme Soviet, a post that conventionally became known as Speaker of the Russian parliament. After several votes at the Fifth Russian Congress in July 1991 no clear-cut winner emerged and Khasbulatov continued in his post as Acting Speaker, and it was in this capacity that he was one of the main organisers of the defence of the Russian White House in Krasnaya Prenya, the seat of the Russian parliament during the coup.

Khasbulatov was confirmed as Speaker of the Russian Supreme Soviet by an overwhelming vote on 28 October 1991 at the resumed Fifth Russian Congress of Deputies. In November President Yeltsin was granted special powers to convert the country to a market system, and in that month he nominated a 'government of reforms' in which, though formally led by Yeltsin himself, Yegor Gaidar played the leading part as Deputy Prime Minister responsible for economic reform, and from June to December 1992 as Acting Prime Minister. On 2 January 1992 the government launched its own version of 'shock therapy' economic reforms, marked by rapid price rises, a squeeze on credit and subsidies in order to reduce the budget deficit and to stabilise the rouble, and the limitation of state support for industry. Khasbulatov vigorously condemned this approach and called for the government's resignation, setting the scene for a period of intense conflict. The Russian Congress refused to confirm Gaidar as Prime Minister and, following a crisis of the whole constitutional order in Russia during the Seventh Congress of People's Deputies (1–14 December 1992), when executive and legislative authority came into direct collision, Khasbulatov's skilful handling of the situation led to the emergence of a new Prime Minister, Viktor Chernomyrdin, a man more sympathetic to the plight of state industry and more in tune with Khasbulatov's own views.

With a consistency that can be traced in this book, Khasbulatov remained one of the keenest critics of neo-liberal economic reform and insisted on the need for greater social protection of the population at a time of economic crisis. He sought to ensure a degree of parliamentary control over the government, and warned against the expansion of presidential power at the expense of the rights of the legislature. The struggle between the executive and legislative branches of Russian government was more than a struggle between personalities; it reflected a profound debate over the nature of power in post-communist Russia.

This, then, is the background to the materials presented in this book. The first part consists of a series of interviews conducted before the coup and the second consists of Khasbulatov's account of the attempted coup of August 1991 and his role in it. The third part is made up of Khasbulatov's thinking on the state system of Russia in its first year as an independent post-communist state in which he provides a vigorous defence of the rights of parliament and advocates the separation of powers and the development of Russia as a genuinely federal state.

ON THE EVE

The majority of the interviews took place in late 1990 and into early 1991 and were published in full in Russian in late 1991.[1] This English version has abbreviated the text, and for convenience the material has been grouped thematically, but broadly following the sequence in which they were given. They provide a unique historical insight from the perspective of one of the leading participants in the struggle for Russian statehood.

On 12 June 1990 the First Congress of People's Deputies adopted a Declaration on Russian Sovereignty, a turning point in Russia's history and the signal that Russia henceforth would try to develop its own policies within the framework of a renewed Union of Soviet Republics. The struggles that ensued are vividly described by Khasbulatov in the first part of this book, focusing on the failures of the Soviet governments led by Nikolai Ryzhkov, and then, from December 1990, by Valentin Pavlov.

Khasbulatov discusses the reasons for the failure of the Soviet economic system, the stifling dominance of the bureaucracy and the absence of genuine economic dynamism, and places his analysis in a larger theoretical context: the inapplicability of Marxist approaches in the twentieth century, the absence of private property, the stifling role of the bureaucracy, and the failure of total planning. Khasbulatov's urgent calls for economic reform and a thorough change in the nature of property and the system of management ring clearly from his responses. His study of the Canadian economy demonstrates that some of the new generation of Russian leaders know the world outside the Soviet Union, though Khasbulatov is careful not to idealise the existing market systems of the West.

Khasbulatov describes the struggle with the centre and reveals the unstable role of Gorbachev in the death throes of the old system.

Gorbachev went back on his earlier commitment to support a radical reform drafted by Stanislav Shatalin and Grigori Yavlinsky, the so-called '500 days' programme, presented in September 1990. Khasbulatov is scathing of the role played by Leonid Abalkin, appointed minister responsible for overseeing economic reform by Gorbachev. The rejection of the plan led to a deepening crisis and the so-called 'winter offensive' by conservative forces from late 1990 into early 1991, marked by Eduard Shevardnadze's resignation as Foreign Minister on 20 December warning of a coup, and the use of military force against the Baltic republics in January 1991 in which fifteen people were killed in Vilnius. Pavlov was appointed Soviet Prime Minister in December 1990, to replace the lacklustre Ryzhkov, but his flamboyant campaigns against alleged currency speculators and his amateurish attempt at price reform only exacerbated the Soviet economic crisis, further alienated the republics, and drew Khasbulatov's justified scorn. Pavlov went on to join the coup plotters in August 1991.

Disillusionment with Gorbachev's leadership prompted Yeltsin to call for his resignation on 19 February, and was accompanied by a wave of labour unrest culminating in miners' strikes in March–April 1991. On 28 March 1991, the opening day of Russia's Third (Emergency) Congress of People's Deputies convened by the conservatives to oust Yeltsin, Gorbachev sent in troops to surround the Kremlin and to intimidate the democratic forces in parliament. However, the popular response was swift and resolute, and in a foretaste of the resistance against the coup, 200,000 people demonstrated in Moscow despite the display of military hardware. The Congress not only endorsed the policies of the Russian leadership, but gave Yeltsin extra powers and prepared the way for Russian presidential elections.

Gorbachev, realising that his alliance with the conservatives was undermining his own position and alienating world public opinion from the Soviet Union as a whole, effected yet another of his sudden shifts, and at his dacha at Novo-Ogarevo on 23 April he signed an agreement on economic and political reforms, the so-called 'nine-plus-one' statement, between himself and the leaders of nine republics, Russia included, committing them to a range of stabilising measures, but above all to the attempt to find a formula for a new Union Treaty for the USSR that would balance the interests of the republics and the centre.

The interviews in the first part of the book cover this tumultuous period. Khasbulatov is careful to explain that Russia had no intention of undermining the Union, but instead sought to place it on a new and genuinely federal footing. He insisted that the break-up of the Soviet Union would be a disaster for Russia and the other republics, tied by innumerable economic and human links. Yet the powers of what he calls the 'centre' had to be undermined so that the central bureaucracy, which acted as a sort of unconstitutional 'sixteenth republic', would lose its grip and devolve powers to the fifteen actual republics making up the Soviet Union. Khasbulatov's draft Union Constitution (see Appendix) provided a model for a devolved confederal system but one which allowed the Union authorities sufficient powers to lead a single state.

The Russian Republic faced its own problems in creating a genuinely federal system, described by Khasbulatov in the text. He played a leading part in devising the Russian Federal Treaty, signed in Moscow on 31 March 1992, which sought to make Russia a genuinely federal system for the first time, a federalism that applied not only to the national republics of Russia but to the whole country as well, including its regions.

A portrait of the destructive genius of Gorbachev presides over the first part, constantly undermining the very forces that might have helped him secure his own objectives of a modernised economy in a renewed Union within the international economic and political system. Thus the text provides a commentary on the decay of Soviet governance. This was a period of great difficulties, yet one of great optimism that a new and more rational economic system could be devised and that equal relations between all the existing republics in the Union could be established. The interviews provide a vivid portrait of the last days of the Soviet regime, and demonstrate that the results were very different from these intended by either Gorbachev or the democrats.

The crisis that threatened to engulf the government and economy of Russia, exacerbated by conflicts with the Union centre and Gorbachev personally, stimulated the creation of a strong executive in the form of presidential power. On 12 June 1991 Yeltsin became Russia's first democratically elected President with 57 per cent of the vote, and it was with the confidence that the popular mandate gave him that Yeltsin faced the coup.

THE COUP

It was in his capacity as Acting Speaker, representing legislative power, that Khasbulatov confronted the attempted coup of August 1991. Together with Yeltsin and Ivan Silaev, the Russian Prime Minister, on the morning of 19 August Khasbulatov drafted the 'Appeal to the Citizens of Russia', which declared the actions of the State Committee for the State of Emergency (SCSE) illegal and unconstitutional, and thus provided a clear rebuff to the attempts by communists and hardliners to reverse the course of history. The defence of the White House, the seat of the Russian parliament and government at the time, has now entered history as a critical moment in the rebirth of the Russian people as independent creators of their destiny.

The accumulating tensions depicted in the interviews now came to a head, and the coup was a last desperate attempt by parts of the centre to maintain the Union and with it their own power and privileges. A draft Union Treaty had been worked out in consultation with the leaders of the union republics following the 'nine-plus-one' agreement of April 1991, and the plan for a signing ceremony on 20 August with Gorbachev and some of the leaders of the republics set the timetable for the coup.

The materials presented here include the most important documents adopted by the Russian leadership during the coup, as well as the minutes of the meeting of the USSR Cabinet of Ministers on 19 August and an interview with Pavel Grachev, commander of the Soviet air force during the coup and later appointed Russia's Minister of Defence. Above all, an account of Gorbachev's gruelling encounter with the members of Russia's Supreme Soviet on 22 August is here provided in full, the meeting at which with a stroke of the pen Yeltsin suspended the Communist Party of Russia, and thus put an end to seventy-four years of party rule.

POWER

The coup was followed by the disintegration of the Soviet Union and the emergence of Russia as a separate state. The end of the communist system placed responsibility for the nation's destiny in the hands of a new generation of leaders, of whom Khasbulatov was one of the most prominent. His analysis of the problem of power and post-communist governance is provided in the third part of this book. Written in late July and early August 1992, the book was published in Russian in September 1992.[2]

The tensions between the two main branches of power, the legislative and executive, are vividly revealed in Khasbulatov's discussion of 'Power'. The earlier alliance with Yeltsin gave way to conflict as Khasbulatov vigorously defended the rights of the legislature against what he perceived as the encroachments of presidential power. The Russian constitutional system was being remade and, though heavily amended, the old 'Brezhnev' Constitution of 1978 remained in force up to 1993. The central question was whether Russia would be a presidential or a parliamentary republic, or some kind of combination of the two. With a protean Constitution, the separation of powers and the relationship between the executive and legislative branches of government developed through conflict rather than through regulation and law. Only in December 1992 did the two sides agree to maintain the status quo until the referendum on the adoption of the new Constitution in 1993.

The text provides an extended discussion of federalism in the Russian context. To many observers it appeared that the disintegratory tendencies that had destroyed the USSR would continue and lead to the break-up of the Russian Federation itself. Khasbulatov firmly opposed secessionist tendencies in Russia, and he played an important part in the achievement of the Federal Treaty of 31 March 1992, although only eighteen out of the twenty national republics of Russia signed, with Tatarstan and Khasbulatov's native Chechen Republic standing aside. The Treaty attempted to provide Russia with a genuinely federal system in which all of Russia's eighty-eight administrative divisions, and not just the nationality areas, were granted certain rights and specified competencies. Khasbulatov was writing at a time when the full implications of the Treaty had not yet been worked out, and there remained a fundamental instability as long as Russia failed to adopt a new Constitution.

KHASBULATOV AND RUSSIAN POLITICS

Russia's national and state renaissance is one of the most important events of the late twentieth century, and Khasbulatov's works are an important contribution to our understanding of this process. Following the coup Russia entered an almost interminable crisis of power. For several months government was marked by drift and lack of resolution, and Khasbulatov insists that preparations for the renewed Fifth Congress in late October 1991 galvanised the executive authorities into action. Despite criticisms of Yeltsin's managerial style and his choice of advisers, in particular Gennadi Burbulis, the Congress assigned yet more powers to the presidency. The sense of betrayal and lack of responsibility on the part of the presidency peaked when Yeltsin arbitrarily agreed with the leaders of Ukraine and Belorus to the dissolution of the Soviet Union on 8 December 1991 without having sought the views of parliament on such an epochal step.

The Russian parliament under Khasbulatov sought to act as a balance to the arbitrariness of presidential rule, and at times appeared to set itself up as a rival to the presidential system. Parliament and Congress indeed emerged as the major opposition to Yeltsin and the neo-liberal policies pursued by his chief minister, Gaidar. Parliament appeared to act as a brake on the reforms, passing illiberal legislation on such issues as exchange controls and land reform. All this forced Yeltsin to resort even more to devices that could circumvent resistance, such as rule by decree. Khasbulatov was severely critical of the President's wide powers and the independence of the presidency from parliament, and, through the ability of parliament to veto government appointments and policies, sought to subordinate the government to parliament.

While parliament was often critical of Yeltsin's tendency to authoritarian rule, defended by liberal reformers as the only way to drive the reforms forward, parliament itself was often criticised as undemocratic. The majority of the deputies elected to the Russian Congress in March 1990 were from the old communist *nomenklatura* appointments system. Some 80 per cent of the deputies from the 1,068 constituencies (though only 1,061 were elected) were communists, and the overwhelming majority occupied managerial posts of one sort or another. The unity that the Congress exhibited in the struggle against the old regime, when democrats and officialdom voted together to uphold Russia's state sovereignty and economic reforms, disintegrated once the communist system collapsed, and the weight of the conservative majority now made itself felt. A 268-strong Supreme Soviet or parliament (with 401 deputies working on a permanent basis) was elected by the Congress, and this two-tier system impeded the development of genuine parliamentary procedures. The full Congress met on average twice a year and took the crucial decisions on constitutional and economic policy, while the Supreme Soviet handled current aspects of legislative and political activity.

The absence of a party system and the atomisation of Congress into numerous shifting fractions enhanced the role of the Speaker. Khasbulatov was called upon to play a dual role: as the representative of parliament in the wider political system; and as the leader of parliament in legislative affairs. The checks and balances that Khasbulatov called for in national politics were often notably absent in the running of parliament itself. The embryonic nature of Russian parliamentarianism, the weakness of organised opposition parties, and the plentiful scope for the development of patronage relations, all promoted the emergence of a type of politics in which conflicts took the form of a struggle between the institutions of the post-communist polity rather than within parliament itself.

Parliament under Khasbulatov emerged as an institutional actor fighting against overweening presidential power. Thus the pattern of post-communist Russian politics took on some of the characteristics of early modern European history, when parliaments challenged the prerogatives of the Crown. The protean nature of Russian politics, with a multitude of weak parties and shapeless social forces, exaggerated the role of individuals and emphasised the struggle of institutions to find a place in the post-communist sun. The ability of Congress when in session to alter the Constitution almost at will gave the exponents of parliamentary rule enormous power, and Yeltsin's claim that they had abused this power to stall the reforms and to undermine Gaidar's government led to the constitutional crisis of December 1992. Until a new Constitution is adopted the fundamental question of power in Russia remains open. Despite the ambivalent character of a Congress and parliament elected when the communist regime was still firm, the defence of parliamentary privileges and the rights of the legislature mark an important stage in the maturation of Russian democracy.

Khasbulatov emerged as one of the leading figures in post-coup Russia, and one of the most controversial. His attempts in 1992 to bring the printing works of the *Izvestiya* newspaper concern under the control of the Russian Supreme Soviet aroused bitter criticism. The democracy that Khasbulatov defended in society at large appeared lacking in the operation of parliament itself.[3] Power was increasingly concentrated in the hands of Khasbulatov's supporters leading the two chambers of the Supreme Soviet, and the position of Sergei Filatov, the independent-minded First Vice Chair of the Supreme Soviet, became increasingly untenable.[4] Khasbulatov set great store on the principle of personal loyalty, and increasingly felt that he had been betrayed by Filatov.[5] Within parliament Khasbulatov's apparent abrasiveness led the leader of the parliamentary group 'Reform', Leonid Volkov, to claim on 2 September 1992 that Khasbulatov regularly exceeded his authority, and other deputies accused Khasbulatov of authoritarian methods of rule and of issuing regulations that violated existing Russian legislation.[6] Leaders of the reform coalition in parliament called for Khasbulatov's resignation, arguing that the Supreme Soviet had a tendency to usurp the functions of the government. They noted that the man Khasbulatov appointed to head his forecasting and analytical group, Vladislav Achalov, was none other than a former general who, as Deputy Minister of Defence, was deeply implicated in the coup of August 1991.[7] The movement among deputies to remove Khasbulatov from his post was, however, brought short by the growing confrontation with the executive authorities. Following Yeltsin's accusations on 10 December 1992 at the Seventh Congress that 'What they [the conservative forces] failed to achieve in August 1991, they decided to repeat now and carry out a creeping coup', and that 'The Constitution, or what is left of it, is turning the Supreme Soviet, its leadership and its Chairman, into the all-powerful rulers of Russia', Khasbulatov tendered his resignation, considering that both his own and the Congress's dignity had been insulted, but was reinstated by an overwhelming vote.[8]

Khasbulatov's relationship with Yeltsin is more ambiguous than might at first appear. The former consistently sought to find compromises, and to find a common way through the troubles besetting the country. His at times excessively florid condemnation of Gaidar and the 'government of reforms' created in November 1991 obscures his moderating role in parliament. At times of crisis, as in August 1992 when the conservatives appeared poised to attack, Khasbulatov and Yeltsin met to discuss common approaches, and indeed the two men met or spoke on an almost daily basis. In the tense period leading up to and during the Seventh Congress of People's Deputies, Khasbulatov again played a central role in trying to find a path of compromise that would both moderate some of the vitriolic criticisms directed against the President's policies from the floor of the Congress and temper some of the extremism of Gaidar's policies, while at the same time neither undermining the presidency nor what he considered a more humane path to the market. Khasbulatov interpreted President Yeltsin's emotional outburst at the Congress as a betrayal of the assistance that Khasbulatov had rendered him in many difficult political moments since the two had been elected to the top posts in the Russian parliament in May 1990. Khasbulatov emerged as the clear victor at the

Congress, with increased power over ministerial appointments, the dismissal of the detested Burbulis and some other of Yeltsin's acolytes, but above all with a new Prime Minister more accountable to parliament and espousing the type of economic policies that Khasbulatov has long advocated. How he and parliament will use their new powers remains for history to judge.

Richard Sakwa
Canterbury, 21 December 1992

NOTE ON TEXT AND TRANSLATION

Dates, places and brief explanations have been added, with the author's permission, into the text to avoid intrusive notes. Care has been taken to ensure that most events are explained by the text itself, and the role of most people is similarly explained.

The first part was largely translated in Moscow, while Parts II and III were translated by Peter Meades and his associates at the University of Kent at Canterbury.

The work of Oleg Alexandrov in Moscow on preparing the Russian version of the text is gratefully acknowledged. It is due to the splendid work of Elizabeth Dorling and her associates in the secretarial office of Keynes College, the University of Kent, that the text was able to be prepared so quickly; many thanks to them all. Above all, the support and confidence in this project by the politics editor at Routledge, Gordon Smith, made possible the fruition of this work. Without his constant support, this unique insight into the death of the old regime in the USSR and the birth of the new system in Russia would not be available to the English-speaking reader.

NOTES

1 Ruslan Khasbulatov, *Rossiya: pora peremen (besedy na Krasnoi Presne)* (Moscow, Megapolis-Takom/Russkaya Entsiklopediya, 1991). The interviews were conducted by Oleg Alexandrov and Sergei Semenov.
2 R. I. Khasbulatov, *Vlast' (rasmyshleniya spikera)* (Moscow, Tsentr delovoi informatsii Ezhenedel'nik 'Ekonomika i zhizn', Russkaya Entsiklopediya, 1992).
3 Otto Latsis, 'Power is a Secret', *Izvestiya*, 28 August 1992, p. 3.
4 Maria Bogatykh, 'Kak toskuyut ruki po shturvalu' ('How hands long for the helm'), *Rossiya*, no. 36 (94), 2–8 September 1992, p. 1.
5 Interview with Sergei Yushenkov, coordinator of the Radical Democrats fraction of deputies, *Rossiiskie vesti*, 10 September 1992, p. 2.
6 *RFE/RL Research Report*, vol. 1, no. 37 (1992), p. 76.
7 Georgi Ivanov-Smolenskii, *Izvestiya*, 3 September 1992, p. 2.
8 *Rossiiskaya gazeta*, 11 December 1992.

Part I

ON THE EVE

1

PERSONAL

Can you tell us something about your childhood?

I spent my childhood years in a small village, Poludin, in the north of Kazakhstan where we, the Chechens and Ingushes, were exiled in February 1944 on Red Army Day. Our family, my mother, two older brothers and sister, were deported with our relations and neighbours, and settled next to about three dozen families of Volga Germans, Koreans and Tartars. The village became a real multiethnic community. Russians, however, predominated, and many were descendants of the nineteenth-century political exiles, the 'People's Will' revolutionaries, Social Democrats, Plekhanovists and Anarchists.

Our exile lasted for about ten years. I cannot recall a single incident of ethnic conflict or ill-feeling throughout the period despite the fact that all of us were deported peoples. We were all in the same boat, living in equal poverty, with shortages of everything, particularly bread, because 'work-day' credits could not usually be exchanged for supplies.

Like other young boys, I did all I could to help mother and my family in their everyday chores. Mother worked as a milkmaid on the local collective farm. I can remember drawing buckets of water from a deep well, watering the cows, cleaning the cowsheds, looking after the calves, digging potatoes, and gathering loads of firewood, often in 40 degrees of frost. I worked just the way the rest of the villagers did.

The local bosses consisted of a couple of field-gang leaders and the collective farm chairman. They were stern but fair people, and in times of extreme hardship they would work next to the collective farm workers. They treated mother fairly, praising her as the best milkmaid in the village.

Other women, Russian, Kazakh, German, Korean, worked their fingers to the bone, toiling side by side with my mother. My first school teacher, Vera Vladimirovna, would often make the 5-kilometre walk to see our family at home. What made her devote her time to a kid from a family of 'criminals'? She could easily have had me expelled from the school. Today I understand: she taught me not only the 'three Rs', but she also tried to introduce me to human values which know neither ethnic boundaries nor government decrees. It was the 'equality of the poor', but it was in no way morally poor.

I stayed in the village attending to my peasant chores until I was 13. By that time that I had developed within myself strength of body and mind, though it was a tough place to live.

Following Stalin's death we moved to live closer to our relations, who lived not far from Alma Ata. I had to quit school after the eighth grade to look for a job, and I became in turn a building worker, a concrete layer and a freight handler. In my career, work came first, academic studies second.

How long have you been living in Moscow?

It has been almost thirty years, time goes so fast. I have long felt myself at home in Moscow, and I have taken the city's problems to heart. I have not, however, lost my former ties with my homeland, the Caucasus, the Chechen–Ingush Republic, the city of Grozny.

What about Kazakhstan?

I have visited Alma Ata only a few times since, but I cherish my memories of the city. I love Kazakhstan, and I love the Kazakh people living in that huge country.

Where did you get your higher education?

At Moscow University. I studied willingly, but I never strained myself. I studied law, but when I was halfway through my university course I began to question the nature of our state system, the character of our democracy, our so-called public (or rather government) ownership in which nothing belonged to any particular individual. I then began intensive extra-curricular studies during which I combed through virtually all the Russian translations of the works of Marx, Engels and Lenin. I then tried to look into the sources of Marxism by reading every book on the subject that was available in the libraries including works by Adam Smith, David Ricardo, G. W. F. Hegel, Ludwig Feuerbach, Immanuel Kant and Robert Owen, not to mention the French encyclopaedists. I then realised that Marxism and Leninism were not simple theories. I would have made my choice already by the end of my studies in the University Law Faculty but for my involvement in Komsomol activities. Public work distracted me temporarily from my thinking about the 'nature of the state'.

And how did you become an economist?

My thoughts led me to a study of fundamental relationships, that is, economics. From Marx and his theory of surplus value I came to study Ricardo's and Smith's economic ideas. I agree with Adam Smith: the state should do nothing in economic affairs except act as a night watchman dealing with defence, law enforcement and taxation (the fiscal function). Slowly but surely these ideas are winning public recognition in this country. One does not have to 'stamp out' Marxism, but simply realise that Marx's economic doctrine rested on concepts devised by his illustrious predecessors who had nothing to do with Marxism. We were stupid enough to reject any kind of rational economic thought so long as our ideologists told us it was not compatible with Marx's doctrine. I think Marx himself would be appalled at the way we have messed up his economic teaching.

When did you finally realise the nature of our society? When did the 'perestroika' of your mentality begin?

I am not one of those who lived with illusions for a long time, and my eyes were not opened suddenly, one day in April 1985, when Gorbachev launched perestroika. My childhood experience was based on a feeling of terrible injustice; after all, my family had been deported quite illegally. I remember being surprised at seeing no tears in the eyes of a classmate on the day in 1953 when Stalin's death was announced. For my part, I knew exactly why I wasn't crying: because my people and my family had been humiliated and degraded. My father, however, devoted his life to strengthening the Soviet system. Despite being poorly educated, he rose to become a collective farm chairman, a champion of the collective farming movement. My father's brothers were all in the war. Two of them came back as Red Army officers, the other two were killed in action.

I had no illusions preventing me from understanding that the deportation of my people was an unjust and arbitrary act by the authorities. For this reason I consider myself among those who were mentally ready to accept the democratic reforms.

In addition, my studies at university and my work experience played their part, particularly being in contact with young people and having to face stiff questioning. As long as you are asked sharp questions, you soon find it impossible to wear rose-tinted spectacles, unless you are a dinosaur. And, of course, my professional studies and trips to foreign countries stripped me of any lingering illusions.

What countries had you visited before the spring of 1990?

Quite a few. I travelled all over Eastern Europe when I was still a young man. During my postgraduate studies I repeatedly visited Canada, Denmark, Holland and France. My doctoral dissertation was devoted to government regulation of the Canadian economy. I studied the government sector, the organisation and management of private, joint-stock and state-run companies, and the role played by foreign capital in national economic development. I took a great interest in such issues as the development of new territories, working out regional programmes, the regulation of agriculture and military procurements. What was a military market? How did state-run corporations operate in a market economy?

The study of Canada's economy made me look into the problem of municipal ownership. I began to study the organisation of municipal bodies of power, community planning and local government. I fell in love with Canada, and I still have vivid memories of the people I met there. Moreover, the country bears a strong resemblance to Russia, especially its rural areas. I then turned my mind to Western Europe and the USA, and for over two decades I studied market economies, which included a comparative analysis for which I visited many Western countries. At first, I couldn't help being amazed at their high living standards. Being an economist, however, I soon realised that their living standards were the direct result of motivated work, extremely efficient management based primarily on personal incentives, and a mixed economy based on private property. Motivated work, that is the key, when the desire to live well is appreciated by public opinion. Wealth and prosperity increase a person's social weight, giving him a higher social standing, making him more confident of himself and honest and instilling into him altruistic values. Nobody goes green with envy merely because somebody else is rich; there is little room for envy because of equal opportunities. If you want to get rich, go ahead, gain knowledge, work hard, explore career opportunities and you will inevitably have success commensurate with your abilities, be it business or science, teaching, law or medicine, anything. These are real possibilities. This explains why nobody throws stones or scribbles obscenities on a luxury car just because they do not own it.

It was amazing to observe life in Western cities and towns. They were so clean and neat. In the morning, bottles of milk or paper bags with food would be placed by delivery boys at the doors of many family homes. People in the street would just pass by and it would never occur to anyone to break or steal anything. This observation made me doubt the theory that class struggle is an inevitable fact of human society. All this was totally impossible in my country. When I returned from abroad and plunged into everyday Soviet life, I would be told that the West was 'decaying' and that the USSR was prospering, a view that depressed me terribly.

The double standards of behaviour and morality, the total absence of any substance in our ideology irritated me. It was probably my good luck that I took up the study of capitalism, for I have not written a single article or book that I am ashamed of today. I did criticise capitalism, but I criticised the actually existing drawbacks. Some people believe today that the market economy is an ideal model. A market is, however, plagued by numerous shortcomings, and I criticised them. A market economy is brutally competitive, ruled by the laws of economic survival. Everyone should be aware of this and harbour no illusions.

In general, I refrained from advocating any economic reforms in the Soviet Union, for there were no tangible opportunities for that. But as a university lecturer, I told my students the truth. Indeed, I would some-times be rebuked for excessive criticism. Criticism was allowed within certain limits; for example, one could criticise the contradictions within economic laws. What I did was to juxtapose life in the West with that in the Soviet Union. And of course, I had to use an allegorical or ironical language in so doing.

After April 1985, I became increasingly interested in voicing my opinion through the mass media. I wrote for major newspapers and magazines, making comparisons in the attempt to achieve the practical implementation of constructive elements of a market economy, such as the principles of price-formation, suggesting that we should be using world prices and not those arbitrarily set by economic bureaucrats. I tried to be heard, but the results were meagre.

It was only on one occasion a couple of years ago that I did score a point by achieving the implementation of my idea of municipal ownership (thanks to Academician Abalkin). Being at the time a member of the scientific council of the USSR Council of Ministers Committee for Social Development, I was able to have the basic idea included in a bill passed by the country's parliament. But there was nothing new in what I had suggested!

Municipal life had apparently existed before the emergence of a first state. Primitive societies, such as tribes, used to have common posses-sions: pastures, for example. This common ownership was regulated by a type of primitive law or social rules varying according to the group. This primitive economic regulation and community rules later evolved to become part of the municipal practices adopted by medieval towns. We, however, totally ignored and rejected those practices. Today, we are witnessing an attempt to rely on common sense, and hopefully a time will come when we can return to true local government based on age-old historical experience.

It must be said, however, that this problem is not so simple. As I see it, we have been trying to substitute soviets (councils) for the once-omnipotent Communist Party committees. The question is whether these soviets are what Vladimir Lenin thought them to be, and whether in the seventy-four years of their existence they have become an effective

7

structure capable of performing the role of municipal bodies which have existed for millennia? Instinctively, many people realise that the idealisation of soviets and delegating to them vast powers is neither democracy, nor a way of involving citizens in real economic, political and cultural life. The municipal authorities and local government in the West are far more capable of exercising the people's will.

We keep repeating 'all power to the soviets', but we do not think about the real meaning of what we are saying. We know only too well that the soviets have never had full power, and it is unlikely that they will ever have it. Parallel bodies of local power dominate; the Communist Party committees.

When did you begin to write on present-day economic issues?

My first article worthy of mention appeared in *Pravda* in June 1986, triggering a discussion about the problem of prices which continues to this day. I am proud of that publication. Unfortunately, my forecast is being translated into practice to the very last detail by the government of Prime Minister Valentin Pavlov, the 'theoretician' of administrative price hikes.

Did you travel much about the country before becoming an MP?

Unfortunately, the place I visited least was my homeland, the Caucasus. I only went there during my annual holidays. I have always been fond of the mountains, but I also like plains, forests and river banks. I should add that I travelled all over the country as a member of the Komsomol Central Committee. It was a very interesting and dynamic job, though I was in it for only slightly over two years. But I still have vivid memories of the people whom I met in Kamchatka, Magadan, Naryan–Kar, central Russia and Central Asia.

Now that you have risen so high, have you forgotten your old friends?

I have not, and it was only a short time ago that we celebrated a sort of a jubilee, the 25th anniversary of our graduation from the Law Faculty. We had a get-together to mark the occasion.

What about your family?

I have a wife, a son and a daughter. My wife works as an economist at an enterprise. My son is a student of economics. We are a family of economists, except for my daughter who is still at school.

What is your family budget?

I get a salary of 850 roubles, about the same as I used to get when I was head of a university department and wrote frequently for the press. I have therefore had a substantial salary for the past 10 years. My wife gets around 200 roubles, my son is still a student, and my daughter goes to school. So, you can easily work it out.

What are your views on the role of family in this society?

I think that it is strong families that make a strong society. The disintegration of families is accompanied by moral degradation, a rise in the crime rate and a number of other negative consequences associated with falling living standards. Today, at a time when the mass media enable Soviet teenagers to compare their life with that of their peers abroad, they soon realise they are just dragging out their existence, not living in the full sense of the word. Hence the dissatisfaction with themselves and with society as a whole, and the many psychological breakdowns. The weakness of many families stems from appallingly low living standards. In this country, making families stronger is a top priority, especially in the Russian Republic where the birth rate is falling catastrophically in most regions.

We must not forget one thing: the fate of women, the mainstay of any Soviet family, is horrible in this society. There is hardly a Soviet family that could survive unless the woman worked, often in appalling conditions, to increase family income. But that is only half the story. It is the married woman who shoulders the burden of looking after the children, attending to her husband, doing the housework, plus constantly hunting (the word 'shopping' is inappropriate) for basic consumer goods and food. Morally and physically, women in Soviet society live under extreme pressure.

Is the transition to a market economy bound to have a favourable impact on the 'primary unit' of society?

Yes, because it would create normal living standards and make the man feel himself the head of the family. In a market environment, a person is given the opportunity to earn as much as he is able to. Personal wellbeing increases family wellbeing and eventually that of the state, which would be able to perform its social functions with greater efficiency. What we must create is not merely a market economy, but a welfare market economy. Poor individuals make poor families and these make a poor state.

Let us turn to you again. What kind of recreation do you prefer?

It is difficult to say. Frankly speaking, it has been a long time since I had

9

any rest. I am so busy these days that I cannot even dream of that. The only thing I can afford is an occasional game of chess with my son. I like skiing, but in recent years I have not had a chance to go: I have been too heavily involved in my scientific and teaching pursuits, and nowadays I have to devote myself to my parliamentary duties.

The Prime Minister of Russia, Ivan Silaev, can often be seen in a swimming pool, and Boris Yeltsin on a tennis court. What do you do to keep yourself fit?

Nothing. I rely on my natural resilience. I am generally rather strong physically, but I know it won't last forever.

They say that the Chinese follow the principle: if you work hard you must rest hard. Would you like to adopt that principle?

Resting hard, well no. That is not my cup of tea. If I could, I would rather opt for working in moderation and relaxing in moderation. Whenever I am free from my public duties, I like to bury myself in books and articles.

Reportedly, you used to work for 12 hours a day prior to becoming an MP, and you now work for 16–18 hours. Is a shorter working day anywhere in sight?

No, not yet.

What is the role of television in your life?

I have few opportunities to watch television since I leave my home early in the morning and come back late at night. If we regard television as a window onto the world, I would say that no amount of television could give me more than I actually receive from my daily meetings with people and their letters to me. I receive countless visitors and have reception hours every day. At 7 or 8 in the morning, when I arrive at my office, I see people waiting for me outside. I do not try to pretend that I do not notice them. When I leave my office, sometimes at midnight, there is still a crowd waiting. People's Deputies also try to see me, and I have no right to turn them away or to ignore their requests; I get countless telephone calls from chairpersons of regional soviets, who seek advice and often assistance. Sometimes they demand a meeting with Yeltsin, but if he is not available, they say, OK, let us talk to Khasbulatov. I then step in, trying to listen and help.

Every such meeting is something of a shock to me. I have, for instance, talked to mothers of soldiers who have been killed while doing their national service. What could be more distressing? Their sons dead, these women try to do everything they can to prevent other boys from dying. As a result of such conversations and letters, parliament issued a decree to recall Russian servicemen from the Transcaucasus, even though MPs realised that this decision was controversial. One thing is clear: mothers, fathers and loved ones of peacetime draftees want their boys back healthy and fit, not crippled or dead.

Different people come to see me. Very often, however, I emerge from such meetings blushing, conscious of how little our people ask for. They ask for bread, meat, they want to have shoes and clothes and decent homes. They don't have any of these things. I am not to blame for their tragic fate, but I am nonetheless ashamed to look them in the eye.

You are no longer merely an academic, but a prominent political leader as well. Could you tell us about your political roots?

I trace them above all to the Law Faculty of Moscow University in the first half of the 1960s and the subsequent decline of Khrushchev's reforms. I recall seminars at which we would have detailed discussions of the theory of the state, democracy, civilisation and society. There were some really first-class professors, representing the old school. They are all dead now. It was only natural that we students should believe we were living in an almost democratic society compared with Stalin's era. Living standards were very low but we considered them adequate, particularly when we recalled our hungry childhood. There was nothing else to compare them with.

Khrushchev's downfall in 1964 was followed by reactionary changes which affected the life, above all, of the children of once-persecuted families, some of whom were my fellow students. Being the university's Komsomol leader affected the way I thought. Komsomol was ordered to expel from its ranks a number of students who took part in the December 1965 Pushkin Square demonstration to protest against the country's un-democratic Constitution. The small demonstration was quickly dispersed and its participants were persecuted. The 'higher-ups' wanted them out of the Komsomol and eventually out of the university. The fate of our fellow students was in our hands. After we decided not to expel them from Komsomol (or from the university), we came into serious conflict with the local Communist Party committee and the university administration. Admittedly, we finally succeeded in saving our fellows from the danger of expulsion, after having been repeatedly accused of 'conformism', 'revisionism' and so forth. It was probably our first major political lesson although we did not realise it at the time.

The real test probably came later, during the election to the USSR parliament in spring 1989, when local authorities did all they could to keep reform-minded candidates off the ballot, and then during the campaign to elect Russia's parliament in spring 1990. The competition was stiff in Grozny: I found myself running against strong candidates, major industrialists, a local broadcasting committee chairman, and the Second

Secretary of the regional Communist Party committee. I encountered much greater difficulty in organising my election campaign than my opponents, for they were 'locals' and my home was in Moscow.

My assistants in the campaign and myself took care strictly to abide by the election rules. By the end of the campaign I developed a competitive spirit, of the sober-headed sort. I would not have won the election but for the help of the teaching staff and students of Grozny University and of my alma mater, the Moscow Institute of the National Economy, professors of various Moscow universities and a group of Moscow journalists. One factor in my favour was that my publications on contentious socio-economic issues were familiar to the general reader. With an effective campaign organisation, it eased my way to victory. The students and the teaching staff of Grozny University, who had actually nominated me for the election, did not spare themselves to support me throughout the campaign. I owe them a lot.

Do you mean to say that your election campaign was your main political 'school'?

For me, it was a real school of political struggle, and, indeed, of political skills. Many said then that Khasbulatov and his team had imitated Western methods; one story even had it that my election team and I knocked out my opponents in one fell swoop. There were many rumours about me at that time, though, in truth, it was enough not to tell lies to the electorate and to promote a clear-cut anti-crisis platform.

In other words, in trying to enlist the support of the masses, one can have empty pockets, but not an empty head?

Certainly, and our pockets were empty indeed. But we had ideas. At first, the voters were sceptical: they regarded me as a 'metropolitan' professor trying to climb the career ladder. But after we had analysed the situation, mapped out a programme, and outlined ways of tackling major problems, I did not encounter a single audience with whom we couldn't find a common language. Overall, I made 220 public appearances during the campaign. People would tell me: 'We share your views, we know you by your publications, and we are going support to you.' I can still feel their support to this day.

Were your opponents playing by the rules?

It was not as straightforward as that. People tried to persuade me to stand in a rural area where victory might have been easier. I insisted that I would fight my campaign in the city of Grozny. It was a hostile environment in which the Communist Party committee and the local soviets all went out to bat for the city's higher-ups.

We would go to a factory and and arrange a meeting, but when we came back at the appointed hour the next day we would discover that our opponents had been one step ahead: the city's Communist Party committee had warned the factory manager, the Communist Party secretary and the trade-union committee chairman to keep out of sight. I would then ask for permission to see the workmen on the shop floor, and would go in and start talking to the workers. After a short time more workers would gather round, and soon there would be a crowd of two hundred people. Some of them would later become my ardent canvassers.

What were the voting results?

In the first round I expected to receive some 52–5 per cent, but the actual figure was 47 per cent. Apparently, some 5–7 per cent of the votes had been rigged. The same thing happened in the second round, in which I attracted some 72 per cent. The Second Secretary of the Communist Party regional committee hid himself from the voters and soon disappeared from the race. He tried to get the Communist Party machine to work for him. I would tell my voters 'I have the feeling that we have to fight the giant ghost of the System.' I do not want to say anything bad about the above-mentioned Communist secretary; I have known him for at least twenty years since we were in Komsomol together.

Does culture come as part of politics, and what traits must a politician possess?

Politeness, professionalism, competence and general culture are the inalienable traits of a politician. Politics is a sophisticated art. It involves making important and wise decisions which affect the functioning of all the elements of the state. A high degree of political culture is therefore an essential requirement.

What does this mean? Among other things, it means a high degree of professionalism. Political culture is impossible without a solid professional background in the domains that politicians devote themselves to. What are these? International relations, economic issues, and so forth. It is not compulsory for a politician to be an expert in medicine or education, but it is essential that he be quick-witted and possess a broad spectrum of knowledge. This is only one side of what is meant by culture.

Culture cannot, however, be confined to knowledge alone. A cultured person is a well-read person, conversant with the history of culture and contemporary cultural life. Culture has always been associated with refinement. A cultured person is always a well-mannered person.

Without giving up his own views, a politician should try to find decisions acceptable to the majority. Parliamentary debates demonstrate not only that many speakers lack good manners, but that they also lack culture. The ability to express one's views is one thing, but to impose them on the audience is another. Hence the attempt to exert pressure disrupts normal parliamentary procedures.

According to Academician Dmitrii Likhachev, the things he dreads most are semi-culture and semi-refinement.

I can only agree with Academician Likhachev, the epigone of Russian cultural thought, the last of an almost extinct generation of the genuine Russian intelligentsia.

Ersatz culture is widespread in this country. Our universities, schools and kindergartens are totally unable to breed a cultured person. We only have a handful of university-level institutions whose graduates can boast real education and cultural sophistication. This situation stems from the 'residual' education funding principle, squalid academic facilities and the miserable pay of the teaching profession. University lecturers and school teachers alike are condemned to look for additional sources of income to keep body and soul together. Occasionally, an individual manages both to preserve their true human self and to become profoundly educated. Were it not for them, really sophisticated and cultured individuals, it would have been even more difficult to launch the reforms and to attempt to transform the political and economic systems.

The inner culture of an individual is important. An individual does not always have the opportunity to gain a profound education, but there are many people who possess a high degree of inner culture. People who possess such an inner delicacy are incapable of hurting other people's feelings, by word or deed. It is essential for people not to lose the human dimension, especially if they are high achievers.

There are some very fine people among the MPs, showing great responsibility in exercising their parliamentary duties. But then you come across a man who had known an MP before, and he tells you that the MP he had known earlier as an ordinary guy has now turned himself into a 'dignitary' inaccessible to ordinarily mortals. The man he is referring to is surely an unrefined, uncultured person. To be able to preserve one's own self and to be true to oneself is not so much an art as an innate quality, the surefootedness of an intellectual who understands life.

What is your attitude towards Marxism as a doctrine?

It is difficult to give a short answer. All of us who received a fundamental education and embarked on an academic career studied Marxism thoroughly enough to get an idea of its main principles. The question is, however, what kind of Marxism? As I see it, we were treated to a Stalinist and later a neo-Stalinist brand of Marxism. Marxist doctrine includes quite a few valuable ideas and concepts which ought to be further developed or revised, such as the question of private property.

It was once instilled in us that according to Marx private property was evil, though Marx and Engels changed their views on that subject. Thus according to an early work, *The Holy Family*, private property would wither away as soon as workers were no longer alienated from the results of their work. Have we done away with this 'alienation'? Instead, we have done away with private property.

This problem requires not only a philosophical judgement, but also empirical study. It must also be taken into account that Marx and Engels were outstanding thinkers of the nineteenth century, and that their views were true for the political society and economic system of their time. On the whole, they thought of major change in terms of a revolutionary overturn. This is apparently the context in which Marxism, as a doctrine, is to be viewed. Without doubt, the ideas of Marx and Engels should be respected for presenting an integral system. The world has known few thinkers who could produce a system of views, a sweeping doctrine of historical development. This doctrine, however, rests on realities that have long since become history. The claim of the discovery of some universal laws applicable to all times and epochs has turned out to have no substance. The realities of the twentieth century have been far more complicated than could have been imagined by Marx while he sat in the British Museum Reading Room or by Lenin when he travelled from one European capital to another.

Do you think that the works of Trotsky, Bukharin and Preobrazhensky can enrich Marxism?

I have much respect for these politicians and I think they must be given their due, but I do not think their works should be used to enrich Marxism. How can you enrich a heritage left to you? Marxism should be seen as a nineteenth-century social ideology. There are other trends that ought to be studied, such as the ones established by John Maynard Keynes, John Kenneth Galbraith, Joan Robinson and Ludwig Erhard. An educated person should be aware of different outlooks and be able to use them both in theory and practice.

The outstanding Russian Marxist, Georgii Plekhanov, dreaded not Lenin himself but half-baked Leninists, the dark forces which followed in his steps. What do you think about that?

Yes, indeed, many disciples of Marxism-Leninism were real monsters. It is my deep conviction that it is those characters who unleashed the Civil War, the fatal consequences of which had been foreseen by Plekhanov.

The war devoured the best of those few Russian and European intellectuals who had followed Lenin. Once the Civil War was over, it was these shady types who grabbed government posts at all levels. These elements have been ruling the country ever since, derailing all efforts to stabilise the economic and political situation in Russia.

Plekhanov stressed that if the October revolution led to a Civil War, its creative potential would be destroyed. In this sense, Plekhanov proved himself a far more sagacious politician than Lenin. Not only did the Civil War weed out the ranks of the reform-minded activists, but it also frightened away the country's intellectuals. It diverted the country's socio-political evolution off the path the world had long been travelling, sending it down an unknown road. In my writings I termed it 'state-monopoly socialism'.

You probably recall the words of Academician Nikolai Vavilov, the outstanding plant biologist who struggled against the destruction of scientific independence in the 1930s: 'We will not betray our principles even if they burn us alive.' Do you think there are many people today who could say this about themselves? Has fear been eradicated?

I think that fear remains, and in a big way, too. It stems from the atmosphere of overall uncertainty and misgivings about the future. We have a vast segment of the population in this country living from hand to mouth. These people fear voicing their opinion. People are afraid of their superiors, of losing their job, a prospective pay rise or the opportunity for summer leave. On a smaller scale, a person may be afraid of not being allowed to leave office one hour earlier to pick up a child from the day-care centre. People fear everything and everyone. Fear is lodged deep in all of us.

People like Vavilov are therefore few. But the words you have quoted can be repeated hypocritically by the authorities and their yes-men, for the 'principles' they advocate, the false principles, are exactly what gives them power over people and the state. When the hour strikes to 'be burned alive', you can be sure they will send others to burn for them.

What were your feelings after you had been elected to so high a post?

It was a rough time, and it still is. It's difficult to preside over the Congress and parliamentary sessions. Above all, because of my poor knowledge of the audience and, to a certain degree, shyness. However, the awareness of being personally responsible for the work of parliament and the fate of the country leaves no room for indecision. After I began to get to grips with the situation, which did not take long, and to know the MPs better, the pressure eased, although the problem of self-control remained. It became easier from the organisational point of view, not the sense of responsibility.

As you might have noticed, our MPs are smart characters. A minor failing on the part of the chairman is like a boomerang. They hit back instantly, often calling you names. The atmosphere is a far cry from that of Communist Party meetings where the Secretary could do what he pleased and the assembly would go along with it.

Are your voters conscious of your being heedful to their needs?

I am trying to be helpful to my republic. Being an all-Russian leader, however, I must pay attention to the needs of people in all regions. I am not in a position to nanny 'my' republic, despite its being my electorate, my homeland and the birthplace of my friends and relatives. I only wish I could visit the place more often.

Was the new mood of openness and reform a decisive factor in your political career?

It definitely was. It should be stressed that despite the evolution of Mikhail Gorbachev's policy, in my view he will enter history as a consistent dismantler of the administrative-bureaucratic system. There is no doubt that he has great achievements to his credit. We would, however, like to see the leader of a great power a more consistent policy-maker, not an opportunist; an exponent of the people's will, not a mouthpiece of a single party and its functionaries. He has been unable to meet these expectations, and I do not so much blame him as sympathise and feel sorry for him.

2

RUSSIA, SOCIALISM AND THE TRANSITION

There is a pile of books on Ruslan Khasbulatov's desk, all devoted to Russia. One can see Alexander Solzhenitsyn's *How to Rebuild Russia*, Nikolai Berdyaev's *Russian Destinies* and his *Origins and Essence of Russian Communism*, Ivan Bunin's *Cursed Days*, Maxim Gorky's *Untimely Thoughts*, and also an array of Russian newspapers and magazines, and a number of foreign publications.

Two books, from the early twentieth century, caught our attention: *Secret Thoughts* and *To Fathom Russia* by Dmitrii Mendeleev. The books were not published throughout the Soviet period: the views of the outstanding chemist were ignored for ideological reasons, and they are not even mentioned in the lengthy entry devoted to Mendeleev in the latest edition of the *Large Soviet Encyclopaedia*.

'To be able to make a professional judgement of the current change in Russia, one must have a good understanding of the country,' says Khasbulatov. 'Busy as I am, not only do I have to keep an eye on current affairs, but I also have to dip into the works by Sergei Witte, Peter Stolypin, Mendeleev, Berdyaev, Solzhenitsyn, anyone who has in one way or another written about Russia's problems. Contrary to Tyutchev's dictum "One cannot understand Russia with the mind", we have to use our minds to understand the country.'

How would you define the essence of the period we are living through?

Mendeleev's term 'Russia's transitional state' accurately defines the current period. In my view, we are abandoning the 'communist' mode of production for a system based on common sense, perhaps a genuinely 'socialist' one? I would not call it 'capitalist', although that is one of the labels which is being pinned on us. One thing is clear: it is not going to be a communist society, but a drastically different society, characterised by a consumer-led economic system.

18

We are in the process of changing the political system. Albeit slowly and inconsistently, we are finding our way back into world civilisation. We are embarking on the path of international development which, at the end of the twentieth century, distinguishes little between different modes of production as the world moves on to a universal economy and a global economic system, at a time that tyrannies fall and economies unshackle themselves from the paternalism of the state.

This transition has driven the country into a general crisis: political, economic and interethnic. The crisis has affected cultural life, morals and human relationships.

When you think about the crisis, does your sense of history help you in assessing it?

My sense of history? The history of my country and abroad? There is a saying: 'Cognition comes through comparison.' In my books, *Socialism and Bureaucracy* and *The Bureaucratic State*, I dwell extensively on pre-revolutionary Russia and the period of the New Economic Policy (NEP) in the 1920s, when Lenin made concessions to market forces, and in particular to the peasantry. Before World War I and the February Revolution of 1917 this predominantly agrarian country lived quite well, and the sound monetary system endured a war that lasted three years. This seems to prove that the economy was in good shape.

From 1903 to 1911, the Cabinet and, subsequently, the Council of Ministers, was headed consecutively by Sergei Witte and Peter Stolypin, whose names are associated with the monopoly on alcohol, monetary and agrarian reforms, the construction of railways, sweeping education programmes, the policy of enlisting the support of the bourgeoisie and the reliance on wealthy peasants. For nine years the Russian government was led by two outstanding statesmen about whom we know little.

Stolypin continued Witte's policy of promoting private ownership and reforms in every sector of the economy. He would say: 'I am promoting a forward-looking programme. I ardently believe in Russia's brilliant future.' The two statesmen put Russia's national economy on to a path of smooth development, and their treatises, laws and reforms still offer many useful ideas. Their efforts to help Russia keep pace with world developments were cut short by a terrorist's bullet and the October 1917 uprising. The twelfth attempt at Stolypin's life was successful, making one wonder what the odds were against him when he said: 'They need great turmoil. We need a great Russia.'

The bourgeois and proletarian revolutions, the imperialist and the civil wars destroyed everything that they had created. Nevertheless, the skills and ability to work remained with a vast professional group, and NEP was based largely on the experience gained during Russia's pre-war economic boom. The introduction of NEP allowed the swift regeneration of productive forces. Per capita meat consumption in 1922–3 was much higher than it is today; high-quality meat, too. This country has proved the unviability of our model of socialism, state-monopoly socialism. Today's crisis was programmed by history's U-turn in October 1917. It should be noted, however, that the subjective factor, the unpardonable errors that have been committed in the past six years, have worsened the situation further still.

The totalitarian system eradicated all kinds of opposition. It had a mortal fear of any dissidence and therefore never published books by authors whom the world had long recognised as great scientists. The system recognised Mendeleev, but only for his genius in chemistry, and it deprived the people of his political thinking. His book *To Fathom Russia*, for instance, went unpublished because long before the revolution he wrote 'The State must not turn towards socialism, i.e., towards the beginning of its end.' Many of his ideas are still instructive and appropriate for our times. 'The cause of our poverty is perfectly clear', pointed out Mendeleev. 'It lies in our preoccupation with primitive trade.' Has anything changed with respect to our exports? The same raw materials go for export, while the rest is pumped into the defence industry. Here is another of Mendeleev's ideas:

> In industry, it is the representatives of the educated class who play the primary part, contrary to what Marx or anyone would teach us .... Industrial development cannot be promoted other than through an enormous effort in which the entrepreneurial spirit is combined with risk and judgement.

But there is no room for the entrepreneurial spirit in a state-run economy. Take, for instance, his geopolitical view of Russia as an integral organism linking Europe and Asia. The sense of history stems from the desire to come to terms with modernity, and it compels one to turn to the works of all those who devoted themselves to understanding Russia. To be able to overcome the crisis, one needs a sense of history.

The crisis has hit every aspect of life. The public blame the government for their woes. Is the government alone responsible?

There is little use in blaming anyone, although the personal factor is very important, of course. Even if the country's leadership consisted of gifted and sober-minded professionals taking the country's numerous troubles to heart, it could only resolve certain tasks. No cardinal change is, however, possible without a total overhaul of the existing system of government and economic management.

This being so, what we are witnessing today is both a governmental crisis and a human tragedy: members of the Cabinet and government leaders are trying to resolve insoluble tasks. What makes me say that? The central government is an inalienable part of the command planning system which has long become hopelessly obsolete. This system, deep in crisis itself, is pulling the whole of society into an abyss.

Government structures, such as the State Committee for Supplies (Gossnab), the State Planning Committee (Gosplan), the Ministry of Finance and dozens of other ministries have for decades towered over the rigidly centralised economy. In a free market environment this system does not work, the economic ties break up, and the steering wheel slips from the hands of the Communist Party and government *apparatchiks*. Meanwhile, the government, unable to come to terms with the hopelessness of this system (or unwilling to lose control) is trying to tackle new problems by resorting to old methods of exerting strong pressure from the centre.

For this reason, we in the Russian parliament and government try to avoid 'squaring the circle'; it would be taken as an attempt to interfere with the policy of the centre, to reduce the powers of the latter to bolster the powers of Russia. We would immediately be accused of trying to demolish the central government so that we can create the same system at the republican level and, in so doing, transplant central bureaucratic structures into republican bodies. Needless to say, this is the opposite of what we are trying to do.

What ideological dogmas ensure the viability of the bureaucratic structures? The chief principle of socialism, 'from each according to his ability, to each according to his work', apparently operates.

Yes, this principle is definitely at work. You have done this much, so your remuneration is this big. Everything is dosed with precision. The implication is that someone has the authority to determine how much you've done and how much you should get for it. Who is there to perform this function? By all appearances, it is the state. The state, that is, the ruling party and ruling bureaucrats, put themselves in a privileged position whereby they can exert pressure, dole out and cut off resources and benefits. It is only natural that this should provide disincentives to normal work. The state completely ignores economic freedom and hence the rights of the individual. After all, the right to entrepreneurial activity is one of the essential human rights.

You mean the right to be the master of one's own abilities?

That's right. One's own abilities, talent and one's own labour. Unfortunately, the principle 'from each according to his abilities, to each according to his work' has permeated our economic relationships and system of remuneration. I think it is one of the chief causes of the grave crisis we

21

have found ourselves in now that the administrative-command system is collapsing.

Simultaneously, it signals the end of the socialist idea?

It is certainly a crisis of the socialist model which we have chosen as the terminal point of our movement, the Marxist-Leninist brand of socialism which we had tailored to our mentality. Lenin eventually abandoned his early attempts to interpret Marx the way he saw fit. The period of NEP did not last long, but it showed clearly that Lenin had begun a serious revision of the socialist idea and fundamental Marxist postulates, and was about to admit that no socialism could be built unless the right to private ownership was recognised.

As far as I can remember, he never admitted that openly.

He did not, but his empirical efforts proved that. Because he did not dare to revise the doctrine, he talked about a temporary retreat and the short-term character of NEP. Gradually, however, he changed his mind about the temporary retreat as he realised that it would take much longer. In this connection, I think that the evolution of Leninism needs accurate definition and chronological dating. There were in fact three stages: before the October Revolution, between the October Revolution and NEP, and after NEP. It would, however, be wrong arbitrarily to interpret quotations relating to different stages of this evolution. Scholars who study Marx's legacy know that diametrically opposite views were expressed by him when a young man and a mature scholar. As far as Lenin is concerned, we are nowhere near understanding the historical truth about him. And we are unwilling to learn from his recantation.

In other words, it is an ideological crisis? The fall of ideological pillars?

Yes. Of the two roads that make up Marxism, the Social Democratic and the Bolshevik, the latter is apparently a dead end. Lenin was the first to realise that. What was he to do? He began to apply things similar to what we are trying to introduce in Russia today: economic freedom, private ownership, enterprise, foreign investment, and consequently the political rights which stemmed from the economic freedom. From this perspective, I can see a certain resemblance between the NEP period and the present-day situation, although I disagree with those who say that we are living through an identical time. In the early 1920s, when Lenin tormented himself looking for a solution, the crisis was only beginning, a far cry from what we are witnessing today. Inspired by the Revolution and victory in the Civil War, people were eager to build. They had faith; now there is none.

The Second Congress of People's Deputies in December 1990 saw a bitter struggle over the reintroduction of private land ownership between two distinct parties: representatives of the administrative-bureaucratic system, on the one hand, and exponents of grassroot interests, on the other. Unless the right to private ownership is recognised, there will be no enterprise and no free market.

It has been instilled into us from our school days that ours was a special road. Do we have to 'reinvent the bicycle'? Why don't we learn from foreign experience?

You are right about what you say about foreign experience. We could well take a lesson from Canada. Canada's provinces enjoy much greater rights compared to our constituent republics. Regrettably, Canada's experience cannot be readily implemented in this country, there are too few opportunities for that. The point is that we find ourselves in circumstances where time has accelerated; yesterday is past, today is coming to a close, what does tomorrow have in store for us? From day to day, one lives in anticipation of a political, economic or an interethnic explosion. Nobody wants to show patience, to think things through or to listen to anybody's advice. That's our trouble.

The central administration keeps hitting us below the belt in an 'unsportsmanlike' fashion. They use treacherous tactics in the attempt to maintain their dominance. President Gorbachev issues decrees virtually on a daily basis: let Russia go to the dogs, but it must remain under his control in the shadow of the Kremlin; it must be reduced to its knees, and its new leaders forced to surrender and pay homage. This is a Tsarist mentality, or more accurately an Asian brand of Tsarism adapted to rule under the red stars of the Kremlin.

In these circumstances there is little point in talking about drawing on world experience or using civilised methods of arranging our life here. When management tries to change the operation of a single factory they risk breaking the law and the constant threat of prosecution. What does it take to implement advanced experience in such an atmosphere? It takes a radical change, something that no director has the right to initiate. Nothing much has changed. Plants have enormous rights on the micro level, but the political squeeze that is being put on them on the macro level bars them entirely from drawing on foreign experience. Therein lies the cause of the crisis. Reliance on private incentives and market forces are the only ways of overcoming the crisis.

Take the draft Russian Constitution. No sooner had we studied and summarised existing constitutional experience and published the draft Constitution, than the Communist Party and official propaganda condemned it, even before the public could read it properly, labelling it as an attempt to restore capitalism. As a result, the draft Constitution was traduced and the public was told it was a bad draft because it was directing the nation towards capitalism.

For six years the government has been trying to 'rescue' the country from a dawning and eventually a full-blown crisis. We all know the results. What is the reason for the failure; the unworkable system, government incompetence or the inability of particular leaders?

It is only too obvious from the professional point of view that neither Nikolai Tikhonov, nor Nikolai Ryzhkov, nor the incumbent Prime Minister Pavlov were the right people to head the government of so huge a country. Even in this system, the Prime Minister must be capable of controlling economic processes, coordinating the efforts of the republics and reorganising the government in good time. Where are we now? The Ryzhkov government tried to impose its anti-crisis programme on parliament. One after the other these programmes failed. The plan suggested by the Shatalin–Yavlinsky team was rejected. The government finally managed to pilot its 'Guidelines for the Transition to a Market Economy' through parliament – a totally unworkable plan with no provisions for a balanced transition to a market economy, for decentralising the economy, promoting horizontal ties and specialisation, and so on. Nothing is being done to restructure the economy, and the conversion of military plants to civilian use is proceeding very slowly.

What does the government do to foster privatisation? Nothing. The old economic ties no longer work. Plants are trying to deal with the situation on their own: they simply do not meet production targets, and there is no one to discipline them. The government is no longer capable of disciplining plants or supplying them with resources. Those factories which decide to set their own targets and promote truly economic ties with their partners are promptly rapped on the knuckles. Presidential decrees issue as if from the horn of plenty. In short, the country's enterprises are in trouble, and the budget is creaking under the weight of bloated defence spending (35–40 per cent of budget expenditure).

One cannot but feel sorry for production managers driven to despair by decrees, ordinances and decisions which run counter not only to common sense, but to existing legislation as well. And all this comes under the slogan of 'building a law-based state'! Government policy hinges on the issue of power. The swift and energetic promotion of a free-market economy would inevitably result in depriving the state of economic controls. The state would then have to devote itself to political matters, its primary function. Economic issues would naturally then be handled by employers, employees, business people, new-style economic managers and trade unions. This would put the functionaries of nearly 100 ministries out of a job. They are now trying desperately to prevent this from happening. My question is: What was the point in re-establishing the same 100 ministries? The answer is clear – to prevent the republics from gaining greater responsibilities and to stop enterprises and enterprising individuals from gaining economic freedoms.

The authorities would not hesitate to let the state and the economy fall apart if that meant retaining their powers. They seem to think that by hanging on to their posts, they are rescuing the country. Not only are they not rescuing the country, they are prolonging the agony and aggravating the crisis, which is increasingly affecting production, trade, the monetary and the banking systems, in fact, the whole economy. From a different perspective, one has the impression that 'higher-ups', the central administration, do not realise the need for radical change, for a radical renewal of governing structures as a whole, as when Ivan Polozkov, the First Secretary of the Communist Party of Russia, said recently 'It's the wrong time for reforms.'

In this country the government has always been an executive body: the Communist Party gave orders and the government obeyed. Hopefully, the Communist Party will no longer be at the helm. That gives the government an enlarged role, doesn't it?

In the first place, Communist Party functionaries are trying to regain their erstwhile powers, at least some of them. Party *apparatchiks* remain a mighty force in Russia's constituent republics, regions and territories. Secondly, the role of the government should be drastically enhanced and reshaped. As you said, the government and the Communist Party used to operate like backup teams: as often as not, the failures of one team would be corrected through a directive issued from the other, mostly from Communist Party committees at different levels. Now that Communist Party bodies have lost many of their powers, and the CPSU Central Committee no longer acts as if it is the central government, its bodies should be staffed with highly competent people and it should have clear goals and ways to achieve them. The government we have now is unsure of itself, and, on my part, I am unsure of whether it really wants reform.

As a result, the country is in a mess. Top-level decisions, such as presidential decrees and laws of the USSR are openly ignored. In other words, there is a growing gap between the lower echelons – plants, regions and republics – and the central authorities. An example of the disintegrating government system is the conference of plant directors, held at the end of 1990. Censuring the government, the directors urged, 'Give us back the administrative-command system, for we are used to depending on the centre for supplies, to turning them into some kind of products, and to distributing the finished merchandise among the consumers. Give us back the old system!' That plea was justified: plant

25

directors are now under enormous strain. Economic ties are falling apart. Regions and territories fail to make deliveries, and plants breach contracts for lack of raw materials, parts, and so on.

There is another aspect to this problem: they lack an economic mentality and the entrepreneurial instinct, and they are unable to take advantage of the economic freedom that has been bestowed on them, and they have difficulties finding partners. It is only natural that they should be longing for the good old days when raw materials and parts would be supplied to them automatically. The old system did work. For this reason the directors demanded that Gorbachev should go back on his reforms, and criticised him sharply for destroying the old system.

You mean to say it was a viable system after all?

Yes, the old economic system was viable within certain bounds. Economic ties based on administrative links worked at the time when the country's economy was not so complex as it is today, and when plants were different. At a certain point, as the system reached the peak of its performance, those ties began to disintegrate because executive bodies could no longer oversee such a sophisticated organism. The economic functions of the state have their limits as well, beyond which the controls malfunction, like any overloaded information system. Market-related ties should replace the huge broken web of the planned economy on self-regulating lines, though with active assistance from the state whose task is to create the prerequisites for a market economy.

Although the conference of plant directors mentioned above was dominated by calls for restoring the old system, sober voices could also be heard saying there was certainly no going back to the old system, and calling for swift and calm transition to free-market relationships. We in the Russian parliament favour this standpoint, for it is through joint work that we see the path to a free economy and an end to the prolonged crisis.

How is the notion of ownership applied in this country?

There should be different kinds and forms of ownership, such as public ownership, share-ownership schemes, private ownership, cooperative ownership, alongside various forms of economic activities. The emphasis should be placed not so much on the reallocation of existing assets as on the promotion of a 'parallel economy', new non-state economic structures that are the harbingers of a market economy. We should be promoting small businesses. I spoke much about that in the past. No market economy is possible without a vast network of small businesses. Slowly but surely, they will begin to heal the country economically. Small businesses are the backbone of any Western economy.

As privatisation gains speed, actual powers will move to capital-owners, and not to persons who control the state-owned assets.

Certainly. The collapse of the government ministries is inevitable. The State Committee for Supplies (Gossnab) and the State Planning Committee (Gosplan) will disintegrate, and the State Committee for Prices (Goskomtsen) will either have to be disbanded or reorganised. These ministries are staffed with tens, or maybe, hundreds of thousands of bureaucrats who do not have the slightest idea of how to create private capital and who have hitherto obstructed those who have. The Pavlov Cabinet has therefore restored the old structures, camouflaging them with new names; the former Gossnab will henceforth be called the Ministry of Supplies.

What will become of all those people when the system collapses?

People have already begun taking care of themselves. Many of them have become heads of various companies. Ministries are being reshaped into concerns, and former bureaucrats are turning themselves into bankers and joint venture bosses. Economically, the bureaucrats are adapting to the new environment. I do not think that a change in the name of Gosplan or Gossnab means a change in mentality. Their philosophy stems from the rather bizarre concept of a 'regulated socialist market'. Nothing good will ever come of it. The only solution is to let the constituent republics implement independent economic policies, leaving the central administration with the role of coordinator. So long as this does not take place, the economy will continue to descend into slump. The economic crisis has now reached a point at which the productive forces as such are beginning to disintegrate, something unheard of in twentieth-century economic history, and living standards are therefore rapidly deteriorating. The flimsy measures (not very competently introduced) on the part of the government have further aggravated the situation, triggering, for example, the unrest by coal miners.

The system has remained essentially intact?

We are suggesting that this system be drastically overhauled. At the core of our programme is the idea of replacing the old system with a highly efficient management and regulation machinery. The whole system across the country should begin a coordinated move towards the free market by promoting horizontal ties. We conceived of a new Union, above all, as an economic community that would be held together by horizontal agreements and a system of contracts. The new relationships would be governed by firm discipline, a ban on infractions and would be based on a master agreement between the republics as well as a single decision-making format.

Within such a scheme, the centre would have its sphere of competency and the republics theirs. The transition period would need a concerted pricing policy, and the contractual obligations would be the same for every republic. Privatisation schedules would be mapped out for every particular sector, region and republic. This would have saved us, promoted mutual confidence and put the renovated Union on a solid base. The horizontal ties would have become stronger in the process of economic change. The country would have been building a national economy – something we have never had in the Soviet Union. The ministerial structures had long divided the economy into feudal-like domains. Regrettably, at least six months have been wasted: the recent statement signed by nine republican leaders and the USSR President has recognised the principles underlying the '500 days' programme.

Does the talk about the threat of a dictatorship have any substance?

It surely does. Any further decline in living standards will facilitate the possibility of a dictatorship. The would-be dictator may not be wearing a marshal's or colonel's shoulder-straps. The question of dictatorship is a question of the system. Had the system been built on the basis of the objective processes which began in Russia after the 1861 peasant reform (followed by Stolypin's reforms) and were resumed during the NEP period, Russia would have been a prospering country with a mixed economy, market forces and a mature democracy.

Mendeleev wrote about a late-twentieth-century Russia as a country populated by 350–400 million people and boasting advanced industry and agriculture. Stolypin set the goal of turning Russia into a great power. 'We need fifteen years of peace', he said, 'in which Russia will overtake the world.' The NEP stimulated the revival of the country's economy and made Russia's prosperous future possible. Had NEP survived, there would have been neither an imperial mentality nor an imperial policy, and consequently no bloodshed in Tbilisi, Baku, Nagorno–Karabakh or Vilnius. The latter would not have grown into the Baltic crisis and eventually into the crisis of the USSR presidency.

The crisis is one of the new presidential power. No sooner had the presidential regime come into existence than it found itself in a deep political crisis. How come? The reason is that presidential power rests on an authoritarian ideology whereby everything is regulated from the centre downwards. Such is the intrinsic logic of the system.

I would like to stress one more point. The country's reactionaries took advantage of the muddled ideas advanced by Igor Klyamkin, Andranik Migranyan and some sociologists about the onset of a conservative wave, the growing reaction in society and the alleged longing for an 'iron hand'. Liberal thinkers play an outstandingly reactionary part by providing an alleged social basis to attempts to install a dictatorship in the late autumn of 1990 and winter of 1991.

According to the new Premier, it is the fault of individuals and not of the system.

That's right. In August 1986, one such individual, Valentin Pavlov, became Chairman of the State Committee for Prices. He held the post for three years, contributing to the destruction of the pricing mechanism. He was right: it is the fault of individuals, not the system alone. Having made a mess of the pricing mechanism, he became the Finance Minister. It took him only two years to mess up the country's finances as well. This only serves to corroborate what he is saying: it is the fault of individuals, and he is one of those to blame.

It is quite amazing how the man who undermined the pricing mechanism was placed in charge of the country's finances. After having inflated the money overhang by 150 per cent, he was appointed Prime Minister. What will be his next target, I wonder? Predictably, the remains of the Soviet Union. He scared the Western business world by accusing it of a conspiracy against the USSR President. It's outrageous. To be frank, my heart sank when the President nominated him for the Premier's post. All this only adds to our desire to take control of Russia's economy, to be able to prevent such individuals from destroying our motherland completely.

So, the situation is cheerless. Where are we today?

At the edge of an abyss. Crisis, or, more to the point, crises: political, economic, interethnic and moral. If, hopefully, there is still a chance, urgent measures will have to be taken to stabilise the situation and to get the country moving. The transitional period is the result of the above-mentioned crises.

3

IN POLITICS AND GOVERNMENT

Now that the First, Second and Third Congresses of Russia's People's Deputies have been held, how do you assess the progress made?

Russia has been making headway. Before commenting any further I would like, however, to talk about the First Congress of People's Deputies in May–June 1990, for it was the starting point of the entire process. Media coverage of the event stressed the low professionalism of the delegates and the high degree of confrontation between different fractions. This judgement, however, is superficial, for it takes no account of the fact that every delegate attending the Congress was more than merely an exponent of his own ideas, feelings and views. Both at the Congress and the parliamentary sessions each MP represented the environment in which he had developed his campaign platform, and which influenced their subsequent behaviour.

It would therefore be an oversimplification to divide the delegates into conservatives and democrats. Every delegate represented his voters and tried to pursue their campaign promises and to promote newly emerged interests. The struggle that took place at the Congress mirrored the complex pattern of relationships in our society. The society that was once simplistically divided into the working class, peasantry and intelligentsia discovered that the real social stratification is much more complicated. This was confirmed both by the Congress and parliamentary sessions.

Step by step, the Congress surmounted the difficulties, common points emerged and positions evolved towards agreement, and the numerous debates and votes were not in vain. We have become used to calling for the consolidation of the progressive, sober-minded sections of society, but as soon as delegates began to look for agreement, people would condemn them for 'sitting here and milling the air, discussing trifles!'. But those were not trifles. The Supreme Soviet is a legislature, and whatever the situation, a legislator must voice his position on a new bill by taking part in discussion and the clash of opinion.

30

The election of the Supreme Soviet Chairman, his deputies and Russia's MPs, as well as the voting on the new bills, were long-drawn out, but a necessary stage on the way to cooperation. Tangible results are in evidence. The First Congress and later convocations adopted a series of major documents, such as the Declaration of Russia's Sovereignty, decrees on the separation of the diverse functions of government on the territories of Russia and the USSR, a provisional decree ensuring the free functioning of Russia's People's Deputies. Various bodies and institutions were set up, such as the Constitutional Commission, the Supreme Economic Council, the Central Bank of Russia, the Bank for Foreign Trade, and the Committee for People's Inspection was abolished. The Russian Supreme Soviet passed bills on ownership, pensions, land reform and many other issues. These were concrete measures enabling the Supreme Soviet, the government and local authorities to embark on the path of sweeping reforms.

Immediately after the adjournment of the Congress, however, the country found itself in a changed situation: the USSR President made a U-turn in his policies by flexing his presidential muscle, for example, in the Baltic states, and exerting extra pressure on Russia's policy and Boris Yeltsin. The Communists of Russia faction resorted to 'uncompromising' tactics. They coerced the legislature into convening the Third Extraordinary Congress of People's Deputies in March 1991, a month ahead of the scheduled date. All this seriously aggravated the political situation in the country.

How would you describe the role of parliamentary Speaker?

A Speaker extinguishes, prevents and triggers conflict. Ideological factors are certainly at work, since there are now some twenty political currents, parties and groups registered with the authorities. Can you imagine the interaction between these diverse ideological trends, the discordant chorus of voices assaulting you from the left, right and centre? The Speaker has to pay regard to the difference of opinions and try to reconcile conflicting interests.

The range of opinion in the country ranges from the Memorial anti-Stalin association to the Pamyat chauvinistic Russian nationalist group. Does this make it any easier for those in the centre?

It makes it even more difficult. A centrist does not belong anywhere, he is an 'alien'. Normally, I try to be guided by common sense. Whenever an issue arises that affects the interests of conflicting groups, or when part of a bill or a decision has to be changed to take into account the views of a parliamentary faction, I try to draw a clear line. This, naturally, arouses the anger of the conflicting parties who attack me from both left and right.

It should be said, though, that the notion of a centre, left wing or a right wing is very blurred and complicated. We do not have centrists in the European sense of the word. In Russia both the left and the right try to claim the middle ground of moderation and tolerance, but these are not sincere attempts.

For instance, after Mikhail Gorbachev emerged triumphant from the Twenty-eighth Congress of the CPSU in July 1990, the Soviet press trumpeted the victory of the left. In my view, however, it was not the left which had won but it had been a game between the right and the ultra-right. In these circumstances, the victory of the General Secretary could hardly be considerd the triumph of the centre. Although Gorbachev emerged undefeated, it was the right, not the conservatives, but the re-actionaries, who scored the real victory.

Whenever the centre shifts to the right, or excessively to the left, it ceases to be the centre, although formally it continues to be called that. The centre must, indeed, be somewhere in the middle of public opinion. In trying to define the true centre, not just the parliamentary one, one must take into account the entire spectrum of public opinion, the social tendencies and the overall political mood, for if parliament is dominated by right-wingers, its centre will shift too far to the right to be able to reflect real opinion in society. This is a complex process, especially in these times when a year of reforms is worth a decade of the stagnation period.

Russia's political scene is dominated by two major political forces: the Communists of Russia and Democratic Russia. Do either of them have decisive influence on decision-making?

There are actually many more political forces, the political spectrum is very broad. The correlation of forces on the floor of the Congress is made up of a left centre, a centre proper, a right centre, a Social Democratic faction, a Republican faction, quite a few political currents in fact. To some degree, the Communists of Russia group helps to make centrist decisions, as it checks the influence of the left and forces the rest of the legislature to find compromises, a middle ground that would be acceptable to the majority. More often, however, their influence has a restrictive effect on the legal acts passed by parliament.

All political parties are afflicted by a destructive tendency in which the ideological aspect is absolutised, and the interests of the grassroots are ignored in the drive for victory for victory's sake. I am particularly worried about the reactionary developments in the top echelons of the Communist Party of Russia. They are dangerous, very dangerous. Take, for instance, the recent attempt to unseat Mikhail Gorbachev from his post of General Secretary of the CPSU. He was rescued by the leaders of the nine union republics with whom he signed the 'nine-plus-one' agreement on 23 April 1991.

Representatives of the Russian Communist Party Central Committee have more than once behaved aggressively during Congresses. Experience, however, demonstrates that most of our MPs can find the correct solution in a critical situation. The Communists of Russia should think twice before attempting to undermine the prestige of the Russian Parliament and the Russian Government.

The Communist Party, many say, has brought the country to economic ruin. The position of the centre is clear. We are also aware of the stand that Russia takes on the Communist Party. Today, the issue of privatisation has come to the fore. What is the Russian parliament going to do about communist property in Russia?

This issue is now being discussed in detail. Quite a few deputies have come up with their own ideas of how communist property should be privatised and nationalised. The question of removing economic issues from the jurisdiction of Communist Party committees has come to the fore. This is made all the more urgent because of the way in which several large CPSU committees have recently been transferring money into joint ventures with foreign companies and indulging heavily in financial activities, often using the old fist-slamming methods and violations of the law. Needless to say, this has nothing to do with the Communist Party's recent tilt towards its 'educative' mission. The desire of some Russian communist leaders to turn party committees once again into the 'leading force' of society is evident. Beneath the surface, the issue of communist property is harder to read, for it has a tendency to merge with organised crime networks.

Are you a Communist Party member?

I am. I have the feeling, however, that the party, particularly the leadership of its Russian branch, is ceasing to be a Marxist-Leninist party at its core. Russia's Communist Party committees have been deeply penetrated by autocratic elements, and this is causing the party's prestige to decline sharply. So long as government functions are performed by party functionaries, there is no place for a party as such. It becomes part of the state structure.

People were brainwashed into believing that a communist was the 'paragon of moral virtue', and that the Communist Party was the 'vanguard', but this belief is being quickly eroded by the sobering realities of our time. It was Polozkov and his team who accelerated this process by indulging too overtly in the struggle for power, without hesitating to resort to the most vicious of means. Being a faithful Marxist, I thought then that perhaps communists ought to build another, parallel party which would become an alternative to this degenerated and unMarxist party. In this respect, I think that the Communists for Democracy movement in the Russian parliament, led by Alexander Rutskoi, has a great future. It is this movement alone that can save the Communist Party from complete historical annihilation.

Let us return to the subject of parliament. Have any methods been devised to check on the fulfilment by MPs of their campaign promises?

During parliamentary committee and commission sessions, as well as at the Supreme Soviet staff meetings, we analyse electors' mandates and the MPs' campaign promises, systematise them and then monitor their fulfilment. Relevant materials are then handed over to the Supreme Soviet Presidium and to the government. Not all of the campaign promises can be easily fulfilled, of course. Suppose a deputy has promised his electorate to build a school and improve the squalid community facilities, but since they have no funds at their disposal it is rather difficult to implement. We do what we can to assist deputies, but we have very limited resources.

For instance, in my campaign platform I stressed the need to recognise the right to private ownership, to develop small businesses, to build a mixed economy, to place local councils on a firm financial footing to enable them to implement social-welfare programmes by granting them broader rights to tax local business profits, and to give the republic greater economic freedom, above all the economic freedom of enterprises, the basic element of a market economy. To be anywhere near competitive in the domestic market, Soviet industries should be re-organised. Once a market economy takes root, enterprises will stop seeking profits by jacking up prices and falsifying accounts, and instead, they will become consumer oriented. As you can see, my programme was associated with the development of the Russian republic as a whole.

Is your platform being put into practice?

Not exactly the way I would want it to. There is stiff resistance to the '500 days' programme. The President of the USSR, who had originally favoured the programme, has shown indecision and we find ourselves in a difficult situation. Nevertheless, the Russian parliament has assumed a firm stand and we have developed a Russian programme of economic reform and we are trying to implement it.

What kind of relations exist between the Russian and the USSR parliaments?

The Russian parliament has proved itself a constructive force, particularly as it has passed a package of laws aimed at giving people economic freedom. The Russian parliament has already recognised the right to private ownership, and the peoples of Russia have given us their support despite the negative reaction on the part of the Union leadership. There has never been any danger of popular anger directed against the Russian parliament or government. Land reform, the problem of Russia's revival, the issue of separating communist, government and economic powers, all these things are being tackled. The Russian parliament has shown more resolution in trying to build a civilised state than the USSR parliament, a stand that is often resented by the latter. After all, Russia is a sovereign state, and it is high time the Union centre realised that.

It is not appropriate for me to criticise the USSR parliament, but, in my view, we in the Russian parliament have responded to reality far more effectively. Unfortunately, many of our decisions do not reach territories and specific persons, or if they do, reach them in a deliberately distorted way. Even in Moscow the mass media provides virtually no information about the work of parliament. One of the most glaring examples was when Boris Yeltsin had to wait two weeks before he was allowed to appear in a live broadcast for forty minutes, instead of the one hour he sought. Compare that with the powers of, let's say, the President of Kazakhstan, or any other regional leader. We found ourselves facing an information blockade, and it is only recently that the situation has begun to improve.

And look at how long we have been fighting for the creation of a Russian television service that would use the broadcasting facilities of Central Television's Second Channel. The USSR President gave his consent, but the matter remained deadlocked. One day, after a Federation Council meeting, Ivan Silaev and I tackled the President on that subject. His reply was: 'Let us establish the budget first!' We understood that what he meant was: 'You stop being stubborn about Russia's contribution to the USSR budget, and I will allow you to set up your TV company.' We proposed a budget, but no Russian television is anywhere in sight.

The new Chairman of the All-Union Broadcasting Corporation (what a name and what powers!), Leonid Kravchenko, tried to stifle the traditionally Russia-oriented Second Channel by filling it with programmes from other channels, apparently to reduce the time available for Russia-related items. Kravchenko declared: 'We are in no position to accept claims for the division of property [implying that Russia was the claimant]. Everything that has been created at Central Television has come from the USSR budget.' They are doing everything they can to step up the information blockade of the Russian parliament and government, to be able to tell people later that we waste our time. We, however, are not going to let this happen. My greatest hope lies with the press: I think that already in a few months' time we will be publishing thousands of booklets explaining Russian laws. We have to computerise the addresses of all rural settlements, rural, urban and regional soviets, and to send our materials to all these destinations directly. Our newspapers are not very effective because of their small circulation. We have been told that local Communist Party committees gave orders to destroy print runs, to prevent them from reaching readers. In fact, we find ourselves in an unprecedented situation in world history: a legitimate government in opposition.

The ideal situation would have been one in which local newspapers would be controlled by democratic forces, but regrettably the situation is different: the press has largely remained in the hands of the Communist Party and they naturally fear the truth and do not wish to back the new authorities.

Compare the two Congresses, the All-Union and the Russian. Although delegates to both Congresses came from virtually the same constituencies, the Russian Congress fought to the bitter end to steer radical reforms through the republic's legislature, whereas the USSR Congress impeded the reforms. It is a tragedy for the Russian people.

It is explicable: the elections in Russia were held on more democratic lines and were really free elections.

Yes, this is true. Nonetheless, Russian and USSR deputies come from the same electorate, and they were elected by people who shared the same views. A people's deputy should be sensitive to the views of the people who elected him. During my campaign in Grozny I would be asked at virtually every meeting: 'What is your attitude to Vlasov?' Yurii Vlasov was previously a local Communist Party secretary and, at the time of my campaign, Chairman of Russia's Council of Ministers. I would say: 'I don't know him personally.' They would reply: 'But we know him only too well. If back in Moscow you start supporting him, we'll have you recalled.' That's the way it was. When the First Secretary of the local Communist Party was trying to convince the Chechen–Ingush deputies to support Vlasov, not Yeltsin, I told him to count me out. Why did I say that? Above all, because my voters trusted me and I was not in a position to break my promises.

The election to the USSR Congress of People's Deputies was held one year before the Russian elections. Many USSR MPs had been given support 'from above' and not 'from below'.

This is all very true, but they still hold their posts today and they cannot ignore the views of their constituents. The electorate supports Russia's policy, not that of the centre.

We don't have a clearly defined procedure for recalling a deputy, do we?

We don't, but we have consciences, don't we? Admittedly, conscience is a complex notion. We have drafted a law which lays down the procedures for the recall of deputies, and hopefully it will be passed soon, enabling voters to make effective use of it. Incidentally, the passage of this law was obstructed by those deputies who pay no heed to the needs of their voters, they are used to listening to communist bosses.

The rejection of the '500 days' programme has a dual impact on the centre and on the republics, and both parties find their freedom of manoeuvre restricted. The centre keeps strengthening its command methods, and Russia takes more resolute steps towards the free market. This discrepancy cannot but affect the stand of parliament and its MPs.

That is indeed happening. We are being prevented from consistently enhancing the economic freedom of individuals and enterprises. The reforms we have proclaimed are being stifled, and our laws are being obstructed. On the other hand, our activity has almost completely blocked the attempts by the centre to interfere in Russia's affairs by using old command methods. As a result one law contradicts another. Regrettably, responsibility for this dangerous state of affairs is being laid at the door of Russia's leadership.

Every politician has moments of dissatisfaction with himself as some of his projects remain unfulfilled. Have you experienced such moments, particularly as regards your parliamentary career to date?

I found myself in a situation devoid of any transitional phase and any choice. My new job demanded immediate action, and together with Boris Yeltsin, I had to take the reins of the Supreme Soviet and its staff, including supervision over soviets across the country. It was now my duty to make major decisions or to take part in decision-making, as well as to negotiate with the central authorities at all levels. I cannot say that I am completely satisfied with my work. The laws and decisions we pass are really not so bad, but they get blocked all the way through. One gets the feeling of bumping into some kind of a soft but impermeable obstacle, like a pillow or a heap of cotton wool. It takes tremendous effort at times to implement a simple decision.

In 1990 we established the Russian Bank for Foreign Trade, but it only started to function as late as 1 January 1991. How come the delay? There was no vacant building. The Moscow City Council wouldn't give any. Isn't Moscow a part of the Russian state? Oddly enough, the leaders of the Moscow Council are reform-minded people. This is the grim reality.

The situation is very complicated. During the harvesting campaign in summer 1990, both Yeltsin and myself had to intervene to eliminate countless bottlenecks: there would be shortages of fuel, tractors or trucks or, when trucks and fuel were available, there would be shortages of storage space, and so forth. The country's aggregate grain yield was 237 million tons, but at the same time we buy 30 million tons of grain from foreign producers, of which 15 million tons go to Russia. Meanwhile, the grain crop in Stavropol, Krasnodar and Rostov regions was 25 million tons. Of this amount, only 15 million tons were turned over to the state. Where the remaining 10 million tons are is anyone's guess; while we continue to import grain for hard currency. I call it irresponsibility and mismanagement. Someone must be held accountable for that. Why the Russian leadership should bear responsibility for the complete incompetence of the centre is not clear. Local authorities do nothing to improve the situation. Inept as they are, they are also blocking our efforts. But look how good they are at cooking up schemes. It all makes me sick.

Given the tensions within Russia's Supreme Soviet, it has nonetheless attracted quite a few USSR MPs. Is there any explanation for that?

In part, it can be explained by the fact that the centralised bureaucratic system has remained sturdy and invulnerable at the USSR level. From this point of view, the USSR parliament represents some sort of isolated superstructure towering over the virtually intact administrative-bureaucratic system. Gifted politicians who emerged on the USSR political scene found themselves on a kind of Olympus, so high that they found themselves cut off from real control and opportunities for adequate decision-making. They display their skills at oratory and come up with original ideas, but these ideas are as short lived as shooting stars in the sky. Concurrently, the real powers, the President, the government, the countless ministries, the Communist Party structures, the military–industrial complex, continue to operate untouched. This being so, the activities of the country's supreme legislature become irrelevant to the real bureaucratic world.

Developments in Russia took a different turn. Immediately after Boris Yeltsin was elected head of the Russian state, he took energetic measures to fill his government with reform-minded persons. How far have we progressed and how well we have been doing is another question. Regrettably, the difficulties we are encountering have proved to be far more severe than we had anticipated. We never thought that forces opposed to reform would aim so overtly to achieve Russia's disintegration and disunion.

Do you mean to say that Ivan Silaev, Yurii Skokov, Mikhail Poltoranin and other USSR deputies were attracted by the opportunity for direct participation in the revitalisation of Russia?

Exactly. In their turn, they drafted in other deputies. We are looking for gifted people, we offer them top jobs and help them fulfil their career aspirations. We receive many applications from interesting and capable people who want to promote the reforms. To be frank, revitalising Russia is an extremely difficult and complicated process. Russia is overlain by the central government, and central structures impede our efforts to implement the reforms.

This being so, what is your forecast for the future?

For all that, I am optimistic. Despite the difficulties, our programme of reforms has already been playing an outstandingly constructive part, both directly and indirectly. After all, we compelled the central authorities to be more vigorous. They are afraid of being left behind, so they have to act. In this way, we are accelerating the transition to a market economy. We also set an example for other republics. This should not be under-estimated.

In your view, will the next election, several years down the road, give us new, resourceful leaders?

It is difficult to tell or to make any forecasts today because the economic situation is still deteriorating. People have an unprecedented aversion towards government in general. A situation in which the democratic forces will refuse to support the new Russian leadership cannot be ruled out. It may occur if we fail to halt the economic landslide. I am worried about the coming spring, the sowing season, the condition of the railways, fuel and energy resources, food supplies, the availability of essential consumer goods. The recent tobacco shortages came as a shock to me. How was it that all the tobacco factories came to a standstill all at once? And every time, the failures and disruptions are allegedly caused by 'objective factors'. There are rather too many 'objective factors'.

Or, take for instance the coal-miners' strike, which nearly brought the President to the verge of impeachment and could have entailed far more grave consequences. Last year, the Soviet Union had a record grain crop. At the same time, we imported huge amounts of grain from abroad. All the same, bread disappears from the shops. Why? I get the sickening feeling of witnessing an unfathomable, intricate and coordinated process occurring on a nationwide scale. What is behind these economically inexplicable phenomena? What is the origin of the artificial shortages?

39

Or maybe there are forces who want the situation in Russia's major cities to become worse, merely to say afterwards: 'look at them, new leaders, they simply can't run this country'. Isn't there some evil scheme behind it all? It worries me a lot.

Politics is a creative profession. Creative work means self-fulfilment and personal achievement. What is your personal contribution to the work of parliament?

That is a difficult question. I am probably one of those parliamentary leaders who see their personal role in piloting through parliament whatever constructive ideas might be proposed by MPs. A parliamentary session can easily be wasted on fruitless discussion, therefore much depends on the chairman. If he conducts the session in a precise and well-organised manner, a hard working day may result in the passage of a much-needed law. The role of the Speaker is to consolidate forces, to pacify conflicting parties, to show them approaches they had failed to see, to make them abandon personal ambition for the sake of the common cause. To say nothing of the day-to-day chores which remain outwardly invisible.

Does this mean that you specialise in building compromises?

More to the point, consensus. Any decision is the result of overcoming a conflict; conflictless decisions are rare. I look at debates and discussions from the point of view of resolving conflicts. To express opposite views will only make sense if it ends up in a compromise.

Are there any lobbyists in the Russian parliament?

The place is just swarming with them.

How far can a lobby sway the work of parliament?

It depends on the particular lobby. For example, we decided to recall Russian conscripts from army units operating in the Transcaucasus. One of the reasons for this was the protest campaign waged by soldiers' mothers, particularly those whose sons had been killed there. This movement of soldiers' mothers is a classic example of lobbying. Except that the word 'lobby' sounds out of place here. Nonetheless, the soldiers' mothers' movement has strongly swayed the conduct of MPs, the voting and the entire atmosphere on the floor of parliament.

Here is another example of lobbyism. Let us say, there is a struggle to appoint a cabinet minister. One worthy candidate is turned down after another. How come? There is an influential faction which is eager to have 'its' candidate appointed and it therefore rejects the candidates nominated by the Prime Minister. This is what I call a negative lobby. Regrettably, negative lobbying has increasingly taken hold of late. It is probably one of the inevitable costs of democracy.

Do lobbyism and democracy complement each other?

They are interrelated.

What kind of people are emerging on the political stage today?

Different people. On the one hand, a truly honest person may become a political figure; on the other, a demagogue, a classic bureaucrat and windbag may find a way onto the political scene. There are, regrettably, only too many examples to corroborate that. Demagogues and prattlers sell gold bricks by promising people rapid prosperity. At the same time, they attack Yeltsin, Khasbulatov, Silaev, without stopping for a breather. Nowadays both an outstanding person and an outstanding ruffian have an equal chance of becoming political leaders, or mediocrities ride the crest of the wave of a mass public movement, which keep rolling over the cowed voters.

Does any kind of 'natural selection' take place?

Demagogues have to step aside, after all. People who have to deal with the real economy and finance, banks and management, come in their place. This is a time for effective people, but the trouble is, however, that there are too few of them, and we have too few professional politicians.

Which of the two phases of perestroika, the first or the second, has been more difficult, or posed the greatest challenge to its leaders?

Definitely the second. The first wave of perestroika brought with it the air of freedom, and the new atmosphere gave rise to people who demanded broader democracy and economic reform. They did not have major constructive ideas, but they were the first to demand change. The economic situation at that time was more or less stable. It was not so bad, really; the real crisis was still ahead. The impression was that the process of reform and the demolition of centralised structures would soon bring about a blooming not only of democracy but in the economy as well. The champions of the initial phase of reform were therefore prone to euphoria. They were sure of themselves, and made fancy speeches and enjoyed the sound of their own voices.

The initial phase of perestroika, however, turned out to be wasteful of time, ineffective from the point of view of social policy and economic change proper. Because the first phase dragged on for far too long, not only did signs of an economic slump appear, but also productive forces began to disintegrate. As a result of extremely ineffective government policy, the destructive process began to dominate. Those who act today must not only overcome the economic disaster that has been gathering for decades, but they must also tackle the burden of errors that have been committed during the six years of perestroika.

We are faced by a nation driven to despair. Boris Yeltsin was right when he said during his trip to the Far East that unless we raise people's living standards, they will raise us on the end of pitchforks. The sense of crisis and insecurity never leaves us. This feeling of real danger never occurred to the leaders and the popular figures of perestroika's initial phase. This mortal danger is caused by the growing popular discontent felt across the country. Aware of growing popular wrath, I sometimes give in to despair, feeling incapable of promoting any change for the better. From this point of view, we find ourselves in far greater difficulties than the pioneers of the reform. We, therefore, draw little pleasure from our new 'station' in life.

Does this imply a double accountability?

It's probably quintuple: we are answerable for pre-perestroika blunders and our own failures and oversights. We shall be held accountable not only for our own errors, but also for those of the previous leadership, and possibly for the errors committed by earlier generations. It should be said, however, that neither Boris Yeltsin nor myself look for excuses in advance. We see it as our duty to find answers to many thorny questions, to break the deadlock and to take well-timed and resolute measures to achieve our objectives. Not only must we stabilise the situation, but we must also try to improve people's living standards: people must see the tangible results of a free-market economy about which so much is talked. Now that there has been a major price rise for foods and essential consumer goods, against which we protested, we are doing all we can to prevent the living standards of the poor and downtrodden from falling lower still. We were, however, strongarmed, blackmailed and ostracised, and finally gave in to the pressure from the central administration.

4

REMAKING THE STATE

THE UNION TREATY

You are the author of one of the variants of the Union Treaty's draft. What made you take on the job?

This calls for an excursus into history. We now know that Marxist-Leninists gave little thought before October 1917 to the state organisation of the future socialist homeland. The proclaimed thesis of national self-determination was interpreted in a peculiarly unambiguous manner. Bolshevik-Leninists had a definite view only about Poland and Finland, which as sovereign states should be allowed to secede from Russia. The problem of the possible withdrawal from the future Soviet state of other outlying national areas was not discussed even in theoretical terms.

The Civil War and War Communism made it objectively necessary to postpone the theoretical and practical issues of state organisation. The concrete reality of the period consisted in the centre's rigid rule and the military administration of territories which had been captured or controlled. The end of the Civil War and, especially, the transition to the New Economic Policy, placed the task of building a new state structure to the fore, of establishing a stable political system within the framework of the former Russian state. The views of the leading circles of the party and the state tended towards either the establishment of a unitary state, which Lenin himself shared to a certain extent, especially at the beginning, or towards a confederation of union states, which was supported by prominent figures of the time, above all the leaders of Ukraine and Transcaucasia.

The first Union Treaty of 1992, which was adopted as a result of discussions between the revolution's leaders, in which the sick Lenin took part from time to time, and of tragic conflicts between representatives of the 'centre' and the 'periphery', was quite confederative in form and severely unitary in content. It deprived union republics and autonomous formations of all independence. The idea of 'autonomisation', championed by Stalin, triumphed all along the line.

The rigidly centralised political system was palpably out of gear with the economic system of a free market, which was taking shape under the New Economic Policy. The strengthening of the former undermined the latter. As a result, the economic basis was fused with the social superstructure and regulatory processes were entirely leached out from state, economic and social structures and replaced with centralisation, with rigid administration by directives from the all-powerful centre. No republic could be independent in such conditions; all of them had to make do with residual rights.

This situation could not survive when the neo-totalitarian regime began to disintegrate and republics began to act as independent forces. Tension in this sphere affected the destinies of millions of people. The more complicated the regional problems, the more people suffered, so much so that whole peoples were deported during World War II. The semi-fascist political regime paralysed republics' political and economic activity and excluded a sensible search for the settlement of national issues. The very first signs of democratic development brought about a national crisis in the Union. Peoples who have been silent for far too long now strive for real self-determination within the Union for some, within the Russian Federation for others; still others want to become totally independent and establish national states of their own.

Thus the very first blows at neo-totalitarianism, the involvement of broad popular masses in the democratic process, began the disintegration of the entire political system which was the USSR and which could maintain itself only by absolute power restricted by nothing and no one. Republics have begun to demand their right to self-determination, to economic and political sovereignty. Real or false representatives of the people have at times made exaggerated claims. Parliaments adopt laws which affirm sovereignty, and theoretical concepts sway from idealising the old or the 'new' Union to the idea of withdrawal from the USSR. There is a strong awareness of the need for a cardinal change in the political system, for discussions and prompt decisions, since spontaneous mass events have already begun to neutralise the actions of state power, of its centre.

A draft Union Treaty has been published. You are known to have agreed to it and signed it as an 'ad hoc variant'. But almost half of the union republics took no part in drafting it, and you yourself have many doubts. The All-Union referendum on 17 March 1991 concerning a 'renewed socialist Union' has not done much to clarify the issue. What is the problem?

I must say frankly that the very posing of the question of a 'new Union Treaty' is in my view a fatal mistake. It was a different matter when the question was raised two or three years ago by representatives of the Baltic republics, which had not actually participated in the signing of the 1922 Union Treaty. But since the 1922 Treaty itself had been fully 'dissolved' in the USSR Constitution of 1924, it was quite senseless to resort to it, especially since the Baltic republics refused to participate in the process. It seemed expedient to me at first, since the problem had been posed, to draft a variant of the Union Treaty which could serve as the basis of the unification of all fifteen republics. It was in this spirit that I prepared my version of the Union Treaty in August 1990 (see Appendix).

Events, unfortunately, rendered my draft unrealistic. The centre could not overcome its striving to preserve the old order of things, albeit in a slightly liberalised form. As a result the Baltic republics, Georgia and Moldova were 'pushed out' of the treaty-drafting process. The national republics of Russia were added to the Union Treaty to undermine us and some other union republics, much complicating the problem. But our deputies were somewhat reassured by the fact that the leadership of the Russian Federation's Supreme Soviet showed itself to be firmly dedicated to the Union. There is no question for us whether the Union is or is not to be. We are firm in our belief that it will be. The cardinal question is what the Union and the Treaty will be like.

What provisions of your version of the Union Treaty presented the greatest difficulties?

The relationship between the future Union Treaty and the USSR Constitution. There were three possible solutions: the Union Treaty replaces the USSR Constitution; the USSR Constitution becomes a part of the Union Treaty; the Union Treaty becomes a part of the USSR Constitution.

The concept of a 'sovereign union state' would, in my view, be best suited by the first alternative, in which the Union Treaty replaces the Constitution. This idea should not be oversimplified, since the absence of a Constitution could well lead to the dissolution of the Union. The Union Treaty could serve as the basic and universal Constitutional Act, defining the fundamental norms underlying the new Union of States. The Treaty would acquire stability and durability if only because it presupposes the absence of elaborate details which are characteristic of constitutions in general and of 'socialist' ones in particular, and which may be present, though to varying degrees, in the constitutions of union states. Otherwise the constitutions of union states would have to repeat articles in the single Constitution of the Union of States.

The most serious problem is that of the relationship between the centre and Russia. How should this be developed?

As I have already said, the centre identified itself for more than seventy years with the Russian Federation, which it controlled directly, so that the latter's parliament, government and other institutions were only subsidiaries of the Kremlin leadership.

It never occurred to the leadership throughout the long and sad history of the Union to think of Russia as an integral state with a destiny, history and cultural and spiritual values of its own. The opposite in fact prevailed. That is why the national heterogeneity of Russia was undermined, national cultures and languages were suppressed and the history of the Russian Federation peoples was distorted. The Russian Republic was in fact viewed as an autonomous unitary state formation while Russia's autonomous republics were deprived of all semblance of real autonomy and independence and were rigidly controlled by the centre. In this sense, other union republics had much greater independence than the Russian Federation.

The lack of rights and the grievous condition of Russia itself were results of the deliberate policy of the central administration, which 'dissolved' the republic in All-Union party, economic and administrative structures. This is what made the proclamation of Russia a sovereign state so important. Congresses of Russia's People's Deputies laid the foundation for smooth relations between the centre and the Russian Federation and the latter with its own republics. The key question is delineating power and control functions between them. It is absurd when various levels of power block one another's decisions and actions, and only add to the chaos within the state.

Confrontation is absolutely impermissible because we all strive for the same goal, that of enabling our country to overcome the crisis and to prosper. Though complete understanding has not, regrettably, been attained, I am sure there is a real possibility of moving in a mutually acceptable direction. This was felt especially strongly towards the end of the Third (Emergency) Congress of People's Deputies of the Russian Federation. The statement made by the nine leaders of Union states and the USSR President is in full accord with our policy.

What should be, within the Union Treaty's framework, the mechanism of demonopolisaton, of freeing enterprises from the centre's dictate?

This process needs serious coordination with the Union government because Union ministries control most of the enterprises on Russian territory. Even industries which are inherently suited for All-Union management, including many defence plants, major energy complexes, railways, and so on, should come under Russia's control, as envisaged by the resolution of the First Congress of People's Deputies 'On Delimiting the Functions of Managing Organisations on the RSFSR's Territory (Fundamentals of a Union Treaty)'. We must take very serious measures in order to change the qualitative content of economic policy to enable Russia to switch over to a market economy as quickly and painlessly as possible. Here we set great store on a Union Treaty, on a new Russian Constitution and on the presidential form of government which should seriously strengthen state power in Russia.

Is it true that all international economic links of the Russian Federation still continue to pass through All-Union channels?

Yes, practically all of them do. The independent operations that have been started are insignificant. It seems to me that our firms could extend their operations beyond the Soviet Union's borders, to other countries. We should also be able by now to enable foreign businessmen to organise their enterprises in Russia and to let them enter the world market. It is necessary to begin to sell to foreigners shares of our major corporations, and allow them freely to organise industrial production, banking, insurance and housing construction and let them help us solve food problems. People say that in doing so we shall sell out our forests and our mineral resources, but it is impossible to ruin them more than we have already done. Nor should they be sold out, but put to use. We should conclude deals which would serve to preserve forests, and introduce intensive processing of raw materials such as oil, gas, metallic and non-metallic ores, timber, and so on. Since we have lost the skills, let foreigners show us how to work properly. There is no threat to our independence in this. It is quite wrong to fear that 'capitalists' will impose their control on us. The state is ours and so is the government. We are capable today of sensibly regulating the activity of any Western firm the way this is done all over the world.

We cannot use them ourselves, but as soon as someone tries to sell them we nip the attempt in the bud, appealing loudly to people opposed to a sell-out. We cannot return to the road of isolationism which was characteristic of us after the New Economic Policy. Lenin declared the open nature of our politics and economics, stating definitely that the socialist economy was a part of the world economy. It seems to me that reactionary forces are trying once again to go back to autarchy, in order to make us close up once again, to return to the times of the 'iron curtain'. But I think that the vigorous activity of the Russian government and parliament together with other republics, in particular those with whom we have concluded treaties, will serve as a powerful counterweight to the reactionary line of reverting to isolationism, to autarchy.

Is it necessary to have a 'new' Union in conditions when republics have declared themselves to be sovereign states? What is the 'new' Union to be like?

We should put an end as soon as possible to the dramatic and absurd situation with the Union Treaty. It should be signed as soon as possible, but it is necessary first to remove all the uncertainties which remain in the centre's version of the Treaty. The main question here is the delimitation of the competence of the Union and of the union republics. Then we have to separate the competencies of the Russian Federation as an integral multinational state from that of the republics which are part of the Federation. We should then define the competencies of the regions and territories of the Russian Federation. In this way we shall eliminate contradictions between the laws and other enactments of the state and government. This is in fact how the political systems of all modern states are built, and this is what is required by global experience, the history of states and the traditions of civil society.

Can you define the main demands of the republics, the universal features of the Union Treaty which could suit the fifteen Union states?

The Treaty should become the main constitutional act of the future Union, which can take the form of a confederative union (community or commonwealth) of independent states. This approach is in fact recognised in the statement of the nine Union states and of the President published in April of this year.

The settlement of the strategic question delimiting the powers of the new central administration and of the founding states of the Union must not undermine the independence of the founding states. This is essential for fulfilling the main task of making the Treaty attractive to all. Such a definition would make it possible to identify the basic functions that could be placed under the partial or joint government of the central administration and the Union states. They were reflected in the draft Treaty which I proposed back in August 1990. It is to be regretted that the republics showed no interest in the draft at that time.

How should the Treaty be adopted?

Political practice has established, regardless of the USSR Constitution, the principle of exercising power 'from top to bottom' whereby the centre determined, independently and imperatively, the scope of both its own powers and those of the republics. The proclamation by the union republics of their sovereignty demands a cardinal change of this traditional order.

The sovereignty of the union republics requires each of them clearly to define the range of powers which it intends to delegate to the centre, to Union bodies of state authority and government. The Union states determine the nature and scope of powers which are handed over to the centre in two stages, first at the level of their own republics and second in the course of negotiation with other members of the new Union.

It should be noted that Russia's republics in their turn act in much the same way when they hand over part of their powers to the Russian centre, retaining functions with which they can deal with themselves without detriment to the state, population and other regions (mostly on the basis of powers characteristic of local government combined with certain functions of state authority).

It would be more correct to view the new centre as a totality of Union bodies of state authority and government, whose functions are wholly determined by the Union states through the Treaty-forming process, on the basis of the priority of their rights in relation to the rights of the future Union.

In the course of negotiations Union states define such principles as the rights and equality of citizens, the right of republics to full independence, the priority of their rights in relation to those of the Union, and so on. This could be followed by norms pertaining to agreements concerning the Union's procedures of settling disputes and conflicts and bilateral and multilateral obligations and agreements of Union states.

What is the essence of the contradiction between the centre and Russia in the matter of the Union Treaty?

It consists in their different approaches to the essential purpose of the Union Treaty: the central administration is trying to preserve the power and boundless influence of the *apparat* while the Russian parliament is trying to save Russia from breakdown and ensure the possibility of profound economic and political reforms. Our idea about the level of independence of the Russian Federation is therefore totally different from that of the bureaucracy of the centre.

You have said that the centre exerts a particularly hard pressure on Russia. Why?

Unlike the other fourteen union republics, the Russian Federation cannot pose, even in theory, the question of 'withdrawing from the USSR' since there is nowhere to withdraw to. It was ordained by history that the USSR should be formed by the Russian Federation being joined by other republics which had existed for centuries as independent states. That is why seces- sion from the USSR for many Union states entails the gradual weakening of their economic and political links with the Russian Federation, from which it follows that we cannot be in favour of Union republics leaving the Union. Regrettable as it may be, the central authorities, whose primitive policies encourage centrifugal processes, employs its powerful propaganda machine to lay the blame for the disintegration of the Union, for which it is responsible, on the Russian leadership. But this is entirely alien to our interests.

The Baltic countries, for instance, close or attempt to close their borders with the Russian Federation because they have no borders with the centre, they demand troops to be withdrawn not to some place in the centre but to Russia, and so on, which shows that in the eyes of union republics Russia is the centre. This, and the deterioration of the centre's position in the republics, explains the inevitable growth of another tendency: the Union authorities are stepping up the pressure exerted on the Russian Federation. They believe that their continued existence largely depends on the 'Russian' factor. The centre is bringing pressure to bear on all levels of central and local government in the Russian Federation.

The anti-Russian activity of the top- and middle-level bureaucracy, whose numerical strength is colossal, is particularly destructive. This bureaucracy includes party committees in Russia, the officialdom of ministries and numerous establishments such as concerns, associations and sectoral amalgamations. They encourage separatist ideas on national or territorial grounds, and there is now a real threat to the RSFSR's indivisibility as an integral sovereign multinational state, which formed the USSR together with other Union states.

The attempt to break regional links within Russia raises yet more obstacles in the way of the new Russian authorities' attempts to implement the transition to the market, in particular the attempt to stabilise the situation by consolidating finances and ending the shortage of basic necessities. It is also suggested that the crisis, which is a result of the central government's destructive activity for six years, has been engineered by the Russian authorities.

One gets the impression that the central administration has reconciled itself to the fact that it is no longer able either to lord it over the union republics or to exert substantial influence there. This only adds to the pressure brought to bear on the Russian leadership to make it totally subservient to the Kremlin. No other union republic is subjected to such massive pressure as is exerted on Russia. That is why it is very important that our economic and political reforms be faultless.

There is no doubt that we will be able to solve the economic problems through the vigorous development of market structures. I trust that our fellow citizens will support the Russian parliament and government in these hard conditions. Still, I am greatly worried by the problem of Russia's state structure, particularly by its territorial aspect.

THE FEDERAL TREATY

How can the unity of the Russian state be maintained?

This is a most important strategic task since the central administration has done much to undermine the unity of the RSFSR as a state. It systematically encouraged the autonomies to withdraw from the RSFSR. It is therefore necessary to sort out the system of relations, first, between the RSFSR and the centre; second, between the union republics; third, between the RSFSR and its autonomous republics, to clarify their character, nature, peculiarities, and so on.

It is important to distinguish between interstate and intrastate relations existing in this sphere.

Interstate relations based on the existing Constitution operate, first, between the fifteen union republics as the only founders of the USSR; second, between the union republics, the founders of the Union, on the one hand, and the Union centre, on the other. The Union centre is a product of the first Union Treaty, an agreement between Union states. The founders of the Union centre, which are the only subjects of the Union, have not been reconciled to the fact that the centre has gradually become a self-governing force, and has broken away from the control of its founders. While certain persons among the authorities of the Union states are reconciled to their present status, their peoples demand the restoration of the republics' violated rights, and, consequently, the implementation of an independent state policy.

Union republics are, even under the Constitution now in force, independent and sovereign states which possess constitutional rights for exercising their sovereignty. This alone makes their declarations of state sovereignty constitutionally valid. The declarations make the republics legally quite independent from the Union centre. Therefore the main interstate problem along the line 'Union centre – union republics' is not that of the centre 'recognising' or 'not recognising' the independence of any union republic, for which there is no need. It is logical to conclude that the issue does not belong in the political sphere, since it is settled by the Constitution, and consists in the restoration of the republics' rights usurped by the centre.

Intrastate relations are relations within the RSFSR, between the subjects of the single Russian state. The current interpretation of sovereignty by some national republics goes far beyond their factual (not to mention legal) status as inseparable parts of an integral state. Almost all of Russia's sixteen autonomous republics have adopted declarations announcing their 'sovereignty', or are preparing to do so. Many of them have hastily dropped the adjective 'autonomous' without notifying Russia. It should be said that the leadership of the Supreme Soviet of the RSFSR has been aware of the need to discard the adjective, which was greatly discredited over the past decades. We have already made appropriate changes to some of our legislation, which will certainly be made in the new Constitution of the RSFSR.

I have said more than once that the national-state formations which are granted the rights of autonomous states by the exisiting Constitution of the RSFSR were in reality deprived of them. The culture, traditions and customs of their peoples were cruelly suppressed, their history was distorted and their national intelligentsia was persecuted. Our policy consists in imparting real content to the declarations of sovereignty by Russia's autonomous republics within the Russian Federation. Although we shall certainly help the republics defend their new powers, we are against setting them against Russia. The republics are parts of the Russian state.

It is often asked in this connection: Who undermines the universally recognised principle of a state's indivisibility without its people's consent? Are there not deliberate attempts being made to smash to pieces Russia, a state with a glorious millennial history and a culture without parallel in world civilisation? These questions are not groundless.

The leadership of the Supreme Soviet of the Russian Federation has defined a programme for the substantial elevation of the status of Russia's national formations. In particular, Boris Yeltsin has advanced an essentially universal concept of constructing new power structures 'from bottom to top' in which each level takes on only such powers as it can put to effective use in the interests of its population, and passes to higher authorities powers that affect the interests of the state as a whole.

This is certainly the only way properly to sort out and harmonise all socio-economic and political relations within the Russian Federation, to grant ample powers to the authorities of Russia's republics, regions and territories. This does not mean, however, that dozens of dwarf states with semi-feudal rulers of their own will appear on the RSFSR's territory. All of Russia's republics are its component parts, and its relations with them should be those of the whole with its components if an integral federal state is to be maintained.

In the event of attempts that may nevertheless be made to dismember Russia by separating republics, internationally accepted procedures should be followed. In particular, a referendum may be conducted in order to clarify the will of the people, probably not only in the republic concerned but in Russia as a whole. The people of Russia alone should decide whether they wish to maintain Russia as an indivisible, democratic and prosperous state, or to turn that state into a multitude of semi-feudal, poverty-stricken principalities torn by conflicts and jealousies.

You said that the political crisis may be overcome by the adoption of a Federal Treaty. What are the main points of that document?

In order properly to examine the Federal Treaty we must proceed from certain general but definite considerations.

First. It is necessary to give a precise definition of the subjects of the Russian Federal State – republics, regions and territories. As noted, the restrictive adjective 'autonomous' before the word 'republic' should be discarded. Since it is axiomatic that the republics will remain within Russia, it follows unambiguously that they have limited sovereignty. No state in the world, be it the USA, the USSR, or any other country, has 'full' sovereignty, since all of them obey the norms of international law. Nor do the RSFSR and other union republics possess 'full' sovereignty, since we have agreed that we delegate to the Union some of our powers. The same is true of the Russian Federation's republics. This reality has to be reckoned with. There is nothing offensive in arguing that Russia's republics have limited sovereignty.

But limited sovereignty should have nothing to do with the republic's lack of rights. I think that the new Constitution should reflect the tangible elevation of the republics' status. This does not mean, however, that the RSFSR should become a kind of loose confederation after the manner of today's Yugoslavia. We must not permit the 'Balkanisation' of Russia, which would entail the end of both Russia and the Union.

Second. Questions of the delimitation of powers between Russia and its republics, between their bodies of authority and constitutions, can be reflected not only in a Federal Treaty but also (and primarily) in the Constitution of the RSFSR.

Third. The actual status of territories and regions in the socio-economic sphere should be comparable to that of republics. The special characteristics of Russia's national republics are, first, that they are state formations (republics with limited sovereignty), and second, that they have been historically formed on land where a specific people (or peoples) have traditionally lived. These characteristics allow their identification as national republics.

But subjects of one state cannot be economically unequal (republics and regions), which would immediately affect citizens' rights. Another aspect of the problem is that all of Russia's territories or regions are multinational communities little different from the autonomous regions themselves, which explains why territories and regions demand their economic status to be equal to that of autonomies. There is nothing offensive in this objective demand. Territories and regions should have the same economic rights as republics expressed in forms of local government. This question should be settled in the same way as the delimitation of authority was agreed between the republics and Russia, in which territories and regions retain certain powers and delegate others to the Russian state.

These approaches eliminate basic contradictions between, first, the Russian 'centre' and the 'periphery' (vertical) and, second, between republics, on the one hand, and territories and regions, on the other (horizontal). As regards contradictions in matters of property, which suddenly arose all over the country, they are, to my mind, transitory and are explained by what may be called the 'legislative vacuum'. The adoption of appropriate laws by the Supreme Soviet of the RSFSR is designed to regularise property relations in the market economy and to establish the rights and duties of all bodies (and structures) of authority and the nature of their relations. The subject of the market is not a republic or a region but a free enterprise.

Such reforms will undoubtedly streamline the political system in conformity with the new economic system, the mixed economy. As market (horizontal) links grow stronger they will effectively overcome the protectionism of district and regional soviets and render politically senseless the current attempts by local authorities to affirm their own undivided control over resources, industry, agriculture, and so on. The market objectively demands the elimination of all administrative interference, by the centre, regions or district, which spells the end of a market economy.

The signing of a Federal Treaty would signal that all republics, territories and regions have settled their relations and are part of a single state, the Russian Federation, which acts and operates as a single entity in international relations. This state, which equally protects the interests of all its citizens, no matter where they live – in republics, territories or regions of Russia – is consequently a subject of the new Union Treaty. The question of the Federal Treaty is inseparably linked to the signing of the Union Treaty and the adoption of the future Constitution of the Russian Federation. Our treaty should set an example to multinational republics and indicate ways for the peaceful political regulation of national conflicts.

Unlike the USSR and the Transcaucasian Federation, which lasted up to 1936, the RSFSR is not a federation built on a treaty basis. The autonomous formations within it based their relations with Russian federal structures not on treaty provisions but on constitutional and legal terms. Thus federal states may be formed on the basis of either treaties or constitutional and legal stipulations. The history of the federal development of the RSFSR knows only one instance, that of Bashkiria, when a treaty was concluded with a national entity which later joined the Federation (the treaty was signed by the All-Russian Central Executive Committee and Bashkiria's government in 1918).

The draft of the Federal Treaty establishes the idea of the Federation as a state built on treaties. This idea allows, of course, different interpretations if applied to the RSFSR. Will this process lead to the disintegration of the Russian Federation as an integral state? This exceptionally important question should be kept in mind during the discussion of the draft. The fact is that the RSFSR Constitution does not stipulate the possibility of any of its constituent republics seceding from it. It should be remembered that the principle of secession without preliminary permission is reinforced if the Federation is built on the basis of Treaty provisions.

The situation has radically changed because of the alterations by almost all autonomies of their status and their attempts to establish state sovereignty.

Since the 'vertical' relation between union republics and republics (former autonomies) has not yet been fully defined, the proposed Federal Treaty evidently could be a document that would define and, most importantly, stabilise the status of the RSFSR's subjects and guarantee their state sovereignty (even if it is limited) and delineate the powers of the Federation and its members. The total number of legal subjects with which a treaty may have to be signed is eighty-eight and includes sixteen republics, five autonomous regions, ten autonomous areas, six territories and forty-nine administrative regions and the cities of Moscow and Leningrad.

I would like to draw your attention to the fact that the draft Federal Treaty has the subtitle 'Treaty on the Delimitation of Competence Between Federal Bodies of State Authority and Subjects of the RSFSR'. Thus the parties to the Treaty are entities of different categories: federal bodies of state power, republics (states), autonomous regions and areas, and administrative regions and territories.

The purpose of the inclusion in the sphere of the Treaty's subjects of such administrative–territorial division as regions and territories is to equalise as much as possible their rights with those of republics and other autonomous formations in terms of socio-economic development. But it is also obvious that the granting under a treaty of equal rights to all territorial units of the Russian Federation cannot ensure in practice, in real life, their fully fledged participation in the RSFSR's affairs, since the attainment of this equality is possible only on the fulfilment of three conditions: equal powers not only in the sphere of socio-economic development but also in all spheres of state regulation; equal (with republics) commitments of all other subjects of the Federation and equal responsibility not only in the socio-economic sphere but also for the state of affairs in the RSFSR in general; equal representation in bodies of state authority and government and in other federal institutions and structures.

The most complicated problem in this respect is that of guaranteeing the rights of the Federation's subjects. Laws of state development inevitably predetermine not only the horizontal development of integration processes but also vertical subordination, above all within an integrated legal system which lately has appeared to be falling apart, something which is quite impermissible, though accelerated by the actions of some of Russia's republics. The problem of ensuring the coordination of the Russian federal and republican (former autonomies) legal systems, including that at the level of constitutional arrangments, has been aggravated by the attainment of sovereignty by the former autonomies.

It should be stressed that the draft Federal Treaty identifies two different issues. The first is the delimitation of the objects of competence between the Federation and its subjects. The second is the delimitation of competence between various federal bodies, on the one hand, and various bodies of the Federation, on the other. These are indeed different, though interrelated, matters since competence is an attribute of a state body while powers, that is, objects of competence, are a property of the state, which is conditioned by state sovereignty. The transfer of relations within the Federation to a treaty basis instead of their constitutional regulation does not alleviate and in some instances jeopardises the priority of the legal acts of the Russian Federation on its territory, even if the spheres of powers within the 'Russian Federation and its republics' are separated in some way.

The draft Treaty states that all subjects of the Russian Federation possess state power on their territory within the limits stipulated by the Treaty. Power is a socio-political category which is always and in all cases a derivative of the people's sovereignty, the subjects of which are the people themselves. State bodies which express and execute this power are derivatives of the people, in which the people actualise their sovereignty.

While the subjects of the Russian Federation have the same basic political and economic rights, they may differ in the scope of powers they delegate. It is not quite clear, however, what exactly 'basic rights' stand for, while the classification of political and economic rights leaves un-answered many questions of the social, cultural, humanitarian and ad-ministrative–political spheres. The draft Treaty provides the possibility of differentiating the scope of powers delegated by the Federation's subjects but not the principles and mechanisms of deciding questions involved in delegating powers.

All the subjects of the Russian Federation are granted the right to legislative initiative and financial self-sufficiency. They may establish economic ties with other states and international organisations within their competence or on the authorisation of the RSFSR's federal bodies.

This, however, should not give rise to any illusions since the growth of federal elements and a higher legal status do not and cannot make former autonomies equal in rights with the Russian Federation. The RSFSR remains a federation of subjects with different rights. It is also clear that the rights granted by the Treaty to republics, regions, territories and areas as the RSFSR's subjects cannot be unlimited. This absolute fact stems from the heterogeneity of their constitutional status and the logic of preserving the state unity and integrity of the Russian Federation.

THE CONSTITUTION OF THE FEDERATION

The draft Constitution has been published. What can you say about this document?

Russia has dreamed of a Constitution for decades. Nikita Muravyev, a participant in the December 1825 uprising against Tsarism, wrote a constitution of his own. The Soviet system produced numerous constitutions, including the Constitution of the USSR and constitutions of union and autonomous republics. We had no problems with Soviet constitutions until the question was raised of constitutions of the period of reforms.

How was the new Russian Constitution drafted? There were alternative versions, including Academician Sakharov's constitution. Were they taken into account in the draft?

Let us begin with Sakharov's constitution. His democratic ideas were oriented towards the fate of peoples and the protection of human interests as paramount, and exerted great influence on the draft Consti- tution of Russia. They also influenced the alternative draft proposed by the Communists of Russia group, which also recognises private property. Sakharov's draft as well as our own forced the conservatives to make a major shift to the left. As for the draft proposed by a lawyer of Saratov University, I must say that we would have used it as the basis of our work had we not had a draft of our own. So we have used whatever constructive ideas were offered. We intend to do the same in the future; that is, to take into account everything sensible and progressive when drafting the final version of the document, so that the Constitution may be accepted by all the peoples of Russia.

The experience of other countries was also taken into account during the drafting of the Constitution. This was criticised on the grounds of the Soviet Union's special conditions and experience.

We have quite a well-developed sense of anti-Europeanism. Russia certainly has a tendency towards isolationism. This may be a reaction to the barbaric methods with which Peter the Great imposed elements of European culture in Russia. While he may have succeeded in partially implanting what may be called industrial thinking when he cut a 'window to Europe', the spiritual and cultural fabric of the people remained untouched. As a result we have Russia, which is neither Europe nor Asia but a very special, very peculiar part of the world. That is probably why people of a European cast of mind perished in Russia where their ideas were repelled, a phenomenon aptly called 'woe from wit' by Alexander Griboyedov.

Whenever I hear that we should not use others' experience or learn from it, I always recall the example of Japan. The post-war restructuring of that country showed that the Americans have been able to implement firmly and precisely a European variant of development in a country with a unique and ancient culture. The model took root and incorporated traditional national elements.

The American Constitution has been working for two hundred years. What makes it so durable?

The American Constitution is very similar to the French Constitution. Although the Americans took into account the features of the traditional system of power, which had been largely shaped by the royal administration and the relations which had been formed among the colonists on American soil, they were mostly guided by the French Constitution, which can be seen even from the terminology.

The real life of a democratic society and the French slogans 'liberty, equality, fraternity' were also taken into account. The Founding Fathers were well acquainted with Paris and French culture, and some of the Constitution makers had taken an active part in the revolutionary events in France. Equally important was complete de-ideologisation, the utter lack of subordination to any idea. Finally there was the free spirit of farmers, which had been strengthened during the struggle for independence. The main subject of the Constitution is man, the individual. Since a person on American soil is a free individual, the main thrust of the Constitution is aimed at protecting the individual. The famous ten amendments deal with human rights.

Will the Russian Constitution last long?

It would be fine for the Constitution to be oriented to eternity, like such great documents as the Magna Carta and the codes of Hammurabi, Justinian and Napoleon. But it will be very difficult to do without amendments in a turbulent epoch like ours.

It might not be necessary to change the whole of the Constitution. Certain amendments may be adopted, as in normal societies, normal states, but the main body of the text should be of a strategic and long-term nature.

Who will be the master in Russia?

The question can be answered by the appearance of various kinds of property, since the owner is the master. What was known as the property of the entire people is being stripped of its mystique. The market demands a real master. Property is being personified and in its turn it personifies the question of who is master.

We are accustomed to the revolution's slogan 'all power to the soviets', while the draft of the new Constitution affirms the classic triad of legislative, executive and judicial power. Is there a contradiction here?

58

Yes, there is. The institution of soviet power must not be idealised. We soon understood that the fusion of legislative and executive powers is both anti-democratic and inefficient, so we began objectively to discuss the advisability of having elders, mayors and governors. World experience of municipal government is very useful and is one of the forms of representative power, but we confused it with the power of soviets. The fusion of Communist Party power with soviet power gave birth to an utterly unviable hybrid. Then during perestroika party committees were deprived of real power and emphasis was laid on strengthening soviets. It was proposed at one time to install presidiums within the system of executive power and then, to remove all executive committees and concentrate all power in soviets, which is very much like removing the government and investing the Presidium of the Supreme Soviet with executive functions. The Presidium, whose task is to direct the Supreme Soviet, would possess immense executive authority. Those who worked on the draft Constitution insisted on a system of representative bodies.

Please explain.

In 1905 Lenin came to the conclusion that the soviet which was formed in the town of Ivanovo–Voznesensk could replace such 'bourgeois' forms of power as municipalities.

How do soviets differ from municipalities?

Soviets had hardly any power throughout the history of our state. Power was primarily wielded by the partocracy, only a few executive functions being allotted to executive committees of soviets. When the slogan 'all power to the soviets' was revived (I also actively supported it) we expected that when the soviets acquired the power that had been usurped by city and regional party committees they would be able to use it effectively.

Did soviets actually receive real power?

Power is divided into legislative, executive and judicial branches throughout the world. The slogan 'all power to the soviets' calls for the concentration of power in the same hands, which opens the door to totalitarianism. It is most unfortunate that the implementation of the attractive slogan, for which our grandfathers and great grandfathers fought and for which we struggled, led to a palpably tragic situation. The soviets failed, and the fact that we gave them power did not make them a government of the people.

Gavriil Popov was right when he said that we need mayors; we probably need some other representatives of high power, and we certainly need strong authority.

Is a military reform being prepared? What will happen to the mammoth military–industrial complex and to people connected with servicing officers and men?

We need to distinguish the military–industrial complex from the army. These are two different entities. The independent firms functioning within the military–industrial complex should in the future be privatised and separated from the state and from the military. They should implement their commercial and other deals the way it is done all over the world. The military–industrial complex should be controlled by civil society, by legislators, and meet the army's requirements on a competitive basis.

The military units deployed on Russia's territory will evidently be regarded as a Russian army. I am for the army being a single body under the Union's command. The republics must not pull apart the nuclear-missile potential lest a Saddam Hussein emerges, but they should take part in decision-making, including the control of military–industrial enterprises.

The Russian government should certainly be informed about the army's activity on Russian territory. And I deem it my duty to strengthen good businesslike contacts with the army leadership and the army. Russian people have always had respect for the army. The present-day difficulties of the army reflect what is going on in society. How can any of society's subsystems be exempted when the entire society is in crisis? The army cannot be isolated from what is happening in our society, but the army's rigid structure and hierarchy can make its vices assume grotesque forms. The question of the army requires an urgent settlement.

The adoption of the Constitution will raise the question of the return of Russians to Russia, of our fellow countrymen not only abroad but also in Lithuania, Latvia, Estonia and other republics who wish to return to their homeland.

The treaties concluded with republics provide for normal living conditions not only for the indigenous population but also for people from other republics. We shall insist on the abrogation of discriminatory legislation and will make every effort to protect our fellow citizens outside Russian territory. We should also take care of those who wish to return.

But our potential for receiving people is extremely limited due to the general economic and political crisis, the problem of refugees from other regions of the country, the transition to market relations, and many other factors. Let me mention only one of the problems. The majority of the Soviet servicemen returning from Eastern Europe are young Russian men, officers and warrant officers, who have to be accommodated in Russia.

Officers relieved under the current army reduction programme (their pensionable age is quite low) also have to be accommodated. Formerly the centre could let them settle in practically any city or town of the Union, while now the entire burden is shifted onto Russia's shoulders.

I would therefore ask our fellow countrymen now living in other republics and intending to move to Russia to wait for a while. We need time to sort out Russian affairs. We badly need the '500 days' of which Boris Yeltsin spoke. Although the programme has been rejected by the Soviet President, we hope to improve matters considerably during that period. Then we shall be able to receive our countrymen in a renovated Russia.

We should first of all furnish better conditions for our farmers to enable them to increase the supply of food. Next we shall draw up a detailed programme for accommodating people who wish to come to Russia. We shall have to establish their number, their requirements, connections with relatives and historical roots, so that people will not have to roam the country, wasting time, money and nerves, but would know exactly what awaits them. All this is a matter for the not too distant future.

Is public opinion prepared to accept such approaches?

Formerly the country's leaders had unfailing support in all situations: everybody was unanimously 'for'. Not so now when the public wants to know for whom it votes and what the rating of candidates is. People may rise up in resistance, even if irrationally. Very much depends on the leader, the individual. The same is true of new laws which are supported by some and rejected by others.

What makes the situation in Russia complicated? We have announced a referendum during which enormous pressure will be exerted on the Supreme Soviet and the peoples of Russia. I already have a rough idea of the forms and scope of that pressure. It will be rough going. But the process will also have positive aspects, including the possibility of consolidating the real situation in Russia, including the Declaration on State Sovereignty, the laws which we have already adopted and the directions which we have chosen with the support of the people.

In spite of that support, which is due to the dynamic activity of the RSFSR Supreme Soviet and the government, we nurture no illusions since the important laws which we have adopted and are implementing to ensure Russia's economic independence have not brought substantial results. The centre and its departments still hold in their power Russia's economy, hundreds and thousands of enterprises and their workers. Although much of the financial structure and banking system has been placed under the control of the State Bank of Russia, they continue to operate as they were originally intended. For example, we have not yet secured the participation of our bank in the emission of money.

The central bureaucracy is neither capable of solving all problems nor allows us to solve them. Russia is not governed by us as yet. It is even hard to say by whom precisely it is governed; probably by obsolete, half-dead structures. We are setting up new structures, including market relations, despite the obstacles. The fact is that we can create elements of the market only after we have assumed full control over Russia's economy. We shall be able then to apply purely economic and governmental levers. We are making progress though the process is, as I have already said, very slow and very hard.

People facing the task of cardinal economic changes have to decide what should be done and in what order. Should they break things, modernise them or create them anew? The question now is what should be destroyed and what should be created.

To destroy is easier. We have in fact destroyed quite a lot. The whole point is that it is necessary to create at the same time. We have more than once turned to the Shatalin–Yavlinsky plan, which was an attempt to launch a real reform. The central government evades major changes, it is trying to patch up something, conduct a small-scale reorganisation or reshuffle some elements and links, without affecting the system itself. The centre is accustomed to taking away what has been earned, using administrative, not economic, methods. A thorough-going structural reform means the destruction of the old system and the simultaneous formation of new structures. The Shatalin plan contained both elements. But the implementation of the reform meant the loss of power by the centre, so the programme was buried.

Since our plan (which was intended for the entire country) was rejected we have to adjust our actions to realities. The implementation of reforms (I mean the processes of both privatisation and denationalisation) slowed down markedly. The transition to market relations can be accelerated only if Russia is really ruled by Russian authorities, which is what we are fighting for.

How strong is the opposition in the Russian parliament?

I believe that the substantial opposition in the Russian parliament and in Russia plays a constructive role. It enables us to improve laws amid stiff parliamentary struggle and to attain legal accuracy in our legislative practice. I would not call our opposition reactionary. Its members are conservatives in the good sense of the word.

How was the draft Constitution received by parliament?

There are two diametrically opposed attitudes: some describe the new

Constitution as a challenge to common sense; while others call it the most democratic Constitution in Russia's history. Parliament will have to work hard to improve the draft by taking into account the suggestions of the people, the Congress and specialists, to publicise the results of the draft's discussion, to prove the worth of the decisions taken and to explain their meaning to every citizen of Russia.

What are the most important ideas and amendments offered during the discussion of the draft Constitution at the Congress?

It is simply impossible to mention all the valuable proposals made at the Congress. The main thing is that we are now convinced that we are following the right course and have not missed any significant issues.

We shall have seriously to revise the draft's sections dealing with our republic's state-territorial organisation and Russia's relations with the autonomies within it. We must re-examine especially thoroughly the articles connected with the term 'federal lands'. I have had talks with deputies from Siberia, the Far East and ten national-territorial areas, which account for nearly 65 per cent of Russia's territory and about 6 per cent of its native population. These vast areas are being mercilessly ruined. It has been suggested, I think quite correctly, that national areas should be preserved or reformed into republics on land where the local people live in more or less compact groups. This could help to promote national culture and generally to improve the conditions of the nationalities. One thing that is clear is that we will have to work hard to find solutions to the complex national-territorial problem.

But the most important thing is the conceptual base, the platform underlying the draft Constitution. Nor should we forget that society must be prepared to accept that platform.

How can respect for the Constitution be cultivated?

Constitutions are known to operate directly in Western countries. In our case even official agencies are sometimes guided by by laws, rulings or instructions which often distort the meaning of the Constitution even when they do not contradict it directly.

You may remember the film in which an American policeman says something to a detained person who replies: 'You are violating Article 5 of the Constitution of the United States.' This is an instance of the direct action of the Constitution. If you ask a Soviet militiaman on the beat what he obeys, the Constitution, the law or the service regulations, he will most likely tell you that he obeys his sergeant. Yes, our people often follow the rulings of the 'sergeant', not of the law.

To inculcate respect for the Constitution, to teach people and government agencies to make proper use of their actual rights and fulfil their duties is a very hard but noble task. The activity of Russia's parliament shows that we are taking only the first steps in this direction.

IN THE COMMUNITY OF THE UNION

What are the general features of Russia's relations with other republics?

The fifteen union republics are legally independent, they formed a union of states; I emphasise, not a unitary, an integral centralised state, but a federal union of states established by the 1922 Union Treaty and the 1924 Constitution. In making treaties we naturally proceed from the premise that these independent states have voluntarily delegated certain powers to the Union's centre, to the central administration. Otherwise they are fully independent, sovereign states whose status was legalised by the Constitution back in 1936. Which means that we have, legally speaking, relations resting on the recognition of the republics' independence.

The potential, size of the population and in general the role of every republic in the Union are naturally different, and so also is their political role. There is no denying it, though we do not like to stress it, that the Russian Federation plays the key role in the Union. Russia is surrounded by other Union republics (with the exception of two Central Asian ones) with which it has very long borders.

We must compensate for the growing isolation of republics by strengthening horizontal links among them in conditions when the process of attaining sovereignty is rapidly developing and the political and economic independence of union republics is increasing. Practically every union republic objectively gravitates towards, in fact requires, the conclusion of agreements (treaties) with Russia. Why should this be opposed?

The national composition of the population of union republics also varies, even though the indigenous population is not in the majority in some of them. Kazakhstan, for instance, has fewer Kazakhs than Russians and people of other nationalities. This is probably why Kazakhstan is keen to develop bilateral relations with Russia and, let me stress it, we are promoting these very good relations. Though the situation is quite the opposite in Lithuania, with its predominantly indigenous population, the republic also wishes to conclude a treaty with the Russian Federation. When we conclude political and economic agreements we make provisions concerning the social and legal protection of the non-indigenous population of the given republic, Russians and other people from Russia. What is wrong with this? Why are the Russian authorities so severely criticised by presidential and party circles for this sensible policy?

Now take Moldova. During the tragic events there we had a treaty with that republic which helped to ease the tension. Groups of our deputies began to visit the troubled areas, the newly proclaimed Gagauz and Dniester republics, and took an active part in negotiations and helped stabilise the situation. Even though not all problems can be solved in this way, such treaties are a good instrument for quelling conflicts.

The Slavic factor is a very important aspect of our relationship with Ukraine and Belorussia, which should be used for bringing our states closer together. Our unity with other republics, besides political links and the objective historical community, has also a powerful economic basis. For instance, we have agreed with other Union states on the stable reciprocal delivery of goods and on promoting other forms of economic cooperation in conditions when many economic ties are severed and contractual commitments are often not honoured. Our political agreements serve as the basis for attaining economic ends. I cannot see the logic or reason for efforts to oppose this contractual practice.

Can we say that equitable economic exchange is a common feature of relations with all republics?

Hardly so, for these relations are based on a great number of links which often took decades to establish. I may say, for instance, that we hope that other union republics will soon be able to set up their enterprises on Russian territory, while our economic organisations will appear in other republics. Nor should we forget links between firms, cooperatives and advanced forms of specialisation. The system of market relations reaches far beyond the bounds of equitable exchange. It is, naturally, true that no economic benefit is possible without equitable exchange, correctly understood, and that economic benefit is the prime mover of production and trade, still more of a proper market where all legal subjects are equal and there is no place for the state.

Here is one example. The treaties concluded by Russia during troubled times with Estonia and Latvia were dominated not by economic but by human considerations, connected with the destiny of the Russian-speaking population and people from other republics, to which we were by no means indifferent. And we were also guided by concern for the fate of democracy in Russia and in the USSR.

In our proposals and treaties we insist on the necessity of cancelling discriminatory enactments and of bringing laws and inter-republican treaties into conformity with international norms in the field of human rights. Those who claim that 'Boris Yeltsin has signed plenty of treaties which do not meet the interests of the Russian-speaking population' are wrong, for the protection of the interests of people from Russia living in other republics is the primary and most important component of such treaties.

Their other component is, of course, economic interest. The Baltic republics have been performing quite efficiently, for instance, in agriculture and light industry. Can they be interested in breaking their economic links, say, with Leningrad, Kaliningrad, Novgorod and Pskov? Hardly so, especially since their vigorous attempts to establish national states of their own in conditions of their alienation from the Union are sooner or later likely to be successful. We should therefore promote good and friendly political, economic and cultural relations with them. We reject the attempts of the central agencies to oppose the conclusion of such treaties and object to unfounded and false accusations against us. We believe on the contrary, that the conclusion of treaties between Russia and other republics is an instance of fruitful and mutually beneficial cooperation. This is a policy of common sense, which is logical and stems from people's interests and demands.

How are Russia's relations with Ukraine shaping?

Russia and Ukraine are the biggest states of the Union in terms of both the size of their population and of their economic potential. They complement each other economically and that is why our economic links will develop very intensively. The fact that Russians account for a considerable part of the population of whole regions of the Ukraine, such as Donetsk, is also an important factor in our relations.

Take the problem of the Crimea. When we signed and then ratified a treaty with the Ukraine some argued that the Crimea is a Russian province, a Russian region and that everything should be put back in its old place. Though very painful, this problem is not beyond solution. Passions will subside and the acuteness of the issue will diminish if we are at one economically, if economic links organically interact with political ones. But the Ukraine is not homogeneous. There is a very strong pull for isolation in Western Ukraine. Some insist that since 'Russians have always oppressed the Ukraine, it is inconceivable that equal relations can be built with them. The new Union proposed by the Russian authorities will lead in the end to still greater oppression of the Ukrainian people'. I am positive, however, that these moods will change as our political, economic and cultural cooperation deepens.

We must not ignore another very serious factor. The Union of Russia with the Ukraine and other republics undermines the unitary approach on the part of the central administration; therefore the latter exerts heavy pressure on the union republics and tries to prevent the strengthening of friendly ties among them. The danger is enhanced by the fact that we live in conditions of shortage of everything while the distribution of material and technical resources is largely concentrated in the hands of the centre. The central authorities are thus able to place serious obstacles in the way of the economic development of both the Ukraine and Russia.

We are well aware of these obstacles. There was, for instance, a sudden reduction in the food supply of Moscow and Moscow Region, including deliveries from the Ukraine. Economic officialdom certainly played a role here. Ukraine is also beset by artificial difficulties which are in many ways associated with the deliberate policy of the centre. I know this well, even though I do not want to cite the evidence.

We have a realistic idea of our strength and the extent of our power-lessness, and we are also able to size up the centre's ability to oppose our direct links with the Ukraine, Kazakhstan and Belorussia.

Has the Russian parliament devised mechanisms for establishing contractual relations with other republics?

Not only have they been devised but they are already operating quite effectively. This is a comparatively new development for all of us, but also very promising, for it is the only way to extend economic links beyond national territories. It is well known that capital seeks its profitable appli-cation beyond its national border. Our political and economic actions follow the same direction as the objective processes connected with the division of labour. One of the problems is the lack of negotiating proced-ures, for which people's deputies have justly rebuked us.

Are the contracting parties interested in these relations?

They most certainly are. Specialists in the union republics are experienced people who well know what an economy is and how it should be regulated. Our common approaches to many matters may be new for us but not for world practice. Common sense prevails in many republics. Kazakhstan's President employs the services of a prominent American specialist and the Soviet economist, Yavlinsky, who is the President's adviser. In all the republics market structures are beginning to operate the way they did for centuries without asking the President or his ministers. This should be regarded as normal. When this happens in Russia, however, there is always a hue and cry. No, Russia does not challenge anyone but is simply trying to go its own way, to meet above all the interests of its peoples.

You spoke about Kazakhstan. What problems has Russia encountered there?

The problems we face in our relations with Kazakhstan are more com-plicated than in the case of Ukraine. The fact is that Kazakhstan is a raw-materials republic. For decades the centre used that exceptionally rich republic as a source of primary goods. While Russia itself is a source of raw materials for the world economy, Kazakhstan is an additional provider of primary goods for the Union, for Russia, the Ukraine and other republics. That is why our cooperation with Kazakhstan should promote the policy of diversifying its economy, equitable exchange and equal partnership in our trade. This is quite a difficult task. For instance, the consumer sector and the manufacture of finished products account for only 18 per cent of the republic's economy. Just think of it: about 80 per cent of that economy is connected with the extraction and primary processing of basic materials. Such is Kazakhstan today.

The people of Kazakhstan are certainly dissatisfied with this humiliating situation, for theirs is a country with immense potential. We therefore intend to help Kazakhstan by intensifying our economic cooperation and stepping up production connected with the purchase of raw materials, the consumer sector, machine building, processing agricultural produce and the manufacture of durable consumer goods. We will implement various forms of cooperation and specialisation. Meanwhile, Kazakhstan has immense possibilities in the field of grain production and animal husbandry. Since it cannot consume everything it produces it delivers large quantitites of agricultural produce to the Urals, Siberia and other industrial regions. Though this is profitable for both sides, the balance should change in Kazakhstan's favour.

Our renewed links are built on a bilateral basis. We can very easily enter the world market and we can exchange experience. There are tremendous posibilities for the development of such links between Russia and the Ukraine and between Russia and Kazakhstan. Hence the idea of forming a union of four republics as a promising model of cooperation. Vertical links would be augmented by horizontal ones, which should by no means be regarded as an attempt to undermine the Union.

The first stage of this initiative will link Russia, the Ukraine, Belorussia, Kazakhstan and Uzbekistan, which others can also join. We are preparing a treaty to be concluded with other republics.

In what way will the new treaties differ from the traditional links established by the old system?

There is a fundamental difference. While the old links were directly vertical from top to bottom, not the other way round, the renovated links will develop horizontally and directly among the equal parties to treaties (union states). Not only is the equality of the sides and their interests guaranteed, but international norms as well as traditions evolved over the centuries and tested by time are respected. We want our treaties to be commensurate with world standards.

Our traditional critics and new opponents are puzzled by the fact that Russia appeals to international law and to the United Nations. The latter has been much abused by certain critics. But hasn't the United Nations helped the situation in the Persian Gulf? Why can't we be guided in concluding treaties by the actions of that organisation, by documents which were prepared, among others, by our experts? The United Nations displays before the entire world community exceptional respect for the rights of various peoples and states, big and small. What is wrong with our concluding treaties in keeping with the requirements of the United Nations? The organisation is despised only by dictators and is supported by democratic states. Who are our critics then?

Water, soil and other resources were formerly the property of the Union, that is, of no one. What will the position be today?

When the Caspian Sea, for instance, belonged to no one it was destroyed by everyone. Or look what happened to the Aral Sea. Now that union republics have become independent, though not fully, their peoples realise that no one except them will be responsible for preserving nature, including rivers, lakes and forests. Ecological thinking is becoming (but has not yet become) a dominant factor now that it is applied not to abstract property but to concrete land, water, forests and mineral wealth belonging to a republic and its people both as a nation and as individual citizens. Take the notorious idea of forcing the northern rivers to run southwards, which could be taken up again in an entirely new sense. Let us consider, for instance, the River Ob in Siberia. Water is now Russian property. The authorities on whose territory the river flows begin to regard water as their actual property. This is one, but very important, aspect of the matter, since incantations about friendship of peoples are being replaced by a pragmatic approach, by economic and moral reckoning. Water is in fact a real value which creates benefits and at the same time something pure and sacred, something that cannot be given up to an organisation, bureaucracy, a soulless 'nothing'.

Why was it impossible to implement the project of turning rivers back? Specialists estimate that 60 per cent of their flow would be lost and result in the salinisation of soils and other harmful effects, since it was intended to make the water run not in pipes but along open canals dug in the earth. The project planners reasoned primitively and in fact criminally when they counted on obtaining in the end a mere 3–5 per cent of the total mass of water to be turned south.

The new conditions naturally encourage a new approach based on a sensible intake of water that would have no negative consequences. It is necessary and now quite possible to bring this limited amount of water to the required destination. People will be eager to do this because water has become, for the first time since October 1917, a real national asset. In conditions of the emerging market the category of a national asset being no one's will thus disappear. Such is the main result of the economic reforms and the recognition of the principle of private property and various forms of economic activity.

We should in general give more attention to detailed environmental programmes, increase investments in this area and step up nature protection measures. We should remember that certain things have no market value even in market conditions. One of them is Lake Baikal, a treasure store of our country. The experience of civilised countries shows us the proper way of safeguarding unique natural phenomena. I have analysed the efforts made by the United States and Canada to clean the Great Lakes, which I consider to be without precedent. Salmon, which disappeared about two hundred years ago, were caught in the Thames recently. It is high time for us to start using the experience of environmental movements in civilised countries. We should allocate far more funds for ecology than we ever did before, but the market is cruel in this respect. The history of the primary accumulation of capital demonstrates that society stops at nothing in its pursuit of profit. We should therefore mercilessly combat this tendency. This could be served both by legislation and ecological actions. We must have a special service and specially trained personnel. Treaties concluded by union republics should have provisions concerning the problem of ecological protection.

Is there something special about the treaty concluded with Belorussia?

The Russian Federation's economic relations with Belorussia have always been stable. Our cultural proximity has played a crucial role. Formerly there could be no political relations, of course, between union republics, and neither did we have them with the Slavic republic of Belorussia.

It was no accident that Alexander Solzhenitsyn pointed to the common historical roots of the Slavic countries. This is a powerful prerequisite for the harmonious development of their relations. It is true, however, that the current economic disintegration inevitably breeds contradictions due to the imbalance of trade, deliveries of equipment, and so on. Contradictions which always exist among states are aggravated in conditions of crisis. But civilisation also possesses mechanisms for regulating and settling disputes, which prevent them from developing into conflicts. The intensification of bilateral economic relations will certainly have an ameliorating effect on contradictions.

You have spoken of forces impeding the process of signing treaties with republics. Can you name them?

These are forces oriented to the centre's position, which manifest themselves most vividly in the Baltic countries. *Pravda* and some newspapers wrote even before the Lithuanian crisis about the Committee of National Salvation. What kind of a committee was it? It was a self-styled body which began to give orders to the army. It would be absurd to think that the army could point guns at people without orders. Where is the secret force which we have so far failed to detect? Curiously enough, the idea of national salvation committees and of self-defence detachments was born within the Communist Party of the Russian Federation (it was proposed by Polozkov at a plenary session of the party's Central Committee). Could it be that agents of Polozkov's Central Committee operated in the Baltic republics?

These forces, guided by the centre, refuse to see the sensible nature of our treaties with the republics. They declare everything that contradicts the interests of the central bureaucracy to be anti-popular, harmful and aimed at the disintegration of the Union. As if it has not been disintegrated by the efforts of the centre itself.

We are in fact trying to bring together the disintegrating Union, to gather around Russia peoples and republics which the central bureaucracy estranges and which it separates from one another with the help of tanks and submachine guns and by economic coercion.

The administrative–bureacratic system built its policy on falsehoods. Can this possibly be repeated?

Economic relations cannot be built on lies. The economy brooks no deception. Economic ties established by the market are not directly influenced by the state. If you deceive a partner even once, no one, not even the country's president, can make them continue doing business with you.

The well-known German industrialist Von Amerong told me: 'We have sympathy for you, for Russia, we want changes, but you must understand that even Mr Kohl cannot force us businessmen to negotiate with you until we have evidence of a favourable political and economic climate.' The President or the Chancellor cannot compel businessmen because people and firms are not obliged by law to obey in these matters the will of the political authority unless it is laid down in a legal enactment of that authority. Firms are independent economic organisations, legally known as subjects of the market. Economic independence alone gives them the real possibility of normal profitable operation as subjects of the market.

Are there questions of special interest concerning the Baltic states?

Nearly half of the population of Estonia and Latvia are Russian-speaking people. While we maintain good relations with the republics we must also show concern for the destiny of our fellow citizens, which is also reflected in the treaties.

The Baltic republics initially adopted discriminatory legal acts in regard to the non-indigenous population. This may have been done in response to the continuous pressure of the centre or in an attempt to provide better conditions for the indigenous population. Though we do not idealise the governments and parliaments of the Baltic republics and their decisions, we have to reckon with the will of these lawfully elected authorities.

Have we, for instance, always 'liked' the US government? We ascribed to it all kinds of things and accused it of many sins but we never called for its overthrow. Why then don't we (I mean the centre) recognise the legitimacy of the existence of republican authorities? It is necessary to discard these outdated imperial ambitions, to return to common sense and real life and take realities for what they are. We should also take the republics as they are. It is impossible to try to change the way things are in the republics from Moscow, from the Kremlin, only because the policy of the republican authorities does not agree with someone's views. A lot of things may not agree with President Gorbachev's views. For instance, he cannot accept the principle of private property, which is accepted by others. This matter can also be viewed differently. So we came to terms with Estonia and Latvia, which are now reviewing their laws and striking out articles discriminating against the Russian-speaking population. Who can say that this is bad?

Why do relations between the republics themselves develop differently from those between the republics and the centre?

We union republics find it easier to agree with one another because we respect one another, recognise one another's sovereignty and seek and find mutually acceptable decisions. We reject methods of political and economic pressure. Things are different with the centre, which does not wish to surrender its privileged position, to be transformed from a commander with unlimited powers into an executor of the decisions of a Union of Sovereign States.

Let me illustrate what I have said with the example of Russia. During the work of the Russian parliament the centre either ignored laws which we adopted or recognised them only to 'forget' their provisions the following day. This was immediately followed by accusations that we undermined their principles, violated order and interfered in others' affairs. These repeated departures from agreements that had been reached could not but result in mutual mistrust.

Take, for example, the '500 days' programme. Everything seemed to have been settled for agreed actions, yet the President repudiated at the last moment his decision which, incidentally, had been recorded in writing. A great many such agreements were disrupted. We counted, for instance, on hard currency remits for each republic. Since oil, gas, precious metals and stones extracted in Russia bring hard currency we thought we had a right to some of it. We seemed to have agreed with the President on this matter, but later he refused to abide by the agreement.

It was agreed at a meeting on 11 November 1990 between Gorbachev and Ryzhkov, on the one side, and Yeltsin, Silaev and me, on the other, that an inter-governmental commission would be formed in order to put an end to the 'war of laws' in the economic sphere, to make it possible to say exactly which enterprises remained under the centre's jurisdiction and which went over to us. But that agreement was not implemented either. There are many more such examples.

In the final analysis it would have been possible to agree to the priority of the centre had it been capable of efficient management, but the economy was only wrecked further during the six years of perestroika. Therefore we seek to protect Russia's interests from the arbitrary encroachments of the central agencies and to shift economic regulation to the level of republics and regions. Perhaps I have repeated this too often, but my heart aches for it.

After a provisional economic agreement was concluded and budgets were agreed, it appeared that there was a basis for settling questions with the centre in a peaceful manner. We were ready for that. But every day that followed brought a new presidential decree which nullified our programme of reviving the Russian economy. There followed what can be called a frontal assault on Russia. The central newspapers began to bait Yeltsin.

Our relations with union republics are built on a different basis. We cooperate as equal partners, take and give advice and consult one another. I am not aware of any cases of repudiation of mutual agreements. I am not idealising our relations, for we may have differences in the sphere of the economy and probably in the matter of human rights or of the protection of the Russian-speaking population or other peoples of Russia. But I trust that we can settle all these questions with our own efforts. The concord of the republics is a real basis for strengthening the new Union.

What is Russia doing to establish contacts with the Transcaucasian republics?

We are working on and, I hope, will soon sign treaties with Armenia and Azerbaijan, which I expect to play a major stabilising role in these republics. The current situation in Transcaucasia is well known. There is open antagonism, armed confrontation, bloodshed in Nagorno–Karabakh, the tragedy of South Ossetia. Such are today's realities, and that is why we attach such great importance to signing agreements with these union republics. We hope that these treaties will enable us to influence the republics' internal development. We are building a legal mechanism for protecting our interests, which is very important and which is ignored by our opponents.

Our deputies and commissions have visited Azerbaijan, Armenia, Nagorno–Karabakh, Georgia and South Ossetia and were very often confronted with an attitude which could be summed up as: 'Who has called for you? Why do you interfere in our affairs? You are after all just another republic like we are.' When we have concluded treaties it will be easier for us to fulfil serious peace-making functions on an inter-republican legal basis. The fact is that 'inter-republican' here means 'inter-national', and there is nothing wrong with this. Nor should we forget that many people from Russia live in these republics. We shall certainly strive to ensure their protection and their rights.

Our political treaties are accompanied by economic agreements. Our traditional links can be further extended and our interests are interlinked and mutually beneficial. Russia supplies these republics with manufactured goods, food and crude oil.

What are the problems associated with the preparation of treaties to be signed with the Central Asian republics?

We are close to beginning negotiations with Uzbekistan and with other Central Asian republics. Uzbekistan is a republic with a large population, extensive territory and a powerful industrial potential. However, its economy, like those of the other three Central Asian republics, suffers from the single-crop system of agriculture. Uzbekistan has for decades developed cotton growing to the detriment of grain production and even of animal husbandry, which had been traditionally practised there for centuries. The situation is so abnormal that the republic has no bread of its own and has to buy it elsewhere. Who is to blame for the troubles of the industrious, peaceable and kind Uzbek people? Russia is not.

Uzbekistan's problems are colossal. The standard of living of its people is below the average level of the Soviet Union. Our task is to help the republic rationally to use specialisation of production, raise the living standard and change the infrastructure. Uzbekistan is very rich in mineral resources. Russia is interested in accelerating the division of labour and it can help develop the machine-building complex, especially industries producing consumer goods. I think that here we have good opportunities for extending political, economic and cultural links. We have already conducted preliminary negotiations with Uzbekistan's President, Islam Karimov, who has a great interest in a durable treaty with Russia. The President is a sincere, broad-thinking politician.

Is it possible to project the relations shaping on the international scene to what is emerging in our country?

Of course it is. I believe that international economic experience should be fully taken into account in our practice. Inter-republican relations, both political and economic, evolve into international relations. However, this is still not recognised at the level of the central administration, of the country's President, even though this recognition has been officially recorded in the 'nine-plus-one' agreement.

I think that the Union will exist as a confederation, something like the Common Market. This seems to me to be the only way of saving the Union, the general idea of a union, and of civilisation in general. Only such an approach on the part of the centre and of the union republics can guarantee painless and conflict-free development in the future since we have lost the present.

The Lithuanian crisis taught us the lesson of pressure by force. The actions of the centre only contributed to the disintegration of the USSR. As a professional economist I cannot justify the separation of republics, though I fully support their indomitable striving for independence. But I am sure that, if we take the path of common sense and take into account the interests of the majority of peoples who wish to establish independent homelands of their own, we shall very soon see the return of union republics, including the Baltic ones, into a new Union, their unification on the basis of, above all, economic links.

Why should this be so? Because we are economically interconnected. We will not be able to enter the world market singly since the world economy will repel us. We shall find really free economic space during the next ten to fifteen years only on the territory of the Soviet Union. Since mutual attraction will be strong, Russia seeks to prepare the ground on which union republics will be able to become fully independent within the framework of a Commonwealth, a Union or whatever else such a community of states may be called.

5

ECONOMIC TRANSFORMATION

RUSSIA AND THE ECONOMIC CRISIS

What is the central government? A sixteenth republic? What does it stand for?

There is no such a provision, or such a 'republic', in the Constitution. But no matter whether we like it or not, the central government is a reality, our bitter reality. Clearly, it is an absurd reality. The central government has 'seized' so many boundless functions and such vast possibilities of planning and distribution of resources that surpass all reasonable limits. The central government is like a lord, and in this system Russia is not a sovereign republic but an autonomy. We have hardly anything at all. The Russian Supplies Committee, in terms of resources, possibilities and scale of operation, is far inferior even to the Supply Committee of Moscow. The central government is a giant wielding economic authority. It has the real power. Little wonder, the republics resent this situation and demand that it be changed.

First. The republics have become convinced that the central government is powerless to deal with economic problems. So they are asserting their right to their economic resources.

Second. This process objectively leads to more independence for the republics.

Third. The world is in a state of integration. In the West integration processes are developing on a voluntary and equitable footing, on the basis of economic imperatives, through the world market. Western commodity producers are free. They freely cross national frontiers, expanding their production and invigorating integration and division of labour processes. There is the free movement of labour, capital and commodities.

Here the situation is different. If the republics had the central government's support and gained independence, they would move towards each other more quickly. Russia must build its relations with the other republics and the central government as an independent state.

We are signing agreements with other republics, thereby laying the groundwork for a renewed Union and creating a certain degree of economic stability. But our independence is irritating the central government.

Do you mean to say the central government's policy differs from Russia's policy?

At first I felt there would be a unity of goals and methods in the central government's and Russia's policies. But life has proved me wrong. There are contradictions between a movement to the market and a return to planning, between democratic change and neo-Bolshevik and neo-totalitarian coercion, and between economic rationality and administrative rule. The relationship between the central government and Russia is full of these contradictions. The central government's reneging on reforms has cost the people dear. There are no foodstuffs, clothing or other essential goods in the shops. The price and monetary reforms have slowed down economic progress. The army patrols the streets. All this is like a tragic farce.

I would not wish to see any evil design behind all these events, but facts are stubborn and reveal policy. The President and his Cabinet of Ministers remain committed to traditional methods and ideology stemming from Communist Party headquarters in Old Square. Old Square and Krasnaya Presnya increasingly misunderstand each other.

Does the central government coordinate its decisions with Russia?

Hardly ever. Few decisions or actions have been coordinated. Frankly speaking, the central government has imposed an information blockade on us. We are working openly, trying to explain our economic, cultural and international policies. The central government, on the other hand, has made one unexpected move after another, perplexing the world. That is what happened with Vilnius and Riga, and that is how they prepared the monetary reform. True, with the 'nine-plus-one' agreement, I hope we will be able somehow to resolve these differences peacefully.

How is the problem of property treated in the draft Russian Constitution? Doesn't the slogan 'factories to the workers, land to the peasants' mark a return to classic Soviet principles? To whom will schools and hospitals go? If factories are to go to workers, why then not to engineers, designers, technicians? Why not to managers?

I think that what you have said concerning the worker, the manager and the engineer is correct, but let us return to today's realities and their history. For decades we were dominated by state-monopoly ownership, which precluded efficient economic development. State-monopoly property is not geared to people's interests and requirements, the saving of resources and the reduction of the capital–output ratio and of prices of goods and services. The philosophy of planned losses and the neglect of society's interests are inherent properties of state-monopoly ownership, which can be eliminated only by removing the very foundations of this ownership.

State-monopoly ownership reduced the efficiency of social production. The continuous worsening of the quality of goods became a persistent tendency, which undermined the very future of socialism. Total planning within the framework of state property inevitably created and perpetuated a shortage economy motivated only by harsh orders from the centre, the effect of which was in most cases contrary to what was intended.

The inefficiency of our economy had long been obvious to people both 'at the bottom' and 'on top', yet the latter for many years held rigidly to old methods of improving the situation by setting up new ministries, departments and economic units and enrolling more personnel for the purpose of 'management' and 'control'. As a result our national economy has not yet become an economic complex integrated by the division of labour. These processes are thwarted by ministries and departments which sever natural economic ties.

These ministerial and departmental structures, which form the basis of state-monopoly socialism, block all progressive changes in the economy, and isolate it from the world market. They suppress scientific and technological progress and undermine enterprises and their workers. What we call state, or public, property is in fact the property of ministries. The word 'state' serves here as a political cover for the new type of property. All this is admittedly a direct consequence of the ideas which seemed so alluring during the first years after October 1917. The logical development of the principle of state property could not but lead to what we now call the administrative-bureaucratic system.

Thus we actually stand in need, as was the case at the time of the New Economic Policy, of breaking down the existing relations of production. The economic results of the first years of perestroika show convincingly that we can no longer delay or search for compromises. The measures that have been taken are quite insufficient for removing state-monopoly property, fortified by the rigid principles of sectoral organisation, and a radical reform is impossible without the destruction of that system.

What steps are required by the reform?

First. It is necessary to abolish most of the ministries and departments and transfer their enterprises to local soviets, which will form a 'municipal' economy of their own. This will create what may be called a special, third form of socialist property along with state and cooperative property.

Second. The development of cooperative property is much too slow to make cooperation an economic force capable of competing with state enterprises. This is primarily due, I think, to the covert but powerful resistance of the administrative-bureaucratic system. As a result, cooperatives are objectively compelled to engage in matters which are not essential from the viewpoint of social interests. It follows that the development of cooperative property in all spheres and sectors of the economy should become one of the priority directions of the reform instead of being its side effect.

Third. 'Mixed' forms of property (with the participation of foreign capital) are developing much too slowly against extremely heavy odds. There is a bitter irony in the fact that the central newspapers announce with delight that three hundred joint ventures have been formed. Given the scale of our country, this figure may well be equated to zero. There has been enough time to set up at least five to ten thousand such enterprises, which is the minimal amount at which quantity begins to grow into quality. The main obstacles to the growth of these enterprises lie not only in the sphere of production but also of management, which is permeated with atrocious bureaucracy, inconceivable in a civilised country, and the traditional fear that 'something untowards may happen'. Foreign and 'mixed' forms of property used efficiently consolidate the much desired principle of competition in our economy.

Fourth. It is necessary to deprive ministries of the possibility of identifying their activity with that of the state. The worst kind of monopoly is state monopoly, which has a political meaning. To this end, it is advisable to reorganise the work of state enterprises, which will remain within the system of 'central subordination' after most of the ministries are dismantled. They should probably be restructured after the pattern of ordinary firms under a law similar to anti-trust acts. When this is done it will be possible to speak about state property proper stripped of its 'ministerial' connotations. This state property will be able to represent more fully the interests of the whole people and not of sectoral bureaucracy.

A socialist commodity economy is a necessary stage of development of the productive forces of a socialist country which has started to advance economically in conditions of very backward forms of labour and of undeveloped production. It is necessary resolutely to dismantle the state-monopoly structures, whose formation served only to consolidate and stabilise the relations of the transition period.

What are the Russian leaders' views on credits? What do you think of the central government's credit policy?

We need credits, large and small. But the terms are what matters, how the credits are used, and how we get them. I have said time and again that it is utterly useless to receive large foreign loans, place them in our national banks and use them as we please. Our economy is insensitive to dollar transfers. There is another way which is simpler and more realistic, credits for particular projects at an industry or regional level. There are good possibilities for cooperation with Mercedes Benz. They are prepared to give us credits and build a medium-sized factory to manufacture fairly inexpensive Mercedes cars, 200,000 a year. The Soviet side has been inactive in this respect, which is wrong. It is for this kind of project that we need to take credits. As for the hard currency the President is getting, we never see it. We do not know where it goes, though it is Russia and the other republics that will have to pay in the end. The central government is using credits and hard currency irresponsibly. So foreign investors should decide and be clear that they would stand to gain more if they dealt with the republics instead of the central administration.

Is it possible to establish direct contacts with the West? How will enterprises benefit in this respect if they come under Russia's jurisdiction?

Russian laws proclaim economic freedom for them, including independent operations in external markets. They can claim their rights and demand complete freedom from central authorities. If we consolidate our position and provide enterprises with adequate legislation, the foreign-currency situation will change. We aim to separate the economy from the state and make as many state-owned enterprises as possible independent, that is, turn them into market agents. We have no intention of creating 'our own' ministries so that they instead of the central ones can dictate to enterprises.

That would appear more beneficial to the state, too.

Very much so. An enterprise will give part of its foreign currency to the treasury, and keep the rest for its workers and shareholders, and for investment to build up production. In this case, direct horizontal ties between countries, republics, industries and enterprises will be strengthened, providing better conditions for a faster transition to a market. These ties are now hamstrung, for a number of reasons. There is political instability, but, more importantly, it is the wrong choice of economic reforms by the central administration.

The Russian economy has great potential. The West realises this and is prepared to make large investments. Unfortunately, there is a 'but'.

Business people are aware of the kind of policy pursued by the Soviet President and his government, and hold back from investing money. Furthermore, the central government distorts the image of our leaders, including Boris Yeltsin. It gives false information about our laws and enforces an information blockade against our parliament. Russia is not introducing its own currency or creating customs services, but we are doing much to be able to pursue an independent policy. Otherwise reforms will not succeed, and we need reforms. We will have to answer to the people. What is Valentin Pavlov's responsibility? If he is forced to resign, he will take charge of a powerful financial or industrial association and later, like Nikolai Ryzhkov, will contend for the role of 'Russia's leader'. The thing about our top-level officials is their total cynicism.

Why are some enterprises continuing to cling to the centralised structures? Because their managers are often linked to central agencies. The Supply Committee (Gossnab) controls the resources. As long as this behemoth exists, with its unlimited possibilities of patronage, enterprises will cling to it. And these resources are taken away from the republics, especially Russia. So it is necessary to abolish the Supply Committee so that the republics can supply their enterprises themselves. As long as these remain dependent on the central government, they will suffer from burdensome taxes and eke out a miserable existence, clinging to centralised structures. If they pass to Russian jurisdiction, they will gain economic freedom.

Equally, we are trying to regulate relations between enterprises and local authorities. We are creating a tax system whereby local authorities will know what taxes they are entitled to, from what enterprises and how much. And the enterprises must know how much to pay in taxes and to whom.

What, in your opinion, are the causes of current economic problems?

Difficulties and imbalances accompanied the development of our economy at all stages. On coming to power, governments always start by choosing a policy, and it usually does not take long to determine whether it is a correct or a wrong one. A strategic, long-term course is quite another thing. For no matter what President or government comes to power in, say, the United States, its long-term policy does not undergo serious changes. Certain principles remain constant, such as support for business; a commitment to external economic ties and international cooperation; maintaining its currency and its protection throughout the world; attraction of foreign investments, that is, the long-term priorities of practically all modern states integrated into a single system of international economic relations.

The differences in the activities of certain governments stem from the difference in the methods of implementing these long-term goals.

81

Naturally, mistakes are possible, but in a market economy they are not decisive since the principle of private property limits the interference of politicians in the economy. In our country, any change in economic policy immediately affects all our huge economy. Why is this so? Because the economy is integrated into the state apparatus.

Ours is a state economy, a state-monopoly economy. This is the main danger and the key reason for the permanent economic crisis. This means that the subjective factor in our 'socialist' conditions is extremely important. The economy is built into the state apparatus, it is not simply monopolised by the state, but also politicised and ideologised. What we have is an absurdity, an irrational thing, although we have become accustomed to it. All the attempts, therefore, to imbue the economy with an inner logic through reforms encounter tremendous difficulties.

You have touched upon the problem of economic balance. Is it connected with the notion of equilibrium?

Equilibrium implies objective proportions in the structure of the economy, which basically works for the consumer. Balance through equilibrium should replace the activity of the State Planning Committee (Gosplan), but in our country the 'planned system' still takes the place of equilibrium, which means that officials determine the structure of the economy. But equilibrium cannot be established by means of directives but depends on a balance brought about by activity designed to overcome the scarcity of goods. What people buy, how they spend their money, how industry, farming and services operate, what goods people need, what is sold in the market and what not, all these are objective processes which should not be dependent on the whims of somebody in the government. The economy should be freed from the grip of the state. Among the prerequisites of a balanced economy, the economy of equilibrium, are the recognition of the principle of private ownership, the demonopolisation of the state economy, and the formation of market structures and conditions for competition.

Economic equilibrium is a notion first introduced by Alexander Bogdanov, a man of truly encyclopaedic erudition. In 1929 Stalin no longer allowed his ideas to be used in academic debate. At that time economic planning was introduced administratively, which brought suffering to the people and doomed them to poverty. A balanced economy is possible only as a result of the activities of free commodity producers in a free market. Our task is to create such conditions when the economy itself becomes a factor of balanced development, that is, to build up a mixed economy where the principle of private ownership would be fully recognised. Only then will the principle of competition begin to operate, and without this the normal development of the economy is impossible. Any economy, call it what you like, capitalist, socialist, communist, the label is unimportant.

World experience has proved that the state sector can function efficiently based on the free firm. Our system of state management of the economy is a powerful brake on genuine reform and inhibits the modernisation of obsolete structures and their dismantling in accordance with new tasks. Unfortunately, there are few changes in the centre, and everything tends towards the continuous growth of the government apparatus which controls the economy. The merger of ministries does nothing to assist integration processes in the economy. For at least three decades the branch division has obstructed economic reform. Our economy is not a single national economic complex, despite all the statements to the contrary, but is divided into 'fiefdoms', ministries and departments.

The Law on State Enterprises (Associations) of July 1987 is not going in the right direction. It is subordinated to the interests of ministries, which approach the entire national economy through the prism of 'their' interests. So although the ministries and their enterprises always fulfilled their plans, the 'economic health' of the state was drastically worsening, prices were rising, the volume of production was decreasing; there was an increasing shortage of commodities and although wages were rising, the difference was immediately 'eaten up' by inflation and rising prices. The ministries lost the possibility of managing 'their' economies, 'their ministates'. The crisis of the ministerial-branch management of the economy is a real fact of life.

Some blame the shadow economy, which refuses to obey the law. Is there any truth in this statement?

The shadow economy is a normal reaction of society to the abnormal situation in the economy. In my articles written three years ago I started calling it not shadow or parallel, but underground. This economy reached tremendous dimensions and is mostly responsible for the shortages. It has become closely interwoven with the party, soviet, economic and administrative structures which are opposed to the reforms. Above all, they hate the government of the Russian Federation and do their best to set the people against it. Party functionaries have actively penetrated the underground economy by buying enterprises, land, buildings, forming dummy joint ventures and even buying real estate in West European countries.

While the part played by the shadow economy is great, what we are really faced with is the crisis of the economic system based on state-monopoly ownership. If the centre had been able in good time to realise that the crisis was caused by the exhaustion of efficient economic management on the basis of state ownership, we would have been able to adopt the law on ownership and other similar laws not six years after the reforms were started but at least two or three years earlier. I am afraid that even today the Union government fails to realise the necessity of accelerating the pluralisation of the economy and of quickly introducing various forms of ownership and management. Too many words and too few deeds.

The government does not have a concept of economic reform. It is not enough to adopt all kinds of 'programmes'. The government programme should rely on legislative decisions and be translated into a detailed, properly substantiated long-term course, a long-term economic doctrine. But the centre does not have a clear idea of a new economic mechanism. This is probably the reason for the lack of resolution and the half-hearted decisions and sharp changes in government course, as well as for the implementation of harsh measures which do not advance reform and which do not challenge corporate interests (state expenditures, allocations for the military–industrial complex and so on) but worsen people's wellbeing. We are faced with a real inability to draft a long-term economic policy. Consequently, there is no idea of how to emerge from the present situation. At the same time, the responsibility for the disintegration of the economy is shifted on to the republics and, primarily, on Russia.

The reforms exposed the lack of viability of the economic system which took shape in our country. We in Russia are searching for the root causes of the crisis and test economic mechanisms which would make it possible to overcome this crisis. For instance, at the Third Russian Congress of People's Deputies Boris Yeltsin proposed a way of overcoming the economic crisis.

In what republic are the destructive consequences of the economic crisis most strongly felt?

In Russia.

What sectors of the economy are most gravely affected by the crisis? Would it be correct to say that the crisis seriously damaged the defence industries as well?

Defence industry has always been in a privileged position. It received more investment and the process of renovation and modernisation was more rapid and the wages were higher, as were the skills of its employees. Naturally, this industry also feels the effect of the crisis, largely in connection with conversion, which is being carried out irresolutely and unprofessionally, thus jeopardising the programme in its entirety. The situation is rather complicated in this sphere too. Many leaders of the military–industrial complex try to preserve their production intact, just in case. With such a half-hearted approach, there will neither be conversion, nor new production, while the workers suffer. Others in the military–industrial complex are for radical reforms and would like to abandon costly programmes such as the construction of aircraft carriers, tanks and missiles, in favour of civil production. This means that the military–industrial complex deserves our close attention, especially as the majority of its enterprises are located on Russian territory.

What about other sectors?

There is practically not a single branch which has not suffered. The most gravely affected are the light, mining and oil industries, which require constant investments. And where can we get them? At one time it appeared that we led the planet in the space industry. Again a big lie. This branch is in a very bad way compared, say, with the space industry of the USA. All talk about advanced technology and competitiveness is obviously propaganda. To be able to achieve the same results we have to spend much more than the West. Either we have no technologies or very few which can withstand competition in world markets. They still have to be created. How is this to be done? Only through the acceleration of the development of the mixed economy and cooperation with foreign partners. Otherwise we will continue to lag behind and the gap will widen.

What is your attitude to the assistance we render Cuba, North Korea, Afghanistan and so on?

We must render this assistance for we are responsible for the crisis situation in these countries. But this assistance should be purely humanitarian. Why should we supply weapons, moreover, in such huge quantities?

What was the stand of Russia during the adoption of the state budget for 1991?

We have taken the course of payments and contributions and refused to pay direct taxes from Russia's enterprises into the state budget. Still there are a lot of problems here: we are virtually strangled by the central government. For instance, almost the entire currency profit of Russia's enterprises is accumulated by the central administration, which is contrary to our laws and causes serious dissatisfaction on the part of the enterprises and their work collectives.

How will Russia operate in the banking sphere?

Russia's parliament has formed two banks, the Central Bank of Russia and the Foreign Trade Bank of Russia. Although Russia has got a certain freedom, it is far from full. For instance, we have no part in the control over money emission. Our task is to put the banking system in our territory in order: state and foreign trade banks, and commercial banks. Unlike other republics, we do not intend to issue our own currency but we would like to take part in the control over the emission process.

Is the prospect of having our own, Russian, money feasible?

Everything depends on circumstances. If the central government joins us in our efforts to stabilise the economy, then there will be no need for Russia to have her own currency. Another version of the development of events is possible if the central government interferes with our efforts. It would be enough for them to continue with uncontrolled money emission. In this case it is quite possible that we will be forced to consider the question of our own currency. Mind you, I said 'consider', not 'introduce'.

What is it, our rouble? If it is impossible to buy anything with it in our domestic market, to say nothing of the international market, then the level of exploitation of every citizen is increased manyfold. The state takes from people their health, strength, abilities and intellect, and in return gives banknotes which are in effect counterfeit, for they are not money at all. A convertible currency presupposes limits to state arbitrariness and the observance of international rules, the economic protection of people and their economic rights.

What part do wages play in the economic crisis?

In the last fifteen years the rate of wages growth in the country was rather high. By the end of 1990 the average monthly wage exceeded 200 roubles, but there is a peculiar feature to this rise. When the growth rate of wages exceeds the growth of labour productivity, it is bound to lead to the appearance of disproportions in the national economy. Earned money is devalued and the shortage of consumer goods grows. These phenomena have been characteristic features of our economy for a long time. The difference between wages in the higher and lower brackets began rapidly to disappear. For instance, if before the revolution the ratio between the wages of a skilled turner and an apprentice was 40:1, now it is 5:1. Gradually the difference in wages between various categories of workers began to disappear. The levelling (uravnilovka) approach became a reality.

Now we are trying to raise the incentive value of wages. But we must admit that the former, levelling attitude still prevails. The main consequence of low wage rates and the levelling approach are mismanagement, the lack of responsibility, the indifferent attitude on the part of the workers to the results of their enterprises' operations; the absence of stimulants for labour; the absence of the labour market stemming from the state monopoly on the means of production. This means that the state has turned its worker if not into a slave, then into a serf. In such conditions it is difficult to make the worker work well. The so-called compensations accompanying the price reform have further aggravated the situation with wages. Today the sphere of labour relations is pregnant with dangerous conflicts. If the situation is not rectified in the near future, Boris Yeltsin himself will not be able to stop the strikes.

What is Russia doing to overcome the chaos in the economic sphere?

First of all, we are taking measures to improve the entire system of power. We have adopted two laws on the activity of the soviets. According to one of these laws, the lower executive bodies are subordinated to the higher ones, which means that we have restored the hierarchy of the executive bodies of power. Still, this is not sufficient.

We are doing our best to accelerate the drafting of the law on local government and local soviets. Until we improve the whole system of local power we cannot count on the success of our reforms. At the same time, the Supreme Soviet of the RSFSR has extended the economic possibilities of the soviets by giving them the right independently to conclude agreements with enterprises on the basis of economic contracts and to engage in export and import operations. However, central government bodies interfere with these activities of both republican and local power organs.

The process of real privatisation, the separation of the economy from state and political structures, is bound to create practical opportunities for economic freedom as the system of compulsion disappears. Democracy has struck deep roots. The state economy has begun to disintegrate. So it is our task to assume control over the process of the disintegration of the state economy, at the same time rapidly forming market structures and creating parallel, non-state, forms of economic management. There is no other way.

We have to overcome not only the resistance of the bureaucratic forces of the central administration, but also 'our own' republican and local opposition, some of which we have inherited from the past, and some of which are new-born. Many local bodies of power prefer to ignore our laws and blatantly oppose our official state policy.

THE '500 DAYS' PLAN AND BEYOND

The '500 days' programme will go down in economic history and in the history of our country, Russia and perestroika as a programme of great hopes and bitter, tragic disappointments. Is there a mystery in what happened to it?

No, there is no mystery. As soon as we came to power and began to deal with Russia's affairs we felt the urgent need to rebuild our homeland, above all by carrying out an economic reform. Boris Yeltsin won both during the elections and at the First Congress, and therefore his platform was naturally taken as the basis of our work. We began to search for ways of improving the economic situation as soon as possible, drawing up long-term programmes of economic development, planning an agrarian reform and looking for opportunities to take advantage of the techno-logical revolution. Russia's economy is closely linked with the economies of other union republics and these links are of strategic, vital importance in conditions of the state-monopoly economy, burdened by countless shortages. Suffice it to recall how dozens of factories all over the Soviet Union had to stop work when a single factory in Nagorno–Karabakh, the one and only in the whole country producing a certain item, was blockaded. When we say 'monopoly' we usually think of some colossal enterprise. But monopoly is above all an economic system in which even a small factory specialises in the manufacture of articles or parts necessary for hundreds of big enterprises.

Russia's independent advance along the road of reforms will be extremely difficult, though possible, in conditions of an acute shortage of everything that can be manufactured, of monopoly relations. We came to the conclusion that profound structural changes and reforms aimed at establishing a market had to be implemented in close connection and coordination with all republics. When we invited republics to cooperate they responded quite readily, including the Baltic, Central Asian and Transcaucasian republics and Moldova, not to mention Ukraine and Belorussia.

The Chairman of the Russian Supreme Soviet and the President of the USSR had a long talk, the results of which were summed up in an agreement between Yeltsin and Silaev, on the one hand, and Gorbachev and Ryzhkov, on the other, on 27 July 1990 to draft a coordinated programme of transition to a market economy as the basis of the economic part of the Union Treaty. A working group was established under the supervision of Yeltsin and Gorbachev to incorporate the experience of Russia and other republics in a programme to be submitted not later than 15 September 1990.

Senior officials of state planning commissions and academics from practically all union republics and from fourteen autonomous republics of Russia took part in the work. The best minds in the country enthusi-astically participated on drafting the programme. Lithuania, it seems, was prevented from participating by doubts over whether the appropriate agreement would be signed. At that stage the interests of Russia and the centre were represented by the Gorbachev–Yeltsin alliance and by the group including Shatalin, Yavlinsky and other experts. The programme was conceived and elaborated as a Union, not only Russian, project. Although Russian approaches were used, the programme's goal was a Union market, which was then considered quite possible.

But soon after the work started I was alarmed by a remark by Leonid Abalkin, the minister responsible for the economic reform programme, that 'We have to fulfil the assignment of the Supreme Soviet of the USSR' (he meant the finalisation of the programme of the USSR government proposed by Nikolai Ryzhkov and rejected in May 1990 by the Supreme Soviet of the USSR). Abalkin began to cast doubts on the possibility of the satisfactory drafting of the programme under the pretext that Yavlinsky had worked in his government commission and invested his best ideas into 'the other' programme and thus would not be able to offer anything new. Abalkin claimed that the government programme took into account international experience, that it was attractive and had imbibed the experience of academicians and other distinguished economists, and that it opened up immense prospects. It was suggested in general that one could hardly expect anything new from the joint programme of the President of the USSR and the Chairman of the Supreme Soviet of the Russian Federation. Thus did the Ryzhkov government for the first time come out openly against the President. I pointed this out at the time and warned the President of opposition to his course by his government.

I realised that the criticism could hardly have been initiated by Abalkin, the thirteenth deputy of the Prime Minister, but was rather a result of the non-acceptance of the programme by the government. I do not think the President had a clear-cut position at the initial stage, and the attitude of the central government to the programme only crystallised as the programme took shape. It soon became clear clear that its implementation would require a radical reorganisation of the government and the abolition of its powerful monstrous ministries and departments. This would naturally result in a considerable reduction of the central government's powers and the strengthening of coordination between union republics and reform processes. Union states were to form an economic alliance and collaborate through cooperation, real integration and the division of labour by means of bilateral, multilateral and other links. The plan was to create a grouping similar to those existing abroad, especially in Western Europe. This would also bring the republics closer together politically and probably avert the threat of the Union's disintegration. But all this was against the corporate interests of the Ryzhkov government.

When Boris Yeltsin conducted a meeting of Shatalin's group on 1 September 1990, I spoke highly of the programme and suggested that it would be proper to prepare a Russian variant in view of the possible blocking of the project by the central government. I was unfortunately unable to persuade either the Chairman of the Russian parliament or Yavlinsky's group at that time, despite my serious concern about the possible failure of our 'undertaking'. These apprehensions were justified when the President in fact refused to support the programme when it was discussed at an enlarged meeting of the Presidential Council. I spoke very harshly at the meeting, where I argued that the Ryzhkov government posed a grave threat to society and demanded its resignation.

This is how Gorbachev turned away from the market. The Kremlin began to issue 'new variants' of the programme almost every day. They were so numerous they began to confuse even experts. There was the renewed programme, the edited one, Abel Aganbegyan's first version, Aganbegyan's second version, the government (Abalkin's) programme, the President's programme. There appeared in the end, as you know, the 'Guidelines' which the President proposed to the Supreme Soviet of the USSR. Thus was buried the '500 days' programme which, to my mind, was the last historical chance of keeping all fifteen republics within the USSR.

Whom did Abalkin and Ryzhkov defend? Was it themselves or an ideology?

The good thing about Shatalin's programme was that it was broken down into ten-day units, months and longer periods, something that had never been done before, and stipulated precisely: 100 days, 200 days, privatisation of such and such sectors and spheres and reorganisation of the banking system within such and such period and of the financial system at such and such a time. It listed practically all basic actions: who precisely does what, which agencies are to be removed, which are to be retained and which are to be set up anew, who is to be vested with what powers, and so on. The programme prescribed the responsibilities of concrete persons for concrete matters, which was frightening for our people accustomed to having rights but not responsibilities, so that no one is ever accountable for anything. Work or idle, equally without effect, is our classic rule, while the basic principle of the '500 days' programme was that each has a concrete job to do and concrete responsibility and has to work to attain a definite aim.

The programme also envisaged, of course, the genuine independence of union republics accompanied, however, with a substantial strengthening of the centre's executive authority. Republics were ready to hand over to the President more powers than they are prepared to give today because they knew that the powers would be used to implement really effective measures for reforming the economy along market lines. That is why independent actions of local authorities were to be disallowed, the adoption of laws contrary to the reform was to be prohibited, strict discipline was to be introduced and a ban (a kind of moratorium) was to be imposed on all actions running counter to the programme.

We did much work with trade unions to secure their support. All in all, there was an exceptionally favourable and probably a unique historical opportunity for the real consolidation of all socio-political forces. People began to believe in the project and there were signs of a favourable turn of the public sentiment. But the programme was rejected by the central bureaucracy, the party structures and the reactionary forces of the country, which had for decades ruled and controlled without answering for anything and were now afraid of losing power. Regrettably, these forces destroyed Abalkin, whom I have known for many years and sincerely respect. Sad as it is, he played an exceptionally reactionary role in this matter.

The programme required a reduction of government expenditure, in particular, of defence spending. Was pressure exerted by the military–industrial complex as well as the state apparatus?

It was, to be sure, but the most important factor was Gorbachev's indecision. Even the strongest pressure of the military–industrial circles could be overcome at that period when the programme was supported by the people. The military–industrial lobby could not hold much sway if the President was committed and firmly pursued the course of implementing the programme. The will of a state's leader plays an immense role during periods of transition. We have been well aware during our leader's 'reign' of six years of his vacillation, hesitancy and fear of taking on responsibility.

It is one thing to be able to pass between Scylla and Charybdis and quite another to make a historical choice, for which one must have both a vigorous will and a proper sense of responsibility to one's people. Conversely, the ability to find one's bearings in bureaucratic corridors, set people at loggerheads and manipulate requires no great will or wisdom. In fact, leaders of states can hardly be praised for such bureaucratic skills.

'Man, freedom, market' was the motto of Shatalin's programme.

Yes, Academician Shatalin was its chief architect. He, Academician Petrakov and Yavlinsky rallied the country's finest academics and sought to prove that there is no sensible alternative to the market. The choice was either the market or planning by directives in an administrative-bureaucratic system where the state takes on all economic functions. But we have a pretty good idea of the limits of the state as an economic force. The idea of state socialism was effective and respectable only at a certain stage of our development, but it now leads only into a blind alley. Why should anyone stick to old dogmas?

May I remind you that Adam Smith wrote that the role of the state should be limited to that of a 'night watchman', that is, to police duties, while Karl Marx held that the state should take on all economic and social functions. We acted according to Marx when we built an 'economy of a single factory' instead of a mixed, market economy. The inevitable result was total bankruptcy.

You may remember that a process of denationalisation and privati-

91

sation began in Britain in the late 1970s when Margaret Thatcher came to power, and later it spread to America and all other countries. The whole world realised that the state cannot manage a country's economy alone, that competitive forces are required for that. It was thus confirmed that there exists a certain optimal level of the fulfilment of economic functions by the state. The process of privatisation, denationalisation, is now under way in 160 countries, so we are no exception in this respect, but are rather unique in that we offer maniacal resistance to the objective global trend.

Theoretical conclusions as regards this phenomenon, not to be found in our literature, would be easy to make. I have already said that any state, regardless of its social nature, which operates as an economic force, has an optimal limit to some of its dimensions (for instance, the size of the public sector). When this limit (the volume of functions) is exceeded the state is, like any information system, doomed to wither away. It is simply impossible to manage from a single centre a system as complex as an economy, as if it were a single factory. We did not and could not realise the destructive potential of state property, of its enormous scale. That is why the more complex the scientific and technological revolution became, the more we drove ourselves into a corner, doomed our economy to underdevelopment. And that is why Shatalin's slogan 'man, freedom, market' and his programme drew on modern economic thought which sustains world economic practice.

When it became clear that the '500 days' programme had been rejected by the President and the Supreme Soviet of the USSR there remained three alternatives for the Supreme Soviet of the Russian Federation. What are the prospects of their implementation?

The first, isolationism, is not our variant, as Boris Yeltsin said, since Russia bears special historical responsibility for the destiny of the Union. Rulers come and go while Russia has existed for a thousand years. Let us hope that it will exist for many more thousands of years. Russia's historical duty has been that of a gatherer, unifier of lands. It was a gatherer under Prince Ivan Kalita, under Ivan the Terrible and under many other Tsars long before the 1917 revolution. It is therefore impossible for us to take the position of isolation from other Union states.

We are thus left with the other two variants, or their combination. We must find, proceeding from realities, a reforming course that will lead us towards the transformation of Russian society and of the Russian state. This course should include the conclusion of treaties with other republics, the promotion of horizontal links, and of political relations with the republics; privatisation, separation of the economy from the state, land reform, intensive foreign–economic and foreign–political activity;

attempts to preserve and strengthen the rouble, to stabilise the financial situation and to cut expenditure. All these tasks were outlined in Boris Yeltsin's programme presented to the Third Congress of People's Deputies.

Will the economy's entry into the market breed order or chaos? Or will the one be followed by the other?

The entry into the market should not lead to chaos, but we are not guaranteed against setbacks and failures due to our lack of market traditions and of normal traders. It should also be said that our mentality is, mildly speaking, somewhat thievish. All this makes us expect certain difficulties, but not chaos. The market quickly restores necessary proportions.

The saturation of the market with goods, for instance, under the 'shock therapy' plan launched from 1 January 1990 by the Finance Minister, Eduard Balcerowicz, in Poland, was achieved quite quickly. We sought to avoid shock therapy, the sharp soaring of prices, especially in the consumer sphere. We could have succeeded if the central government had supported, not opposed us. In the USSR, the result was shock without therapy.

What is your attitude to the centre's programme of market reforms?

The centre's programme and actions bear the distinct stamp of old approaches. New attempts are being made to bar union republics from active participation in the reform and to give all powers to the central government. The programme pays little attention to the problem of transforming state property, nor is it clear what share of the economy is to be left under the direct control of the state. All the old ministries and departments, of which there are nearly a hundred, are to be left virtually intact. Land reform is probably the most vulnerable spot. It is not clear what mechanisms the centre wants to use to implement the Law on the Land. Yet this is today one of the decisive knots the untying of which could make it possible both to feed people and effect a painless transition of the economy to market relations.

One gets the impression that the centre still lacks a comprehensive concept. In this case it would be logical to use the progressive experience and mechanisms that the republics have already obtained and to urge them to take an active part in the shaping and implementation of the economic reform. We must act without delay while there is still a glimmer of faith left among the people.

What is the essence of the recently prepared new Russian programme of stabilising the economy and switching over to the market?

It is based on the same principles that we were guided by when we approved Shatalin's programme which had, however, to be substantially amended on account of the more complicated situation. The emphasis is on land reform with a particular stress on the more effective use of taxation techniques. We also intend to provide favourable treatment to enterprises placed under Russia's jurisdiction, broaden the scope of economic freedom for people and stimulate the setting up of a large number of small non-state enterprises. It is also planned to reform Russia's political institutions through the establishment of effective structures of executive authority all the way from the presidency to local government.

LAND REFORM

What is distinctive about land reform in Russia?

It should be carried out according to the principle 'land to the farmers'. This would be the best and most democratic way of resolving the food crisis. Certainly, we have faced a lot of resistance from heads of collective and state-owned farms and from party committees at all levels. They are used to ruling without any constraints, like feudal lords, showing contempt for farmers' interests and urban people's needs, only hoping for government subsidies. There is resistance from millions of officials in charge of agriculture. Shortages are good for them. They feel all-powerful, distributing and redistributing funds, raw materials, farm machinery, fertiliser and seed. Hideous corruption is a tradition among them.

A government land committee with local offices has been set up to implement the land reform. But the land committees have met with setbacks in places. Where local soviets take the land reform close to heart, progress has been achieved, with land given to individual farmers, along with machinery and fertiliser. In short, something is getting done, but there have been many negative experiences, too.

If a collective or a state-owned farm misuses the land, the land committee must act with determination, identifying interested farmers and giving them the land belonging to the farm. But it is not enough just to give out the land. Farmers need fertiliser, credits, technology, pedigree livestock. The land committees and the newly established farmer's associations must deal with this vast range of problems.

It is instructive to study Stolypin's agrarian reforms. He is becoming a popular figure again, a legendary reformer of the Russian state. Yet, an even better thing would be to study the experience of Western nations. The basic principle is that the farmer must own the land. The past should be critically re-examined and something added from our times and the experience of other countries. If we develop a dependable mechanism of land transfer, we will take determined action to abolish loss-making farms, those 'lame ducks', dividing them into many individual farms.

Is it correct to interpret the present policies of the Russian parliament and government as aimed at ridding the Russian farmers of nearly 100 years of bondage?

In 1917, despite their promises, the Bolsheviks failed to give the land to the people, even though peasants had fought under their banner only in the hope of getting land. The land was never given to the people in the seventy-four years that followed. The people have remained in bondage. The state has refused to give the land because it understands human freedom differently. Anyone owning land is not a bondsman, to say the least. They have their business, their source of income, and they know how to earn money. Economically, they are independent of officialdom. The existing power structure has denied people independence, telling them when to sow and when to harvest, what wages to collect and so on. Human bondage regarding land rights stemmed from the political system. Land was state property, and the state used little short of coercion to organise farmers' work. It systematically estranged them from the land to a grotesque degree.

Many reactionaries argue that Russia no longer has any true farmers, they have lost their skills and hate to work the land, and are no more than hired labour. However hypocritical, there is some truth to this, but I disagree that the farmer's love of land, the old farming world and farming mentality have been lost forever, or that the people cannot make a new start on their ancestors' land. If they are placed in new conditions, given ownership of the land and granted the possibility of freely disposing of their produce, they will regain their spirits and pull themselves up very quickly.

We aim to change our countryside and give the land back to the farmers. To do this we set out to reorganise drastically the administrative bureaucratic system. Not that we are against collective and state farms. If a farm is profitable and people want to continue working on it, let them work and we will support them. There should not be a wild move from one extreme to another. There are hardly any farmers left as they used to be. A worker of a collective or a state farm is not a farmer but a hired worker. So we aim to restore the farming community, which can be a real pillar of society supplying it with food. Individual farms will work side by side with collective and state farms. We do not insist that these farms be abolished, but they must stop being feudal estates. They will have to change, yielding their place to cooperatives or associations.

PRIVATISATION AND THE MARKET

What about industry? Will the privatisation mechanism enable the workers to take control of the factory and choose the type of ownership they like?

The Russian parliament has at last adopted a law on privatisation, and earlier it passed a law on property. Privatisation is an involved and ongoing process. A factory can be privately owned or publicly owned, it can be a share-holding company, a foreign business or a mixed one, or it can remain state owned. We are trying to create a mixed economy of the type found throughout the world. There have been enough dubious experiments that reduced living standards. In the initial stage, privatisation should steer clear of industrial giants, factories that are important to the nation as a whole. It should focus on services catering for people's essential needs such as retail trade, restaurants, housing construction, and consumer goods industries. Many small and medium-sized enterprises should be established. Here special emphasis must be placed on new construction so as to create a parallel market economy by encouraging non-state economic activities.

It is difficult to imagine the Nurek hydro-electric station not owned by the state.

In many countries of classical capitalism hydro-electric stations are government or municipal property. If you understand the logic of the market economy, you would not insist that the Nurek station or another plant of this kind be privatised immediately. As you know, the Kamaz truck plant is not a state-owned enterprise any more, having been transformed into a joint-stock company. In general, privatisation must be carried out with care and wisdom, without affecting people's interests, but rather by drawing on them. It should not affect the interests of any social group or republic. And, more importantly, it must not damage production or destroy economic ties or we will never overcome our economic problems.

Industrial workers can buy out the factory. But what can a school teacher buy? Everyone has contributed to the common cause.

Our state has been a monumental exploiter. A capitalist gives at least 60 to 70 per cent of the labour value back to the worker, but here the figure is only 7 to 15 per cent. Certainly, this is exploitation not only of someone who creates material values with their work but also of a school teacher, who earns a pittance. The intellectual work of a teacher, doctor or engineer must be fully rewarded so that they will not feel cheated by the market economy. The economy will be more productive, making it possible to pay the school teacher good money. Of course, this is an ideal situation, but it does operate in other countries, and quite effectively, too.

When will the legislative mechanism of privatisation be finalised? When will a person be able to understand how he or she can buy out a shop or a pharmacy?

We have a law, regulations and a method. The market spirit has already been created in society. The problem is disbelief and lack of confidence among people, on the one hand, and resistance from officials at all levels, on the other. A person might reason: 'OK, I'll buy a shop, invest my money and my family's work, and one day I might be dispossessed as a private owner.' Such things have happened many times in our history. So we must make people confident that the reforms cannot be reversed. To this end, practical actions are needed, including new laws. Sometimes we are rebuked as law-makers for adopting too many laws, but the thing is that at some point the number of laws creates stability in which the relations that these laws regulate become truly irreversible.

Many people feel quite cautious about the market. Are their fears justified?

People are told that when the market comes they must brace themselves for unemployment. Just imagine, living in penury as they do, plus unemployment. But there are no grounds for such fears. In Russia, at least one million small businesses should be created if the economy is to function normally. They will need a lot of people and pay good money and even if some go bankrupt, unemployment will be most unlikely to occur. The history of economics proves that whenever the volume of business grows, more employees are needed. When economic booms happen in the West, unemployment usually falls to zero. Why should we have unemployment amidst the growth of business opportunities? It reveals an elementary misunderstanding of the market.

The trouble is there are few market experts among the theorists who are developing the policy of switching to the market. All their lives they worked with 'socialist planning', and now they are putting the market into place without understanding its inner workings and relationships. Of course, there will be unemployment. But when? I think eight or nine years after the market is fully created. Our economy will become increasingly integrated in the world economy and international division of labour, and then it will need profound restructuring. There will be business failures in the private, state-owned, collective and cooperative sectors. But by that time we will have gone through the period of the primary accumulation of capital. The state and the people will have savings. Our soviets and municipal authorities will have sizeable resources. The role of the state will change, with the emphasis shifting towards social protection and its economic role will diminish. I do not think we will be threatened with unemployment until these major structural changes have taken place. On the contrary, if we move to the market more quickly and boldly, we will have considerable labour shortages.

Our unemployment results from the economic crisis and the many wrong decisions by the central government. It has little to do with the market. So people should not be afraid of the market generating mass unemployment.

What should be done immediately to switch to a normal, market economy?

Take any country with a healthy economy, the huge United States or the tiny Denmark, and everywhere the picture is similar. There are eighty to a hundred small businesses to each large corporation. The market economy is driven by impetuses from below, not from above. It creates optimal economic organisation itself, and this consists of small, medium-sized and large businesses. We will have no market until we take purposeful and very serious action to create an extensive non-state sector of small enterprises.

We have a law on leasing, but no genuine leases. The same is true of cooperation, though it is the only sector of the market economy at the moment. We have a law on property, which recognises all types of property as equal, but there is no real equality. The economy remains in the hands of the state. So there are not adequate conditions for the market to be introduced.

We have coined an absurd and vague term 'de-étatisation', which reflects attempts formally to decentralise the state sector. The received term elsewhere is denationalisation or privatisation, but whatever you call it, the meaning is the same. We need to move over to company principles in industry as soon as possible even without privatising the state sector. Every country has a state sector, not only ours. State-owned companies can operate effectively, on market principles. They are separated from the state and do not use political power to achieve their goals.

Let some of the businesses under ministerial control remain state-owned, but they must be free and independent, fully-fledged market agents. But what we do is cling to the old type of management, the ministerial structures. Perhaps they did a good job in wartime or in emergency, but one should realise that they have outlived their usefulness. It is a breach of professional ethics to turn a blind eye to the fact that the ministerial system has historically outlived itself and has long been a brake on development. As for the 'concerns' into which industrial ministries are being turned, they are an even greater evil than the ministries themselves. What we need is competing forces, whereas the 'concerns' only cement the old monopoly. The state must be pulled out of the 'economic game', with its economic role reduced. At the same time we must try to strengthen its social role to protect the people.

What are the reasons for the central government's half-hearted decisions? Does it lack a feel for real life or the willpower to make cardinal decisions?

On this point I can only speak as an economist, not as an individual airing his views. It is obvious that all economic sectors, industry included, are in a critical state. What the Pavlov government has tried to do, especially with its price increases, is to solve purely financial problems, to balance the budget. It was clear, however, that the proposed measures would fall short even of those limited goals. Our financial and economic agencies have always played too great a role, exercising too much influence on all policy, though this influence usually served corporate, departmental needs. The Ministry of Finance, the Committee of Prices (Goskomtsen) and the State Planning Committee (Gosplan) very ably used any idea, even strategy, to further their own interests. In trying to balance the budget, they lost sight of everything else.

This process intensified when the Finance Minister, Valentin Pavlov, became the Prime Minister. Even earlier the Committee on Prices had to all intents and purposes become an extension of the Ministry of Finance. When Pavlov was in charge of the Committee on Prices, the highly unstable economic equilibrium began to collapse. He then took his destructive ideas to the Finance Ministry, and now to the Cabinet of Ministers. Needless to say, it is not a question of personalities. But the Finance Ministry plays a tremendous role, it is an all-powerful ministry. We have highly centralised management, but there is clear decentralisation, confusion and disarray at the top level of government. It is difficult to understand who is responsible for decision-making, if anyone at all.

It seems that what we are most afraid of is the power of capital.

We are most afraid of the power of capital and the power of man. We are afraid of giving the reins to the working person. That is why we refuse them the possibility of using their work freely. Let us remember the tragic situation that developed at the Second Congress in December 1990. A proposal to give the land to the people, even in ten years' time, met with a barrage of resistance. Why? They said that selling the land might strengthen the mafia, cause social stratification, and result in plunder of the land. All right. What about poisoning the land? Or letting it rot? Every year Russia writes off hundreds of thousands of hectares of land, which cannot be used any more. Those things you can do, but you cannot give it to a caring owner who would make proper use of it. Why? Because all talk of the mafia and social justice conceals the economic interests of party and government bureaucrats and of collective and state farm feudal lords who over the decades have grown used to the unquestioning obedience of millions of hapless serfs.

Why do you think that private property is the linchpin of the economic reform?

It is clear that there can be no market without private property. It is a far

99

too important matter to be overlooked, as the politicians of the central administration are trying to do. Orientation towards a genuine, not a declared, pluralism of property has enabled us to take practical action. In the law on external economic activities we equalise the rights of foreign investors with the rights of our enterprises. In other words, we provide the essential government guarantees which the central government has never given in the last six years. Furthermore, we have granted local authorities the possibility of registering joint and foreign businesses. We intend before long to replace permission with registration.

The Russian intelligentsia, working class and farmers are beginning to realise that they are independent, but the central government refuses to accept that. You remember its reaction to our budget in the concluding resolution of the Fourth Congress of People's Deputies of the USSR. The nation's President lashed out at our Declaration of State Sovereignty, refusing Russia the right to independence.

ECONOMIC REFORM AND THE WORLD

How do you see Russia's position between the West and the East?

I feel that European civilisation and culture is wielding a dominant influence in Russia now. Since Peter's times Russia has been moving towards Europe, although the October Revolution, Stalinism and neo-Stalinism checked this movement. Only now the lost trend towards convergence is beginning to gain strength again. It is important that we drop our aggressive ideological doctrines in foreign policy and embrace universal human values and ideas. Russia should be guided by universal humanitarian ideals both inside the country and in our foreign policy. But domestically the ideology of confrontation still remains, sustained by the leaders of the Russian Communist Party.

If the entire country and all its republics move towards market structures and a society-oriented market economy, the market doctrine will enable us to overcome the confrontational attitude towards universal human values. Then our rapprochement with European civilisation will accelerate. In this respect it is important to re-assess the concept of convergence and support Sakharov's appeal for convergence to be accepted unconditionally. There might be zigzags, retreats and vacillation in our domestic policy, but convergence will forge ahead. People want to be closer to each other and do not want to live in isolation, poverty and insults. They must move towards each other. This is the basis of the ideas about cooperation which have deeply permeated contemporary society.

Will rapprochement with the West and a Common European Home become a reality? And when? This could happen when all the major nations become more closely involved economically, when economic ties evolve between our country, including Russia, and other European nations. There must be a network of capital, services, and human destinies. The world market brings countries and people closer together.

A priority area for Russian foreign policy should be the Eastern European region, the former CMEA (Council for Mutual Economic Assistance) countries which the Kremlin has abandoned.

Have your views on international cooperation changed?

On the one hand, we can see that our traditional ties with Eastern Europe nations that refused to remain loyal to the socialist choice are weakening. But on the other, relations of a new nature have emerged, bringing the two opposite systems close together. We say that there are no socialist or capitalist ties. There are specific economic ties. These are either full-blooded or partial, stable ties or incidental ones, long-term ties or erratic ones. Until recently, virtually all our ties of the post-NEP period, however large-scale they might have been, were like 'one-off deals'. The partners had no need for each other. There was no need to fuse production relations. There was no systematic exchange in goods and services, technology, capital, manpower, experts, whatever. There was autarchy, isolationism and inane arrogance as a direct consequence of primitive party propaganda. All those mythical units of payments, transfer roubles, those absurdities.

Only a convertible currency can link our economy up to the world market. Only then will normal relations develop and a real measure of value appear, a universal measure. There is none yet, and instead we are in a very bad economic, financial and food crisis. It is amazing that, in spite of everything, Western business people wish to cooperate with us and develop human contacts. We in Russia must create favourable conditions for them. By making determined efforts to this effect, we can influence the Union as a whole and the nature of our international cooperation. But that is a passive attitude, so to speak. The active approach is to try to enter world markets by ourselves, our direct agreements setting an example for other republics to follow. If not for interference, we would have done that.

The problem is that we have failed to create a dependable mechanism to accumulate foreign-currency earnings. But this will not last long. We must take control of external economic activities, if we are to accumulate sizeable foreign-currency funds. Then we will be able to create favourable conditions not only to make the rouble convertible but to create reliable guarantees for foreign businesses and attract them to Russia.

How will the deduction of 60 per cent of Russia's foreign-currency earnings to the Union budget affect its economy?

This runs counter to Russian laws. We believe that the entire range of foreign economic activities is Russia's prerogative. We must pay certain sums into the Union budget, but we must agree with the central government about their size. That will depend on us, the Russian government. The central administration will be unable arbitrarily to take away from the Russian state what belongs to its people.

Is the foreign trade monopoly an obstacle for various regions and free zones to join the world market?

Of course it is. Over the decades foreign trade has become encrusted with special structures and personnel who export and import no one knows what, regardless of regional needs and national economic needs. We signed large-scale agreements for grain imports, though it was perfectly clear that we would have a good harvest. But the harvest was destroyed, left to rot. The services responsible for foreign purchases are opposed to improved production and storage of grain at home. If God sends us good weather, and our land, which is good, yields a good harvest, their job is to destroy it. For these people national economic needs do not seem to exist. Export and import operations are made to serve their corporate interests. There seems to exist a mafia which has long played buddy-buddy to government, party and economic-management officials.

It is necessary to create conditions in which such multi-billion criminal actions will become impossible because economic relations as such have changed. The system itself must be changed. We have had to establish a Ministry for External Economic Relations, which did not exist in Russia before. The Supreme Soviet has passed laws proclaiming external economic activities a prerogative of the Russian government. We are winning one position in foreign trade after another. I view this sphere as a major lever helping to implement the Russian programme for a transition to the market and to integrate the Russian economy in the global economy. This is one of the main principles contained in the Declaration of State Sovereignty of the RSFSR adopted by the First Russian Congress of People's Deputies in June 1990.

What place can Russia occupy in the world political process, centred as it is on Gorbachev?

We must occupy the place we deserve. No one has the right to conduct serious negotiations affecting Russia's direct interest without Russian representatives. If these are major economic or political negotiations, there must be an authorised and plenipotentiary representative of Russia. I have repeatedly said to Japanese representatives that any negotiations about the Kurile Islands will be pointless if the Russian government and local authorities are not represented.

Would this make such negotiations more difficult to organise?

More difficult, yet more feasible. Russian territory is involved, so why should someone else decide for Russia? We welcome the unification of the two Germanies and I, for one, am no less glad than the Germans are. But in the forty years of cooperation with the former German Democratic Republic we invested large sums in Germany and have the right to get them back. I am sure that if we, Russia, had taken part in the negotiations, we would have received not 10 or 15 billion marks but a lot more, about 100 billion. We would have reached the same agreement if we had pledged to withdraw our troops, say, in five years' time. Then, maybe, the army's problems would not have come to a head and we could have dealt with the crisis more easily. That is, troop withdrawals would have been made dependent on creating a social infrastructure for the servicemen to be withdrawn and for the troops to be relocated. The Germans are reasonable people. But someone was after swift political dividends, as if they could compensate for an extremely primitive domestic policy. And this is a truly momentous decision. It means reconciliation, final reconciliation in Europe, reconciliation between peoples, the unification of Germany, which was a concern for all, and the return of the Eastern European nations to the fold of civilisation. Without doubt, popular diplomacy should have prevailed, and the Russian authorities should have played a role in drafting the agreement. But the whole thing proved a separate agreement between the two leaders, Chancellor Kohl and Gorbachev. We still do not know what lay behind this.

Many experts say that in a number of economic areas China's experience suits us best. Is that so?

I think that is right. Why did China make such a big stride forward, including opening special economic zones? It profoundly changed its economic system and unequivocally recognised private property. There is no market and there cannot be any without recognising private property. Certainly, private property is not ideal but it is a vehicle of economic development and economic progress in general. You should not give it an absolute value, and a mixed economy is a better arrangement. The economic model based on state monopoly has fully outlived itself and there is no point in trying to restore it.

What about the Kurile problem, which has been the subject of so many battles?

The Chairman of Russia's Supreme Soviet, Yeltsin, has developed a quite realistic attitude to the matter, though it might appear outdated and conservative. He is in effect the first of our leading politicians since Khrushchev's statement of 1956 who says there is a problem. He has been accused of many things, even of being prepared to sell our land. What sell out? Yeltsin admits there is a problem and suggests how we can deal with it. Maybe, we are ready for some temporary solution, and only the next generation will be able to solve it. But we are close neighbours and partners and we must take each other's interest into account. So let us create a special economic zone for the two nations, a zone of interrelated interests, and let us deal with the problems one by one. Perhaps, we can agree about joint administration of the zone. We can do something now and leave other problems for the future. It is a highly flexible policy, a wise and realistic policy. There has been Hong Kong, there has been Alaska. The world community has known solutions.

As an economist and expert on foreign economic problems, I appreciate Yeltsin's approach to the problem. Cross-penetration of capital is occurring in the world. In professing to preach internationalism, we used to practise the most abhorrent nationalism. One should clearly realise that no one is itching to buy Russia. What is happening is the joining together of economic and cultural interests. Some people in other countries would simply like to live in our country. They should have the possibility of buying a piece of land in the countryside to build a farm and begin working the land, or of buying an apartment in a city. They want to live and work here, and spend their money. What's wrong with that?

What do the Japanese want to do in the Soviet Far East? They say: you don't have a normal kind of economic activity in the area. Let us do something together. Just let us feel that we are truly safe economically so that in a year or two you won't force us into collectivisation. In this case we would be ready to invest 50 billion dollars. We should give them clear guarantees that their interests will be protected, without them having to bribe local or other officials.

Just look what is happening in Moscow. To buy a two- or three-room apartment for an office, a foreigner has to pay 50,000 dollars and a bribe of 150,000 roubles. It hurts me so when I have to listen to all these things. A two-room office here costs even more than in Japan. We have pushed prices that high. Our pricing policy is such that only very large corporations can cooperate with us, especially in Moscow. We keep small businesses out, and it is they who can often produce a dynamic economic effect.

6

BEYOND COMMUNISM

POLITICS BEFORE THE COUP

It is ten months since the deputies accorded Boris Yeltsin and you their confidence. What has the Russian parliament done since April 1990?

That is not a simple question. People are mostly searching for answers in the economic field. Everyone would like to see economic results, but the Russian economy is bound by millions of invisible threads with the entire national economy, to a larger extent than in any other republic. The economy was virtually dissolved in ministerial and departmental structures lying beyond Russian jurisdiction.

When we proposed the '500 days' programme, we believed that we could move to the market jointly with all the other republics. But nothing came of it. Today, without abandoning the main ideas for Russia's economic rebirth as outlined in the programme, we are having to advance to the market by ourselves. The road has proved much more complicated than anticipated.

In the ten months we have created a fairly firm legislative basis to achieve a degree of independence. Back in June and July 1990, the idea of Russia's state sovereignty was just beginning. In the following months it has taken shape and begun, slowly but surely, to be translated into reality.

Both the deputies and we, Supreme Soviet leaders, tend to criticise our government for proving less capable than we hoped. But you have to remember that this is the first Russian government in the last seventy-four years that has made its mark as a genuine *Russian* government. Previous governments were abject semblances of leadership who would dance to the tune of the central administration. Ours, though not too effective a government so far, has taken determined action to implement the laws we adopt in the Supreme Soviet in order to strengthen the Russian Federation's independence.

This constitutes its strength but also its weakness. As soon as the Russian government embarked on independent policies to implement our laws and decisions, the central administration began to obstruct and condemn its actions in all spheres. In agricultural policy there was the notorious increase in prices for machinery, fertiliser and implements. Faced with pressure from the heads of collective and state farms, the Russian government was forced to raise farm prices and as a result we were accused of having masterminded the price increases. Now where were our 'critics' when the central administration increased the prices of all agricultural services by five to six times. How could a collective or state farm or an individual farmer possibly grow crops or raise cattle in such conditions?

Or take foreign economic activities. Our economy is structured so that the machine-building, smelting and other industries depend on the purchases of various types of plant and equipment from many foreign countries. But when our Ministry for External Economic Relations gives us the licence to buy equipment for industrial facilities under Russian jurisdiction, we encounter all sorts of obstacles. Customs officials, taking their cue from the Ministry of External Economic Relations of the USSR, will one day let the equipment into the country, and the next day refuse to do so. They act like arrogant lords. That is what the situation is like. So one can only admire our courageous Premier, Ivan Silaev, who is doing his best to steer the ship of government across these stormy waters.

The Third Congress in March–April 1991 witnessed the split of the Communists of Russia faction. A new faction, Communists for Democracy, was created. How does this affect the correlation of forces in parliament and in the country as a whole?

As you remember, the split occurred after deputy Alexander Rutskoi's speech. He is an interesting person, an Air Force colonel who served in Afghanistan, Hero of the Soviet Union and convinced communist. You cannot associate him with 'destructive forces'. His speech in parliament was a well thought out and serious move. To my mind, he voiced the sentiments of the majority of party members who resent the aggressive behaviour of the Communists of Russia leaders. You know that most communists are asking the painful question: what kind of a party is this, especially Ivan Polozkov's Communist Party of Russia? Where is it leading us? Many speeches by Polozkov and his supporters testify to a crisis within the party. It seems to me that his appearance on the stage of history as the leader of a ruling party, so to speak, bears proof of its decay and disintegration.

When Rutskoi set out his programme, he in effect created a new platform, Communists for Democracy, within the Communist Party, and thus took the first step towards rebuilding the party. Many communists hope that the party will become such as it was conceived by the theorists of communism who equated the words 'communism' and 'socialism' with true equality among people and democracy. Polozkov's party model is acquiring neo-fascist characteristics. It seems to me that Rutskoi's initiative is vastly important, though it has not been duly assessed by our media, theorists and ideologists.

Rutskoi's platform can ensure a future for the Communist Party; perhaps, help preserve it as an influential social and political force. Otherwise, the party is doomed. Deep down, people are still frightened. We still have a long way to go to achieve democracy, even middle-level democracy. The first shoots of democracy have just appeared. So party members are apprehensive about their future, especially in our quite uncertain present.

In the seventy-four years that the party has existed as an official state entity, many members have developed an abstract yet tangible sense of affinity with official decisions and policies. 'I am a communist', someone would say proudly, though he did not have an iota of faith in communism and its principles. Why did they say that? Because they knew that a person unaffiliated with the party would never make an elementary career. Is not healthy pride inherent in a normal person? Everyone wants to realise their talents and abilities. And party membership would be the first step towards a career in science, industry, higher education, health care, government service.

Who stood the best chance of rising in the world? It was those party members who were inclined to lies, time-serving and hypocrisy. People who sincerely believed in communist and socialist ideals would always remain in the background. They were derided by party careerists who used their party membership to advance themselves. I meet many fine people who had become party leaders, but in principle the party's personnel policy corrupted people. If you did not join the Komsomol, you would never join the party. So you would try to make a Komsomol career to become a party official later. To be appointed head of a factory, an expert had to work in a district, city or regional party committee for some time. An able factory manager choosing the career of a party committee secretary would most likely degenerate as a personality. He would develop a warped morality, his heart turned into stone, with chilly cynicism oozing out of it. But millions of people did keep some life in their hearts, and regarded party membership as a way of helping to rebuild the country. A demonstration is a great thing, but many people realise that it is an instrument to influence the authorities, not an effective way of participating in constructive processes. If life were breathed into party structures, they would enable every member to participate in perestroika.

Rutskoi has realised that the Russian Communist Party leaders have played such a harmful role even in our parliament, preventing us from working normally in the Supreme Soviet. He refused to keep them company and said that the Communist Party had to be changed. It was a unique historical event for the country and the party. If communists support the ideas of the Rutskoi group, I think the party will be able to survive as an influential social and political force. Otherwise, we will find ourselves in a situation similar to that in Eastern Europe, and our society will demand to be rid of party officialdom. And this will happen, if the party's healthy forces turn their back on Rutskoi's platform. I feel this platform has a big future.

The demand to convene a special congress came mostly from the Communists of Russia. Why?

I talked to the four presidium members who had signed a statement criticising Boris Yeltsin and demanding that the Congress be convened. I said:

> You, deputies, misjudge your fellow countrymen's sentiments. They will denounce your attempts to overthrow Yeltsin. They will condemn your conspiratorial methods and blows below the belt. The Congress, even if it is convened prior to the referendum, may produce totally different results than you expect. Deputies will arrive, having experienced the direct influence of local people, and they will adopt totally different decisions than those you planned. So don't hurry. We would do well to convene the Congress after the referendum. Then you will know what the people truly want.

Common sense triumphed in the Supreme Soviet. For one thing, we had the results of the referendum of 17 March 1991 which supported the direct election of a Russian President, and for another we ensured the proper organisation of the Congress and developed serious policy proposals to resolve the economic crisis in Russia.

Yeltsin was highly self-critical in his report. He analysed the mistakes both of the Supreme Soviet, and its presidium, and the Russian government. On the other hand, the Supreme Soviet's Chairman showed the extent of our influence on Russia's affairs, and identified the huge 'blank spot' which lay outside our competence, though it was called Russia. Both in the economic and political spheres we felt the obstruction of our decisions. The first thing we expected of the Congress was to show the people the truth about our activities, our very limited practical possibilities, and the forces that were interfering with our work.

And people did see the real picture and began writing to us. Nine letters in ten said: 'We thought you were in power and in control, so why didn't you want to change the situation? Now we know you are not in power, the central administration remains in command, and locally your decisions are obstructed by the same old secretaries of regional and area party committees. Now we know that your hands are tied.' The First Congress in June 1990 decided that party jobs must not be combined with government positions but the Communist Party is sabotaging this, apparently taking their cue from General Secretary Gorbachev. We adopted a law on the referendum, but whole regions and republics of Russia are ignoring it and remain free from any responsibility.

This huge public pressure on deputies played what I feel to be the crucial role. The reactionaries had to retreat, and Polozkov was forced to call for cooperation and deny any intention on the part of the Communists of Russia to overthrow anyone. I wish it were true, but have difficulty believing it. I have always wanted to cooperate with all social forces, except diehard reactionaries and revenge-seekers. We have always been prepared for cooperation and open for it.

Even when Boris Yeltsin made his statement on 19 February demanding the Gorbachev's resignation, I did not take it literally. That was an emphatic, yet desperate, appeal to realise the extremely difficult situation in which we find ourselves. Just look at what is being done to Russia, its people and its leaders, Yeltsin seemed to say. We have neither an army nor a KGB. Officials are waging war on us, with regional chiefs kowtowing to commands from Old Square. We have nothing but the support of the people who led us to power. This was the message of Yeltsin's speech. And his demand for the President to resign was a tough gesture. But contrary to what some party newspapers said, it was not an improvisation but a considered step intended to alert Russian and world opinion to the abnormal state of affairs.

And it was a very strong move. Certainly, it invited an attack from reactionary forces, and they tried to exploit it. They decided to portray the Supreme Soviet leaders as a destructive force, and called on their supporters in local party committees to collect deputies' signatures in support of convening a special Congress. You know how this was done? A regional committee secretary would summon a deputy and say: 'You sign this. It's a demand to convene a special congress'. That is how it was done.

How, in this context, do you view the deployment of troops in Moscow on the opening day of the Third Congress of People's Deputies on 28 March 1991?

That was an episode and, to my mind, a rather dramatic one, not of power struggle but, I would say, of pressuring Russia's lawful government, elected by popular vote. How does it feel to be a Russian deputy in the Kremlin surrounded by troops and military equipment? It turns out that 50,000 troops were deployed in central Moscow, and the Kremlin was as good as encircled. Now, what for? Naturally, to pressure and browbeat the Congress, which in effect was convened in order to oust Yeltsin.

I think most deputies showed courage. A day or two earlier, the Moscow police were taken from the Moscow Soviet and placed under the control of the USSR Ministry of Internal Affairs. Therefore, both the armed forces and the police were set against the Russian government. Even the vacillating deputies realised that this was no way to live. What sort of Congress of People's Deputies of Russia was this? What were the troops doing there?

The Congress suspended its work and demanded that the President order the troops out of Moscow. With the consent of the Congress, the Chairman of the Supreme Soviet asked me to negotiate with President Gorbachev. I had a rather long and difficult conversation with him. For half an hour I tried to persuade him that Moscow is the Russian capital, and now the venue of a Congress of People's Deputies of Russia. 'Why did you deploy troops around the Congress?' He answered, 'To protect it.' The troop deployment followed a request from twenty-nine deputies who had been criticised at the Second Congress for voting against our programme of economic reform. For some reason, they now asked the President for 'help'. And absurd as it might seem, such 'help' was provided. It was a pretext to try to pressure us. You know how World War II broke out. Gestapo men dressed in Polish army uniforms seized a German radio station in Danzig. It looked as if Polish troops had attacked Germany. A similar political provocation, quite a silly one, was used in our country. As a matter of fact, I think the defeat of the reactionary forces began on the first day of the Congress when under the pretext of 'protecting' twenty-nine scab deputies an army of 50,000 men was called in.

Why did you undertake to mediate?

Well, first of all, I support peaceful solutions in general. The Congress decided not to resume work until the troops had been withdrawn, and I tried to prevail on President Gorbachev to meet this demand. If we had shown fear or lacked confidence that we would win, I might not have been so patient trying to persuade the President. But we were confident that reason would prevail if at the Congress we honestly spelled out our views and explained the objective and subjective reasons for our setbacks and achievements, of which there had been quite a few in our work. So I did my best to persuade the President to withdraw the troops that same day. If he had said: 'All right, there won't be any left after lunch', Yeltsin would have urged the Congress to continue working. As you can see, we were fully prepared to cooperate, regardless of the potential outcome of the forum. Perhaps, weaker people might have tried to exploit the incident to disband the Congress and blame the President for that.

Did you feel the country was waiting for the results of your talks?

Of course. I felt the country was waiting with bated breath. Not only this country, but the whole world was watching that rather tortuous episode of our history. It looked like a tragedy, but to some extent like a farce, too. In those days Moscow truly belonged to its people. Despite the intimidation, some 200,000 men and women took to the streets. I must pay tribute to our deputies who did a great deal to avert confrontation and bloodshed, which might well have happened. It seemed the people who had advised the President to call in troops strongly hoped that things would come to a head. The Congress suspended its work. True, the President promised to withdraw the troops the next day. He was forced to promise that. At any rate, the armour and other units were withdrawn, though they were rumoured to be somewhere in the outskirts. But on the whole both the Congress and the people of Moscow showed good organisation and resolution. Maybe, I must say it again, this marked the beginning of the defeat of those forces that were plotting to overthrow Yeltsin.

The deployment of troops was meant to demonstrate force. What was the meaning of Gorbachev's absence from the Congress?

I think vacillation and indetermination are the best words to describe it. On the last day of the Congress, when it was clear that reconciliation was in the offing, a group of delegates wanted to see the President, and Yeltsin asked me to call him and invite him. This was after Yeltsin's final address when he in effect extended his hand, not for friendship, as some interpreted his gesture, but for cooperation, for normal and businesslike cooperation. Certainly, if the President had come, it would have been possible to call on the miners to stop their strike. I know that Yeltsin intended to say: 'All right, men, let's end the strike and get down to work. You see the President promises his cooperation, and I, too, will cooperate. Together, we'll get things moving and do everything possible to improve your position.' But the President never showed up.

Incidentally, both in the Supreme Soviet and in Congress sessions I do not permit deputies to attack President Gorbachev's dignity. Irrespective of whether he is good or bad, he is the constitutional head of state and must be treated with respect. I will just say that when I talked with him, the President suddenly began to rebuke me: 'Why didn't you send me an invitation in writing? I would have come but you didn't invite me.' I said: 'How come? A deputation was going to see you. I called your aides and left a message with them that we were waiting for you. The differences were being patched up and it would be a good thing if the President was here.'

Perhaps he did not want reconciliation and unity. Perhaps, he wanted to reserve his right to talk about Boris Yeltsin in his usual insulting tone. This had happened many times before. After the road accident in September 1990 when Yeltsin was in Kislovodsk for treatment, I had to make a strong statement in the Supreme Soviet, saying that the President had used inadmissibly insulting words towards the Chairman of Russia's Supreme Soviet, something he had never done with regard to any other republican leader. But for some reason the President uses any kind of words, at times highly insulting and intolerable, towards the parliamentary leader of the Russian state.

So perhaps the President reserved the right to this seemingly independent attitude when our Congress was coming to an end? If so, it is a disturbing sign. Why? Because our society needs unity, especially to cope with economic problems. At the Congress Yeltsin and I convinced even our radical democrats, so to speak, that we needed a Union Treaty. We accepted it as the basis of our work at the Congress, of our own free will. Nobody was imposing that idea on us. We believed that we needed to state in public that we sincerely wished to preserve the Union and that we supported a new Union Treaty with actions, not only with words.

Neither Yeltsin nor I have ever denied the need for a new Union Treaty. What we were opposed to was the content of the draft. On the whole, I would view the President's failure to appear at our Congress and his reluctance to meet the deputies as an attempt not to be bound by his promise for cooperation. And another thing: the President is highly skilful in passing the buck, blaming others for his own mistakes.

When we held very complicated negotiations about the budget, all the leading party press, television and radio claimed that Russia was impeding efforts to formulate normal budget proposals. All right, we came to terms and the budget crisis came to an end. We signed a provisional agreement for economic cooperation. The next item on the agenda was a price rise. We were opposed to an administrative price increase because it would reduce people to poverty. We were accused of obstructing reforms and of torpedoing efforts to rectify prices. Furthermore, Russia was accused of trying to exploit other republics. The Chairman of our Supreme Soviet had to face so many insulting attacks for being flatly opposed to such a 'rectification' of prices.

In the past six years I have written many articles against price increases, Pavlov style. Pavlov launched his rather shallow theory back in August 1986 when he was appointed Chairman of the State Committee on Prices. This was the origin of the idea of a limited price 'reorganisation' taken out of context of economic reform as a whole. A price reform has to be part of a large range of other measures to reform the economy, and it must not be carried out by purely administrative methods. So I said to Yeltsin:

You told the Supreme Soviet that you can't bring yourself up to sign this unpopular decision providing for price increases. But to avoid accusations that we are foiling the President's reforms, let me sign this document on Russia's behalf. Certainly, I will be assuming huge responsibility, but we will avoid the accusation that we are obstructing the central government's 'correct' decisions.

I signed it, but with a heavy heart.

Less than a month later, what consequences did we see? Did we not warn about them? As a matter of fact, similar things have happened quite often in other areas of economic policy. And when our warnings come true, those responsible try to 'forget' everything and set up new traps. It is very difficult to cooperate with a central administration of this kind. Indetermination, treachery and obduracy seem to pass from one central government to another.

Little wonder, at a meeting of the Federation Council on 9 April some participants spoke of the attempts by central government officials to set republics off against one another. It had been alleged the Russia was not paying up in full, which was detrimental to Uzbekistan and Karelia. Similar accusations had been made against Ukraine. The Chairman of the Ukrainian Council of Ministers, Vitold Fokin, said in plain words that the republics would never fight against each other. Islam Karimov, the President of Uzbekistan, said: 'Esteemed Mikhail Sergeyevich, why did you call us here for? Are we going to sign the Union Treaty so that you can create forty-seven ministries again? Isn't it clear that as soon as they are created they will die because we in the republics will not support them?' Leaders of other republics spoke in the same vein. Central television did not show that. On the whole, the republican leaders are highly educated and far-sighted politicians who know only too well the cunning games played by the central economic bureaucracy.

Considering these difficult conditions, what gives you hope for Russia's rebirth?

First of all, I hope that these difficult conditions will at last force the central administration, President Gorbachev and the leaders of the republics to develop common approaches to economic reforms as soon as possible. This must also apply to the recognition of the republics' independence within the areas of their competence. This is bound to happen, but I wish it were understood as soon as possible.

Furthermore, the laws that the Supreme Soviet of the Russian Federation has adopted, even though they are half-hearted decisions, provide a legislative framework for the faster growth of a mixed economy.

I should remind you that an attempt to carry out a coup using parliamentary means failed at the Third Congress. Was that not a success?

Moreover, that victory was consolidated by practical measures, including the dramatically increased role of the Supreme Soviet, the government and the Chairman of the Supreme Soviet, codified in the Congress resolution on the redistribution of powers between these authorities. Therefore, the Supreme Soviet and its Presidium, jointly with the government, can now exercise a more forceful, responsible and purposeful influence on political and economic processes. The Supreme Soviet effectively used this redistribution of powers when it adopted its laws, including the one on the presidency. The same is true of the Presidium and the Chairman of the Supreme Soviet, Boris Yeltsin. At the same time, it urged us to propose serious changes in Russia's political and government structures. We must quickly develop serious changes in the state structure of the RSFSR to help implement the democratic ideas outlined in our policy documents.

Changes in the political system should correspond to economic reforms aimed at bringing about a market. Since the 'nine-plus-one' agreement of 23 April 1991, the fetters have been somewhat eased. I should also like to remind you that the Third Congress, which was convened to overthrow the Supreme Soviet leaders, accorded them political trust, which came as a complete surprise to the putsch organisers. Finally, in the decision itself, you will not find any proposal submitted by the 'co-reporters' or any other extreme conservatives. Does that not indicate the total bankruptcy of those forces that had provoked the special Congress? And it highlights the complete absence of positive ideas on the part of the so-called parliamentary opposition. No one proposed any point to the resolution from Isayev's co-report or from the speeches of Boris Isaev, Goryacheva and others. Frankly speaking, they appeared miserable. And, let us put it straight, any honest person must be ashamed that our society breeds politicians of this kind. Their intellectual depravity is obvious to everyone.

The world is waiting for the further course of events. Can you make a forecast for the near future? How will the situation develop?

Well, I will try, though I must say I do not like making predictions. Everyone knows who is heading for confrontation, inciting it, and laying the groundwork for it. The address is known. It is the central administration, it alone. It is provoking discontent in the outlying regions, in other republics. It keeps inciting revolt by regional party secretaries who also hold the jobs of chairmen of regional soviets, despite the decision of the First Congress that no official can combine these two jobs. The 'regional' officials hold these positions with the direct support of the General Secretary and President. Hence they are led to believe that the worse things are, the better, for the Russian leaders can be blamed for all these troubles and will have to answer for them.

114

I believe that the Third Congress was important in that it definitely dispersed all illusions that we, Russian leaders, are trying to wage a 'war of laws', provoke confrontation, oust the President and so on. I think most people know perfectly well from where the wind blows, and this has been demonstrated by sociological surveys. We can sense public opinion. Nevertheless, in such conditions everyone should, of course, strive for cooperation.

Deep down, President Gorbachev, as I see it, has reconciled himself to the loss of union republics, virtually all of them. So even more fiercely the central administration is pressuring the Russian structures of power, all without exception, something it does not do to the other republics. The central administration is desperately battling for the right to rule Russia. I have long used the term 'dual government' in Russia. But, I repeat, the dramatic Third Emergency Congress of Russian Deputies, which met at a time of growing labour unrest, led to a situation in which it is possible for us to reach agreement with the central administration. The extreme right-wing and reactionary forces, too, are trying to oust the President. Can we sit on the fence in this situation? I do not think so.

There is room for agreement. For instance, it would be pretty easy to agree about the Union Treaty and define the functions that, in accordance with the Declaration on the State Sovereignty of the RSFSR, we are delegating to the President, his Cabinet and the central administration, while we keep the prerogative to implement economic strategies in Russia, and exercise external economic activities. This would be a reasonable and modern approach. But, frankly speaking, I am not sure that the President and his advisers will be wise enough to opt for this conflict-free and least painful attitude. Far from being radical, it is a left-centrist plan, though I do believe in the sincere intentions of the authors of the 'nine-plus-one' statement.

Yeltsin outlined a highly constructive proposal at the Congress, to create a broad coalition government from among the union republics and different political parties, groups and platforms. It must be a responsible government enjoying people's confidence, otherwise it would be unable to implement profound reforms. Kazakhstan, the Ukraine and the smaller union republics are carrying out much more radical economic reforms and nobody is obstructing them. The central party press, far from criticising them, is praising them. But as soon as our banks or government try to do something or voice some idea in the Supreme Soviet, we immediately come under attack and a great deal of pressure.

It is very important for Russia to establish foreign policy priorities. Will this be the West or the East or Latin America?

We must be open both to the West, and the East, and Latin America. I would not phrase the point the way you do. Since around mid-October 1990 President Gorbachev's policies have evolved rapidly. For the preceding five years the President looked to the West and reckoned with Western opinion. In October 1990, it seems to me, he experienced a dramatic change of heart. To him, as a politician and statesman, Western influence ceased to exist. For this reason, I believe, he ventured in January 1991 to take strong action in Lithuania, trying to overthrow the lawful Baltic governments with armed force. Naturally, in these conditions, Russia's role sharply increased, especially when Yeltsin went to Tallinn where he signed treaties with two republics and supported the Baltic demand for troop withdrawals. Russia's Supreme Soviet adopted a statement protesting against the use of force, and it was supported by the Supreme Soviets of other republics, including Ukraine, Belorussia and Kazakhstan. At that time, it seems to me, Russia's leaders and Supreme Soviet became the strongest barrier to the dictatorship about which Sheverdnadze spoke when he resigned. The confrontation between the two governments, the Union and the Russian government, became particularly visible. The climax came on 19 February when Yeltsin called on the President to resign and devolve powers to the Federation Council. It was the time when the reactionary attack on Russia was at its highest and, I believe, the most critical period we had to live through. We had to stand our ground.

After Yeltsin's speech, the President lost control of the situation. The people stepped in. They wondered why Yeltsin had made such a demand. And they began thinking in earnest. After all, Yeltsin had been in power for nine months, and Gorbachev for six years. The point of departure was April 1985. Whatever we might say about the stagnation period, we must note that even the Kremlin gerontocrats of the Brezhnev era were cleverer men. They never allowed the economy and living standards to fall to such a critical point. This means that the men who came along with Gorbachev, especially Ryzhkov and Pavlov, have proved to be dilettantes. There have been many mistakes since April 1985. Who was responsible for creating the infamous agro-industrial complex (*Gosagroprom*)? Agricultural potential, including livestock breeding, has dramatically weakened. Then there was the notorious anti-alcohol war. All right, you combat alcohol abuse but why destroy all the vineyards? The damage totalled 50 billion roubles, not counting the profits lost. It was then that useless money began to be printed, the source of the present inflation. These major mistakes were committed by the President and his government, which has changed little in the past six years. We have no right to forget about it, though we need to cooperate, and very closely, too.

How do you visualise the place of the Union President? I have the impression that Mikhail Gorbachev stands on a piece of shagreen leather. It is shrinking, but the ambitions of the one standing on it are not. Is there a contradiction here? The loss of power by the man who began the movement away from the totalitarian system, but who is now pressed to give up many of his governing functions in favour of the republics is, evidently, a very painful process.

I would not like to paint a psychological portrait of the President. The reality is that the President has enormous powers which even the USSR Congress of People's Deputies does not possess. As a matter of fact, the Congress handed over a number of functions to the President without asking the approval of the union republics. And that became legalised lawlessness.

Sooner or later the President will have to come to terms with the fact that he cannot exercise all of the powers that he has assumed. In the 'nine-plus-one' statement the President officially recognises that those powers he assumed belong to the union republics. I am speaking of the economic sphere in the first place. That is why I think that since the President has signed the statement he must realise that, once signed, the union republics will naturally never give it up. And if the President, after waiting for a while, tries to recover what he has lost, the next time he will find it impossible to rely on the support of such influential forces as the union republics. This should be understood and accepted. And if everything goes in accordance with the provisions of the statement, we shall help the President, and he will play a worthy role in the Union, taking into account the changes to be enshrined in the Union Treaty. It is high time everybody realised that the Union will be the way which the republics want it to be. And the head of the Union state will have exactly the amount of power which the sovereign states will hand over to him. And we are really interested in preserving the Union and carrying out major economic reforms in conjunction with the union republics.

It would do a lot of good if the President came to know how to learn lessons. But I agree that he does not like to admit his mistakes, although he had made more of them than all the Union leaders put together. The economic upheavals we are going through now, were they inevitable? The President should have said, 'Yes, I have chosen the wrong economic policy, for three years I have been talking about the market and done nothing to start moving towards it.' That is the main strategic error committed by the President and his team. And the new Cabinet of Ministers has now taken up those errors and delusions. Naturally, we cannot be guided by such an economic policy.

Let us assume that Gorbachev admits his mistakes, understands everything, and changes his policies. But can there be any certainty that the top leaders of the army, the military–industrial complex covering Russia with its enormous wing, will agree with his choice? We are an extremely militarised country, and many of our troubles stem from this fact.

117

It seems to me you are too pessimistic about these forces. If we take the army, the military–industrial complex, we see that not everything is one colour there either. Large groups in the army are patriotically minded. They will serve Russia and will not oppose Russian policy. There are such people among the generals too.

The military–industrial complex devours enormous funds, nearly half of the budget goes there. But not everything is uniform there either. Many arms factories are ready to develop civilian production, although it is very difficult to stop the giant flywheel set in motion after the war. However, the people working there are not to blame.

Why then did the President's policy take a reactionary turn in the autumn of 1990? He went back on an agreed programme, the events in the Baltic countries, adopting a hostile attitude to 'so-called democrats'; all these events were not accidental. In my view, a right-wing coup was in the making, and the President swayed sharply to the right. As a result of that gesture, he lost his supporters. So where did the danger come from?

Of course, there was pressure from certain quarters, but it was also a reaction to the steps taken by the republics and their policy. The President was looking for ways of stopping their development, *and* that of the Russian parliament, in the first place. Evidently, it was intended to begin in the Baltic countries, to put severe pressure on them and, later, perhaps, on Russia, too. However, the President has always valued world opinion very much, and in that case he was willing even to brush this aside. This still remains a mystery to me. And he tried to use force to halt the Baltic countries' movement towards independence. What follows is the conclusion you are making: the forces putting pressure on the President evidently proved very powerful indeed.

The reactionary schemes were foiled by the resolute stand adopted by the Chairman of the Supreme Soviet of the Russian Federation, the support given to Yeltsin by the Russian parliament, and the support given by democratic movements to the Baltic republics.

And that was followed by a string of the President's actions which even obliging lawyers and legislators could not describe as constitutional. Moscow's militia was subordinated to the USSR Ministry of Internal Affairs, the holding of an authorised meeting in Manege Square was impeded, and troops were deployed on Moscow's streets on the opening day of the Congress. What was that? Boyishness, wounded pride? Or creating conditions for an even sharper political turnabout?

You know, when I learned about the troops, I saw that we had won the struggle in Congress. One should think twice before taking such actions.

It is not serious, it is disappointing that the outstanding leader of pere-stroika – for Gorbachev has done a great deal both for his country and world civilisation – should suddenly believe in the effectiveness of power politics, and even with regard to such a large republic as Russia. In other countries the President would probably have been simply removed from office for such things. However, fortunately for our President, we live in a society which is far from democratic.

And yet in spite of everything I do not support the appeals to remove the President from office now. The Russian Supreme Soviet has con-sidered one of the demands of the striking miners, the idea of holding a 'round-table' conference to form a coalition government. I hope that President Gorbachev will not put off its implementation. I think he understands that the government formed by Pavlov is far from inspiring confidence. Pavlov is compelled to take unpopular actions, but it is all the more vital that the government have prestige. And what prestige does Pavlov have? It was he who wrecked the economy, perhaps he was even more zealous in this than Ryzhkov. At first as Chairman of the State Prices Committee and then as Minister of Finance he wrecked all finances. Since the time Pavlov appeared on the political scene he has had nothing but failures to accompany him.

With the presidential elections coming soon, this will be the first time in Russia's millennium-old history that a head of state will be elected democratically. What forces do you think Yeltsin can count on?

We count on all forces, except for party, government, economic and other officials, that is all but high-ranking officials. We count on the poor people who make up 70 to 80 per cent of the population. We count on our much-suffering intelligentsia who will certainly vote for Yeltsin. And most of the officers' corps certainly support our reforms. It is not true to suggest that the officers and the army are against us. Of course, there are some, but the situation there is not so simple either. Is not General Konstantin Kobets, who has consented to serve Russia, a representative of the high-ranking military? There are many other generals, true patriots, who are concerned about Russia's potential collapse. Are they not our allies, too?

We are trying to improve living standards for officers and their families. To this end, we have set up a Defence Committee which is concerned with the armed forces deployed in Russia. It is responsible for housing construction and other community services. Concerning officers resigning from the army or returning from Eastern Europe, we will be giving them land and helping them with entrepreneurial ventures, or else finding jobs for them or teaching them new skills. Our intelligentsia, our scientists, are they affluent people? I think the intelligentsia are proletarians, too. They have nothing at all. There are industrial proletarians and there are pen and paper proletarians. They want radical change. We rely on Russia's entrepreneurs, but they are just coming into being and remain weak. Our main support is ordinary people, workers, the destitute, and without them we would have been out of power long ago. And, of course, a special role in supporting our policies has been played by the miners and steel workers. They have provided important support for the course of Russia's rebirth and independence.

Recently I was surprised to read an article in a leading paper which again praised poverty: 'A poor person was respected in all times.' The same leaders who have failed to make people rich are again extolling poverty. Certainly, this means the degeneration of the ideas of the 'ruling class', that is, the bureaucratic elite. No, we will not extol poverty. We will try to make everybody affluent and the nation prosperous. Russia needs well-off people confident of the future. A confident person is strong, free to think and voice his or her ideas.

Needless to say, our opponents are officials, top-ranking party, govern-ment and economic officials, and many civil servants. Why? Because they have been directly linked with the ruling regime for decades. They are opposed to democracy in virtue of their office, often for hereditary reasons. They are a clan, a new nobility, a new elite. You cannot make them your allies. Let them be the opposition. Let them criticise us. This criticism can help us fine-tune our policies and eventually arrive at what is called 'constructive cooperation'.

Do you think that those who are now practising speculation will go into real business some time later?

The largest fortunes in the West are said to have started out with speculation, with land deals bordering on the criminal. But decades and centuries later, the first to build up capital began to rule national destinies. They organised revolutions: the first and the second industrial revolution, the third information revolution, the cybernetic revolution. Obviously, the same will happen here. Some of the entrepreneurs and speculators will go bankrupt, others will move into other spheres or 'pass into oblivion' (having built up fortunes), and still others will remain. These, I hope, will usher in a new industrial age for Russia and other republics, I hesitate to say for the country as a whole. For me Russia is the country. I am sure that conditions must be created for normal and honest entre-preneurial activities.

Russian deputies have raised the issue of the home of the Russian parliament, and now of the President, too. Will a special palace be built for it somewhere or will the parliament and the President return to genuine Russian territory, the Kremlin?

It is a complicated problem. I have been warned time and again that we should leave the present building (the Russian White House), because we are under total control and any word we say goes out. We are under absolute control. That is not a secret. The central government has waylaid us, as hunters waylay a wolf with red flags. When I leave papers on my desk, I can often see they have been thoroughly studied. But the thing is I have no secret papers. All my secrets are in my mind. There is nothing in the safe, except for my party card. So I do not really know what it is I should try to keep secret. The building in which we are now has become a true political centre, not a semblance of it as it used to be.

We are holding to an open and frank policy and we do not intend to play tricks, or make intrigues or conspire. As I said, I tend to support Gorbachev because there is no saying who might come after him. But I wish he showed more wisdom and common sense in this truly difficult time of trial for our peoples. I wish he mustered up the courage to say: let us build our renewed country together.

What can help Russia's peoples recover the self-confidence they have lost?

I feel everything begins with a certain number of things a person needs. As Marx argued, before going into politics, one must have the essential things like a home and food, but they are now lacking. Rebirth must start from there. Another factor is economic freedom. If you steal three kilos of something at a factory, you are sent to prison, but our ministers, those bureaucrats, have caused damage costing tens and hundreds of billions and are quite all right. Everything is written off because there is no economic freedom. Because the state takes everything a person produces and gives it to ranking political and economic bureaucrats who are wasting assets they did not produce. Why is that so? Because a human being is not free. Economic freedom presupposes a shareholder, a private owner, an honest cooperator, someone who has a stake in a concrete business, be it the owner or a free worker whose effort is fully rewarded. Only then will the principle 'My home is my castle' apply. Economic freedom is central to any freedom in general, human freedom. Human rights stem from economic freedom. If we logically follow this road, we will begin rebuilding Russia.

REBUILDING RUSSIA

Among recent journalistic works one can hardly find any to match Alexander Solzhenitsyn's article 'How to Rebuild Russia' ['Kak nam obustroit' Rossiyu', in Komsomolskaya Pravda and Literaturnaya Gazeta, 18 September 1990; in English published as Rebuilding Russia (London, Harvil, 1991)] *in its* analysis of Russia's historical destiny. Does this mean that many things look clearer at a distance, from the outside?

I do not think you can consider Solzhenitsyn's article a view from the outside. Solzhenitsyn knows Russia better than anybody else, from within and not from the outside. Behind each of his judgements is his enormous personal experience he tried to comprehend in the light of world culture. Besides, during the past fifteen years he was able to see another nation's way of life with his own eyes, and that could not but enhance his sense of pain for Russia while the events of the past six years could not but heighten his feeling of involvement in its destiny. Take *August 1914* and *The Red Wheel* as a whole, and *The Gulag Archipelago*. Solzhenitsyn knows both the past of Russia and its present-day reality better then anybody else.

Solzhenitsyn's work arouses everybody's keen interest. In what way did it touch you?

Solzhenitsyn speaks about things which are not usually discussed in our country even now, at the time of glasnost. He makes a realistic appraisal of the situation to which we are still trying to shut our eyes. For the first time, without beating about the bush, he states that, evidently, the Soviet Union is not destined to exist any more in the shape it has existed hitherto. It is a bitter truth. Solzhenitsyn believes that the most important thing for us, having recognised the sovereign rights of the Baltic states, the Central Asian and Transcaucasian republics, is to concentrate the efforts of Russia's citizens on rebuilding the Russian state with its thousand-year-old history. This idea is very close to my own views. It is also remarkable that Solzhenitsyn, living far from us, sensed the gravitation of Russia, Ukraine and Belorussia towards one another and raised the question of the possibility of a Slavic community.

What place does the 'Russian idea' occupy in the range of problems raised by Solzhenitsyn?

It is common knowledge that the 'Russian idea' came into being during the dictatorship of Nicholas I. Solzhenitsyn develops this idea in the new conditions. Alexander Yanov describes the time of Nicholas I as a regime of Russian counter-reform and shows beyond doubt that the best minds of those days – Pushkin, Zhukovsky, Belinsky, Gogol, and Tyutchev – proved unable to resist the despotic regime with its ideology of political idolatry. 'The government is the thought of the people, with their spiritual leader, their conscience. The government knows everything, sees every-thing, loves everybody, and can do everything. The principal civic virtue of a Russian is the faith in the infallibility of the government.' This pagan deification of the government was a phenomenon extremely dangerous to Russian culture and was fraught with its degradation, proved in practice after October 1917.

The 'Russian idea' began to take shape among the Slavophiles, who challenged the deification of the state. The challenge came from two standpoints: orthodoxy and injured national feeling. The 'Russian idea' began to degenerate in 1855 after the fall of Nicholas I's regime. The Slavophiles failed to see it and continued their struggle. The development of Slavophilism is linked with the idea of Slavic expansion, in particular, the capture of Constantinople and the creation of the Eastern Roman Empire. N. Danilevsky, the ideologist of Slavophilism, maintained that the most important thing for Russia was not reform but military power so that it could be stronger than Europe. As you can see, the contemporary military–industrial complex has an age-old tradition on which to draw. Another Slavophile idea, about the spiritual 'decay' of parliamentary Europe, was not only a windfall to Marxist eclecticism, but also became the centrepiece of the subsequent strategy pursued by the rulers of Russia and the USSR. According to Danilevsky, to become stronger than 'decaying Europe' we needed a mere trifle, internal monolithic solidarity, the unity of the Tsar and the people, rallying around the government under the banner of the great Russian historic mission. And the old 'formula of freedom' was entirely of no use to us, for to each Slav the idea of a Slavic community should be the highest idea after God and the Holy Church, higher than freedom, education and all creature comforts. Yanov is quite right when he says that from this there is only one step to the fundamental conclusion made by Konstantin Leontyev a decade later: 'The Russian nation was not specially created for freedom.'

In connection with Solzhenitsyn's article I should like to underline two aspects of the Slavophile problem. First, from my point of view, Solzhenitsyn, as a supporter of the 'Russian idea', is undoubtedly closer to the founders of Slavophilism with their criticism of despotism and autarchy. And he is least of all close to the Slavophilism which declared war on the intellectuals, the West, culture. Second, the destructive consequences of the development of the October 1917 coup are undoubtedly linked with the fact that it was in Russia that there occurred a distinctive merger of Marxism and left-wing radical Slavophilism preaching the cult of the deification of the state, expansionism and the suppression of the individual and freedom.

Do you agree with Solzhenitsyn that democracy to us is a means and not an end?

In the final analysis, democracy is just one of the conditions for the normal development and existence of society. However, there are circumstances in which democracy may also be a social objective, where it does not exist or where it is curtailed. In this case the struggle for democracy may become both a personal and a social objective.

Is it not remarkable that Solzhenitsyn sees the family as the main value and the main indicator of society's health?

Yes, indeed, Solzhenitsyn aspires to reshape every aspect of Russia's life in his article. Significantly, its title is 'How to Rebuild Russia'. And the family constitutes the basis here. Incidentally, the constitutions of several countries open with articles on the family. Humanity realised a long time ago that the family is indeed the main cell of society. And it is with the family that a person's morality, ethics, wellbeing, and happiness begin. However, what we have now is practically the disintegration of the family. A destitute society affected by violence and cruelty cannot produce a viable family.

Nevertheless, official ideology has been hammering into us that we had an ideal social structure, and that the people and the relations between them were also ideal. Consequently, the evil became a norm; as it were, the standard behaviour of an individual. Needless to say, this was damaging to the family, in particular, to women, children, youth and old people.

You have written a great deal about property. What do you think this sentence of Solzhenitsyn's: 'Property is part of the notion of the individual and gives the latter stability'?

There can be no individual, no personality without property. Animals have no property but human beings must have some property. A person seeks to make himself throughout his or her life. To say it the way Solzhenitsyn puts it means to make society, to make Russia through making oneself. Man seeks certain comforts of life whether we like it or not. The greedy seek creature comforts to excess, but a normal person seeks to have such things which would give him confidence in the present and the future.

In the section entitled 'The Province', Solzhenitsyn maintains: 'Our way to recovery is not long.' Do your forecasts coincide with those of Solzhenitsyn?

They do, to a considerable extent. The provinces are beginning to sense themselves a living organism, and not a Godforsaken backwoods obeying orders from the centre. Although there are some passive regions still waiting for assistance from the centre, others have been far more active. True, the latter sometimes assumes a destructive nature in our reforms. However, that stems above all from economic difficulties as well as those

124

linked with considerations of the moment. The provinces, seeing the impotence of the centre, are trying to carry out reform on their own, but in doing so jeopardise the actions of the Russian authorities. The provinces are now changing in both creative and destructive ways.

What is your attitude towards Solzhenitsyn's appeal to use the experience of the Russian district councils [zemstvo]?

Now that we are building soviets anew, we should take a closer look at the activities of the Russian *zemstvo*. According to Solzhenitsyn, their experience is a means of developing democratic principles. In the light of our experience we cannot say that our soviets are an ideal form of local government.

Nor can we accuse Solzhenitsyn in any way of imperial temptations. Some alleged that Solzhenitsyn spoke as a Russian chauvinist. I do not see anything of the kind in his article. 'I see with concern', Solzhenitsyn observes, 'that the awakening Russian national consciousness, to a considerable extent, is by no means free from thinking in terms of great power expanses, from an imperial intoxication.' It is apparent that he has no sympathy for chauvinistic feelings. And although he is a true and consistent Russian patriot, in my view, he can see through the merits and shortcomings of a Russian person, a citizen of Russia, first and foremost. So I do not think it is fair to say that he is all in the past. On the contrary, it is to the future that his thinking is projected.

Besides, we can hardly view Solzhenitsyn's article as a political statement. Rather, it is a literary and philosophical essay. Just recall Solzhenitsyn's reply to the US President when he invited the well-known writer to the White House as a dissident: 'I am not a dissident; I am a Russian writer.'

The Komsomolskaya Pravda newspaper reported that Solzhenitsyn's article was a reply to a message from I. S. Silaev, Chairman of the Council of Ministers of the Russian Federation.

Indeed, Solzhenitsyn's article was published by agreement between the Russian Prime Minster Ivan Silaev, *Komsomolskaya Pravda* and Solzhenitsyn. What is more, there was a half-hour telephone conversation between Solzhenitsyn and Silaev on 24 September 1990. Silaev again requested the writer to come to Russia, to be his private guest. Silaev told me that the conversation was friendly and cordial. Solzhenitsyn promised that he would think about it. He said, however, that he would like to return for good because both his heart and soul lived with Russia and its concerns. He would never be able to feel an American citizen. Such was the conversation.

In this context sharp criticism levelled against Solzhenitsyn in the mass media reminds me of the witch hunt in the old days. Why was there such an outburst of anti-democratic tendencies? It seems to me that those criticising Solzhenitsyn play into the hands of people who resent the activities of Russia's parliament and Russia's deputies, seeking to break out of the clutches of the central authorities.

However, does it not seem to you that the attitude towards Solzhenitsyn's article as well as that towards Sakharov's statements in his day stem from their extraordinary nature, their unexpectedness?

Yes, it stems from that, for we live in a world of stereotyped approaches, which are chiefly ideological, while Solzhenitsyn, just like Sakharov, sees life in the light of morality, in the light of man and his interests. And this is so unusual that it is rejected by conventional thinking at first.

Do you think that the Bolsheviks have succeeded in moulding a 'new' man over the past seventy-four years?

They have, no doubt about it. Only this man has proved to be worse than the 'old' one. They did succeed in breeding a 'new' man who is not very educated on the average. A man without any high cultural, moral or material requirements, devoid of any beliefs, including moral ones, a man without any moral barriers. In this sense the experiment has proved rather successful. Only they failed to mould a happy, cultured man, a man of high moral standards, a conscientious man, to use Solzhenitsyn's language. The conditions that bred *Homo Soveticus* proved to be deep-rooted. The half-century of Stalinism and neo-Stalinism resulted in the moral degeneration of the individual. Solzhenitsyn proceeds from the assumption that Stalinism and neo-Stalinism are the greatest evil, and it is this evil that moulded a perverted type of individual.

Nevertheless, the moral climate is now changing. Can the national features of the great Russian type of man such as thrift, industry, tolerance, well-wishing, be restored? Or has it all gone never to return?

Many believe that what was lost cannot be returned. For instance, in reply to the demand to give the land to the farmers we hear people say that farmers are now different, they allegedly do not want land. Vasily Starodubtsev, Chairman of the Peasants' Union, often says that the contemporary farmer is no longer a farmer. I do not think he is is right. I believe that the genetic memory of Russia's people has retained industry, discipline, respect for the elders, and tolerance. But these qualities are hidden somewhere very deep. We need specific economic and legal conditions to bring that memory back to life. And we seek to create such conditions in our new laws. I believe in the rebirth of humanity.

126

Is there a contradiction here? On the one hand you maintain that the seventy-four years have moulded a 'new' type of man, and on the other you believe in the rebirth of Russia's people?

There is a contradiction here. Indeed, a considerable number of our fellow-countrymen have lost traditional morality. But it is not so simple to get rid of one's own nature. That is why if we create new conditions and ensure the action of new economic relations, there will appear real pre-requisites for the rebirth of the traditional features of Russia's people. A true moral rebirth will occur.

Solzhenitsyn deals with precisely those problems which are now the subject of serious discussions. These are the problems of Russia's state structure and the question of the new Union and the new Union Treaty. Can there be a Union Treaty in general? It is apparent that there will not be fifteen republics in the Union any more. It will be a different Union. Even if only one republic dropped out of fifteen, we shall have to speak of a qualitatively new phenomenon. And one can hardly be serious in main-taining that 'the 1922 Treaty will be in force for those who fail to sign the new Union Treaty'. This is yet another absurdity coming from the central administration, and the 'non-signatories' will simply brush it aside. Solzhenitsyn understands all that only too well. After making a political analysis of the present-day nationalities processes, he says that no, there will not be a Union Treaty the way it has been conceived, say, in the centre. Unfortunately, such is the stark reality.

I, personally, stand for preserving inter-republican state ties and for the conclusion of a Union Treaty by fifteen republics. But I understand that it is no longer realistic. The Baltic republics will never join the Union for anything. There will also be difficulties with other republics. It is better to face the fact than pretend that nothing has happened. In this respect Solzhenitsyn's article helps one understand political reality and contri-butes to asserting the idea of national tolerance in social consciousness. Unfortunately, some of the leaders at the centre are captives to the illusions created by their imagination, that is where the tragedy lies.

President Gorbachev asserted that 'Solzhenitsyn's political views are alien to me as a politician; he is all in the past – the Russia of the past, the monarchy, it is unacceptable to me. I feel like a democrat ready to speak, to adopt radical views on the present'. Is that assessment of Solzhenitsyn's views correct?

One can hardly say that Solzhenitsyn is all in the past, that he rejects democracy. Just recall that, after considering various types of the state structure defined by Plato and Aristotle, Solzhenitsyn concludes 'We shall undoubtedly choose democracy.'

APPENDIX

Union Treaty
(drafted in August 1990)

We, plenipotentiary representatives of the peoples of union states, aware of our historical responsibility; expressing the interests, requirements and aspirations of our fellow citizens; recognizing the priority of generally accepted values and of human rights and freedoms; taking into consideration the historically evolved links and the community of the destinies of our peoples and their right to self-determination and free development; and acknowledging our striving for peaceful and friendly cooperation with all peoples, hereby state our readiness to become full-fledged founding members of a Union (Community) of free sovereign states.

ARTICLE I

Section 1

The parties to this Union Treaty and subjects of the Union (Community) are union republics (all fifteen republics are listed).

Section 2

The parties to the Union Treaty agree that the Union (Community, Commonwealth) is a confederative association of states which are sovereign states in international law. The sovereignty of the Community is based exclusively on powers which are defined by this Treaty and which have been voluntarily delegated to it by the founding states of the Community.*

* States (republics) may join the Community as associated members without delegating their powers to the extent required by full membership of the Community. This should be agreed upon with all founders of the Community during the treaty-drafting process and upon the establishment of the Community with a Convention, subject to endorsement by the Community's parliament.

Section 3

All power on the territory of founding states is exercised by these states which enter into treaty relations. The peoples of the republics are the sole source and exponent of state authority in these republics.

Section 4

A founding state of the Community which has signed this Treaty preserves its sovereignty except for the powers which it voluntarily delegates to the Community's coordinating bodies. The laws of each Community member state have priority on all its territory and are not subject to abrogation or arbitrary interpretation by the Community's bodies which are formed in order to fulfil tasks defined by the founding states in this Treaty.

Section 5

Each founding state of the Community has its own citizenship. The question of the Community's common citizenship will be taken up at subsequent stages of the Confederation's development.

Section 6

Each founding state has its own Fundamental Law, the Constitution, which may be amended or supplemented exclusively through the expression of the will of the state's peoples or by representation bodies of state authority.

Section 7

Founding states represent their interests in the international community independently and without any exemptions. They may delegate their powers to the governing bodies of the Union (Community) under bilateral agreements outside this Treaty (subject to ratification by a Convention).

ARTICLE II

Rights and Freedoms of the Citizens of the Union (Community)

The founding states agree that every person on the territory of the union states has personal, property (economic), social, cultural and political rights.

Section 1

Personal rights are the rights to life, freedom and inviolability; to impermissibility of infringement of one's honour and dignity and interference in one's private and family life and secrecy of correspondence;

to inviolability of one's home;

to freedom of travel and the choice of residence;

to leave one's country and return to it without hindrance;

to engage in occupations which correspond to one's wishes, abilities and possibilities.

Section 2

Property (economic) rights are the rights to property (material and intellectual) which is sacred and inviolate, is protected by law and may not be alienated from a person in any way, except for cases prescribed by law;

to participation in the management or administration of enterprises and organizations with which a person is connected by labour and other agreements, including property relations;

to a worthy material life in accordance with international standards.

Section 3

Social rights are the rights

to work, rest and leisure;

to social security;

to medical assistance.

Section 4

Cultural rights are the rights

to bringing up based on humanitarian values which reject propaganda of enmity on class or any other grounds;

to education;

to participation in cultural life and in the moral and spiritual revival of one's people and of its traditions and customs in keeping with the norms of universal human morals.

Section 5

Political rights are the rights

to taking part in running the state;

to the franchise in accordance with the generally recognised requirements of the world community;

to freedom of thought and word, conscience and religion and the possibility to express them freely orally or in writing;

to uniting in political parties, organisations and social movements other rights recognised by the human community.

Section 6

Guarantees of human and citizens' rights and freedoms

The constitutions of the founding states contain legal norms which provide guarantees of human and citizen's rights and freedoms, including protection by court (trial by jury) or by another body prescribed by law.

ARTICLE III

Section 1

Powers of the Community

The founding states of the Community agree that it is necessary in order to ensure

the Community's integrity as a confederative union of independent states and the common interests of their peoples in the economic, political, ecological and defensive spheres, to hand over some of the functions of the Community's founding states to the General Administration of the Community, which is a governing body established by them. The entire system of governing the Community is based on these exclusively delegated powers.

The Community's bodies of authority and government have no powers other than those delegated by the founding states.

Section 2

Objects of Government by the Community

The founding states agree that the objects of direct government (under the control and with the participation of the founding states) by the

Community's bodies of power and government may be: defence (except for functions of control and interior troops); public safety; nuclear power engineering.

Section 3

Objects of Joint Government

The founding states agree that the objects of joint government of the founding states and the Community may be:

environmental protection;

air and railway transport and merchant marine;

defence branches of industry and space exploration;

defence of the state borders of the union states.

Section 4

The Right to Ownership of the Objects of Government

The founding states agree that the transfer (delegation) to the Community of some of powers for the administration of material, financial and other objects and resources does not constitute the Community's property. Property and other means allocated for implementing the Community's tasks remain shared (common or joint) property of the founding states of the Union and may not be alienated by the Community's bodies of authority and government.

ARTICLE IV

Composition and Structure of the Union's (Community's) Bodies of Government

Section 1

Formation of the Community's General Administration

The founding states of the Community agree that a General Administration headed by the Community's President is necessary for attaining the Community's tasks and interests.

Section 2

Election of the President

The President is elected by the parliaments of the Community's founding states for a term of three years and may be elected for another term. Elections are held on the first Monday in December. The President takes office on the first Monday of the February of the current year upon being sworn in (inaugurated) before the members of the Community's Constitutional Court.

Section 3

General Administration

The President forms the General Administration which consists of

a state secretary (for inter-state relations);

a secretary for external affairs;

a secretary for the affairs of defence and disarmament (a civilian);

a secretary for finance;

director of the Security Agency;

a secretary for transport and communications;

a secretary for power engineering;

a secretary for agricultural matters;

a secretary for matters of environmental protection;

a secretary-inspector for human rights;

a state minister who is the Community President's personal representative.

The General Administration forms the budget from contributions made by the Community's founding states and submits it for approval to the Community's Parliament.

The President controls the General Administration within the established prerogatives.

Section 4

Convention

Control of the activity of the General Administration and the elaboration of the Community's policy are effected by a Convention, a Conference of the Heads of Founding States which is convened not less frequently than once in three months. Its work is directed and its sessions are chaired by the Community's President.

Section 5

The Community's Parliament and its Formation

The Community's Parliament has two chambers.

The upper chamber, the senate, is elected by constituencies of the Union's states for a term of four years at the rate of ten senators per union state.

The lower chamber, the chamber of deputies, is elected proportionately to the number of voters of the founding states who are required to elect a total of 400 deputies for a term of three years.

The chambers have equal rights; disputes between them are resolved through conciliatory mechanisms appointed and endorsed by the chambers and their bodies.

Elections are conducted on the last Friday of October of the year of election.

Section 6

To be elected to the senate a person has to have been a citizen of a Community's founding state for not less than ten years and to have attained the age of 30 (27 in the case of the chamber of deputies) by the time of the elections.

Section 7

The Parliament conducts legislative activity within the Community's prerogatives, controls the effectiveness of the General Administration's policy, arranges parliamentary hearings of ministers and other officials of the Community, approves the budget and makes proposals to the parliaments of the Community's founding states.

Sessions of the senate are conducted by the state secretary and those of the chamber of deputies, by a speaker elected by that chamber.

Section 8

The Parliament has the right in exceptional cases to start proceedings for the removal from power of the President or any other official of the Community (impeachment) if obvious signs have come to light of the violation of this Treaty as the basic constitutional act of the Community. In this case the chamber of deputies acts as the prosecutor and the senate as the judge.

The maximum penalty under the impeachment procedure is the removal from office and a vote of censure.

Section 9

The Community's International Court

The International Court is a judicial body which considers mutual complaints and disputes of the Community's founding states. Participation in it is confirmed by a special act of a founding state. The Court's decisions are binding.

The Community's International Court is formed from among prominent specialists in constitutional law according to a special procedure approved by the Convention.

ARTICLE V

The Community's founding states select the venue of the Community's bodies of coordination and control, which may not be one of the capitals of union states.

ARTICLE VI

The Right to Enter the Community or Withdraw from It

Section 1

The founding states declare the right of any of them freely to withdraw from the Community. The necessary decision is made through a referendum by a simple majority of votes of the citizens of the founding state concerned. After the decision has been made a period of one year is allotted for settling questions connected with the republic's withdrawal and the ensuring of normal conditions for the functioning of the founding state and the Community.

Section 2

The members of the Community have the right to cancel the Treaty with a founding state which has systematically violated the Treaty's provisions and obligations flowing out of it. Such a decision is taken by a simple majority of the members of parliament on the initiative of the Convention.

Section 3.

In the event of withdrawal from the Community or the cancellation of the Treaty the founding state concerned shall settle within one year all of its obligations to the Community which does the same as regards its obligations to the founding state unless other provisions have been made by special agreements.

ARTICLE VII

This Treaty may be included in Constitutions of the founding states as norms of their Fundamental Laws which are recognized and respected by the citizens of founding states.

The Community's founding states proceed from the inexpedience of having one (common) Constitution for all the Community's founding states.

ARTICLE VIII

This Treaty or some of its provisions may be cancelled, altered or augmented only with the consent of all parties to the Treaty. The necessary proposal should be made by the founding state concerned to the Convention. The decision is made by the Community's Parliament.

ARTICLE IX

The Union is open for the entry of any state which shares the aims proclaimed by its founders. The necessary request is sent to the Community's President who consults with the Convention and may then submit it to the Parliament.

ARTICLE X

This Treaty comes into force at the moment of its endorsement by the functioning Supreme Soviets of the Community's founding states.

Part II

THE COUP

7

DAY ONE
19 August 1991

DEMOCRACY IN DANGER

I had arrived at my dacha at Arkhangelskoe on the previous evening with my daughter and my niece, having cut short my holiday. My wife remained in the Moscow flat. On 19 August Boris Yeltsin was supposed to conduct a meeting of members of our delegation for the Union Treaty, and the 20th was the date Mikhail Gorbachev planned that it would be signed.

On 19 August I got up at 6 a.m. as usual. I had a quick wash and a shave, drank a cup of coffee and was just about to go outside to where the official car was waiting when the telephone rang. I knew instantly from the intermittent tones that it was a long-distance call, otherwise I would not have bothered answering it. It was Sergei Filatov, the Secretary to the Presidium of the Supreme Soviet. He was on holiday in Zheleznovodsk, in the Northern Caucasus. His voice was extremely agitated:

'Ruslan Imranovich! Have you heard the news on the radio and on the television?'

'No.'

'It looks as though Gorbachev has been forced from power, even though they are alleging that he is ill.'

At this point we were cut off. I switched on the television immediately. The announcer said that Gorbachev was ill and that Gennady Yanaev, the Vice President, was assuming the responsibilities of the President, and also that a State Committee for the State of Emergency (SCSE) was being formed and that a State of Emergency was being declared in certain regions, including Moscow and Leningrad, and that there were eight people on the SCSE: Yanaev, Valentin Pavlov, Dmitri Yazov, Boris Pugo, Vladimir Kryuchkov, Oleg Baklanov, Alexander Tizyakov and Vasili Starodubtsev.

Boris Yeltsin's dacha is next door to mine. Of course I went round immediately.

'Where is Boris Nikolaevich?'

'Upstairs,' answered Naina Iosifovna, the President's wife.

The President was sitting in an armchair, deep in thought. We went into his office and called the Russian Vice President, Alexander Rutskoi, and the Prime Minister, Ivan Silaev, asking them to come to us. And we began to discuss tactics. It was of the utmost importance to grasp the situation. What was happening and where was President Gorbachev? Even at this early stage we reached the conclusion that a coup d'etat was being attempted. To what extent was the army mobilised? What was the role of the Communist Party oligarchy in all of this? And how would the republics, Ukraine and Kazakhstan, react to this turn of events? This was of paramount importance as Russia had signed treaties on political and economic cooperation with these two large and influential republics.

It took us ten minutes to get through to President Nazarbaev.

'Do you know what happened last night and what is your reaction?' asked Yeltsin without any kind of preamble.

'How do you intend to react to these events? It is obvious that this is a coup d'état and that Gorbachev has been forcibly removed from power.'

The entire conversation lasted not more than four minutes. Nazarbaev's answers were in no way reassuring. Above all, Yeltsin remarked that the Kazakh leader's evaluations and opinions were unusually cautious and restrained, and he gave answers such as 'We need to study the situation in more detail', and so on.

We could not get through to the Chairman of the Ukrainian parliament, Leonid Kravchuk.

At that time we thought that the putschists had come to some kind of arrangement with these leaders. As it turned out, things were not as they first appeared. The conspirators, including General Varennikov, the Commander of land forces, and Defence Minister Yazov's deputy, were indeed applying very strong pressure on them and trying to secure their agreement 'not to interfere' in exchange for a promise not to introduce a state of emergency in Ukraine and Kazakhstan. As yet we were unaware of this, but it was already clear that for the time being we could rely only on ourselves. Yeltsin telephoned the commander of the paratroops, Pavel Grachev, and asked him what was going on and whether or not he was going to take repressive action. The general replied that he had been ordered into Moscow to blockade all important points, including the White House, but that he would not take arms against the people. There then followed a brief discussion of the joint tactics we would employ. We chose to adopt a tough line in response to the putschists' actions.

Silaev arrived, along with Ruskoi, the mayor of Leningrad Anatoli Sobchak, the Ministers Victor Yaroshenko and Mikhail Poltoranin, and a few others. We exchanged opinions and discussed what action could be taken against the putschists, whether we should enter into negotiations at all, and if so, whether we should negotiate directly or through some influential mediator. I responded sharply, saying that negotiations were equivalent to capitulation and so there should be no negotiations. We had to adopt a tough line as far as the putschists were concerned and our first document, an appeal 'To the Citizens of Russia', should call upon the people to come out decisively against the conspirators. Agreement was soon reached on this. I was given the honour of preparing this document, taking into account the suggestions and observation of those present at this first meeting, who also constituted our headquarters, the headquarters of the resistance.

We had no way of printing the appeal, and so Yeltsin, Silaev and myself signed a handwritten copy, photocopied it and gave a copy to everyone present, in the full knowledge that we could be arrested for this. Here is the appeal, in which the action of the conspirators is declared to be a coup d'état.

To the citizens of Russia

On the night of 18 to 19 August 1991 the legally elected President of the country was removed from power. Whatever reasons might be given to justify this removal, we are dealing with a right-wing, reactionary and anti-constitutional coup.

Notwithstanding all the trials and difficulties the people of our country are experiencing, the democratic process is sweeping the country on an ever-broadening scale and it cannot be reversed. The peoples of Russia are becoming masters of their own fate. The uncontrolled rights of the Party and other unconstitutional bodies have been severely curtailed. The Russian leadership has assumed a decisive role in accordance with the Union Treaty, striving to maintain the unity of the Soviet Union and of Russia. Our stand on this question has made it possible substantially to speed up the preparation of the Union Treaty, coordinate it with all the republics, and set the date for its signing – 20 August.

Such a development aroused the animosity of reactionary forces and provoked them to try and solve the most complicated political and economic problems by the use of force. Such actions can only be described as irresponsible and adventuristic. Earlier attempts at a coup had already been made.

We have always considered that the use of force to solve political and economic problems is unacceptable. It discredits the USSR in the eyes of the world and undermines our prestige in the international community, returning us to the Cold War era and the isolation of the Soviet Union from the international community.

We are forced to declare unlawful this so-called Committee together with all its decisions and resolutions.

141

We are convinced that local authorities will unswervingly follow Constitutional Law and the Decrees of the President of the RSFSR.

We call upon the citizens of Russia to give a fitting reply to the putschists and to demand that they immediately return the country to a normal path of constitutional development.

It is of vital importance that President Gorbachev be given the opportunity to address the people. We demand the immediate convocation of an extraordinary session of the Congress of People's Deputies of the USSR.

We are absolutely convinced that our compatriots will not allow the arbitrary rule and lawlessness of these putschists, men with neither shame nor conscience, to become firmly established. We appeal to the troops to demonstrate a sense of civic duty and not to take part in this reactionary coup.

We call for a general strike until such time as these demands are met. We do not doubt that the international community will correctly evaluate this cynical attempt at a rightist coup.

The President of the RSFSR   B. N. Yeltsin
The Chairman of the Council of Ministers of the RSFSR

           I. S. Silaev

Acting Chair of the Supreme Soviet of the RSFSR

           R. I. Khasbulatov

19 August 1991, 09.00   Read and pass on to others

While we were discussing our struggle with the junta and formulating the appeal, the President's guard kept us informed about the movements of mobile mechanised units in the area around Arkhangelskoe. People were starting to feel on edge and it was suggested that we return to the White House in Moscow as quickly as possible. Moreover, I had a meeting of the parliament's Presidium at 10.00 a.m. Sobchak asked whether he should stay in Moscow or return to Leningrad and I requested that he be flown home immediately to organise opposition to the putschists there.

I got into the car. My driver, Volodya, suggested that we avoid the main road and leave the dacha estate by a country road through the woods. This we did, and, coming out onto Profsoyuznaya Street, we set off for the White House at terrific speed.

THE DEPUTIES: ORGANISERS OF THE DEFENCE

Almost all the members of the Presidium were there. Their faces were anxious. The hall was packed with deputies and journalists. They were all wondering what I was going to say, but I had absolutely no information, apart from what had been announced on the television and the radio and was already well known to everyone in the hall.

I told them about the meeting with the President and the Prime Minister, read the text of the appeal calling upon the people to take a firm stance opposing the coup and to begin the immediate organisation of a general strike, and I suggested that, firstly, the Presidium of the Supreme Soviet approve this document, and, secondly, that an emergency session of the Russian parliament be called for 21 August with the agenda 'Concerning the political situation in the Republic as a result of the coup d'état'.

A stormy debate began. The putschists were censured and various methods of opposition were suggested. Only two people voiced their disagreement. One of them was the Deputy Chair of the Supreme Soviet, Boris Isaev, who in very ornate language expressed the view that 'first of all we had to examine the situation', 'we should not call a general strike', 'nothing terrible has happened' and so on. The other, Vladimir Isakov, was more direct and categoric in his convictions. He declared that in principle he agreed with the evaluation of events that a coup d'etat had occurred the night before. But it was justified because 'You, Ruslan Imranovich, through the signing of the Union Treaty, were preparing another coup for 20 August.' In February 1991 Isaev and Isakov, along with four other deputies and the 'Communists of Russia' group, had demanded an extraordinary meeting of the Congress of People's Deputies and had tried to remove Yeltsin and myself from the leadership of the Supreme Soviet.

I responded sharply, telling Isakov and Isaev that they were agreeing with Yanaev and the putschists justifying the actions of the SCSE. The morning party papers had printed material with a similar interpretation, justifying the actions of the conspirators. They had also published the declaration of the Chair of the USSR Supreme Soviet, Anatoli Lukyanov, with his criticisms of the Union Treaty.

However, it did not take long for us to pass a resolution on two points: to approve the appeal 'To the Citizens of Russia', and to call an extraordinary session of the Supreme Soviet for 21 August at 10.00. The resolution was the second official document adopted by the Russian leadership on 19 August (the first was the appeal 'To the Citizens of Russia'). The President's decrees came after them. I place special emphasis on this so that the role of the Russian parliament in the suppression of the coup is made clear.

Resolution of the Presidium of the Supreme Soviet of the RSFSR on the Convening of an Emergency Session of the Supreme Soviet of the RSFSR

On the night of 18–19 August, as a result of an unconstitutional coup, the political environment of the country has been fundamentally changed.

In accordance with the Constitution of the USSR, a state of emergency can be declared by the Supreme Soviet or the President of the USSR with the agreement of the Republics, but in the absence of such consent, to be passed by the Supreme Soviet this resolution must have a majority of not less than two-thirds of the members. Since the implementation of a state of emergency has violated the Constitution of the USSR, the actions of this so-called Emergency Committee amount to a coup d'état.

The normal operation of the constitutional authorities of the RSFSR has been brought into question.

In the current situation the Presidium of the Supreme Soviet of the RSFSR decrees the following:

1 To convene a special session of the Supreme Soviet of the RSFSR on 21 August at 11.00 a.m. in the House of Soviets of the RSFSR, the agenda being 'The political situation of the RSFSR resulting from the coup d'état'.
2 The fulfilment of decisions of the so-called emergency committee will be considered as complicity in this crime against the state with all the consequences that arise from this.

Acting Chair of the Supreme Soviet of the RSFSR
R. I. Khasbulatov
19 August 1991

After having adopted this resolution we turned to a host of organisational problems. The members of the Supreme Soviet and its Presidium as well as the majority of the deputies were to stay in the White House, while some were to leave for their constituencies immediately to rally the people for the struggle against the junta.

Immediately after the Presidium session had finished I went into my office on the fifth floor. The windows look out onto the wide courtyard of our building and onto the embankment. It was 11 a.m. I glanced out of the window and saw tanks and armoured cars, and in the distance a huge crowd of people heading for the White House. And I saw them begin to build a barricade around the parliament building. Two lads were carrying some kind of rusty bath. I have to admit that my heart beat fast and my eyes filled with tears. Muscovites had come to defend their parliament and their Russian President. Moscow had risen. Amateur radio stations were already broadcasting our appeal. Why amateur stations? Because we were practically cut off from all means of communication; we had no access to television or to the radio, and our *Rossiiskaya Gazeta* and *Rossiya* had been closed down along with other democratic newspapers.

I have to say that worrying information had reached us earlier about changes in the staffing of officers of the Kantemir and Taman divisions, and also about the cancellation of leave. None the less, Monday 19 had taken us completely by surprise. The column of tanks and armoured vehicles moving along Kutuzovskii Prospect had completely encircled the House of Russian Soviets by 12.00.

The first spontaneous demonstration took place in Manege Square. A paratroop colonel opposite the Moscow Soviet building on Gorky Street said apologetically that the army had been sent in so that there would be no broken windows and no people hurt in the riots!

A large group of deputies came in and once again the question was asked, 'What are we going to do?'

Without answering I gestured for them to come to the window and pointed to the crowd of people heading towards us and the first barricade going up in front of the White House. We immediately agreed to call all the deputies together in the assembly room and work out some general tactics.

At 12.00 between 150 and 200 deputies had gathered. I explained the main tasks as best I could: in order to inform the population about the events in the capital, some deputies would be sent to the airport and to the railway stations to distribute our documents to passengers and passers-by; we had to mobilise the amateur radio stations, look for a printing-press to print our material, arrange for speeches to be made via the radio, and so on. The most important thing was to make contact with the provinces and to convey to the Russian hinterland our firm resolve to restore constitutional order, to distribute our first documents, the appeal 'To the Citizens of Russia' and the resolution of the Presidium of the Supreme Soviet to call an extraordinary session of parliament. There was one more important task, to organise a special radio centre to supply a constant stream of information to those inside the building and those defending it outside. Most of our telephone connections had been cut and our fax machines were not working. We began to get ourselves organised.

At that time we were receiving constant reports about the military units that had been sent to Moscow; they were heading towards the White House and the Moscow Soviet. From our offices we could hear the roar of the tanks becoming louder and louder.

The internal phones never stopped ringing with calls from the President, the Vice President and the Prime Minister; we were constantly exchanging information. While I was coordinating work with the deputies and then contacting the regional capitals (we were often cut off), the President was busy trying to establish whether there was any widespread support for the coup, what the aims of the conspirators were, what had become of President Gorbachev and his family, and what the situation was in the military units and the mood of the officers.

Even while the Presidium had been in session, Lev Sukhanov, the President's assistant, came to tell me that the President wanted me to come to a press conference.

The large hall was packed with journalists. Boris Yeltsin began by reading the appeal 'To the Citizens of Russia' and his first decree, evaluating the action of the putschists. Yeltsin emphasised that it was impossible to broadcast this declaration to the people by television and radio. The putschists had practically all channels of communication in the capital under their control. Therefore he was hoping that the appeal would become known to the inhabitants of the country and to the international community with the help of foreign journalists. The President informed those present that he had spoken with Yanaev by phone and that the latter had 'unconvincingly tried to explain why Gorbachev was no longer able to carry out his duties'. Yeltsin then replied, 'Show me a written declaration or statement by Gorbachev in some other form, in accordance with the Constitution, as no one can believe you.'

Yeltsin went on to say that his attempt to contact Foros, where Gorbachev was supposed to be, had not been successful: 'We could not get through. If he is still alive and at his dacha in the Crimea, then he is completely cut off. I last spoke to him on Friday. He was in good health and preparing to fly to Moscow on the 20th to sign the Union Treaty, and had called a large meeting for 21 August. There was no threat to his health.'

The President of Russia went on to emphasise that the cynical decrees of the Committee threatened that the legally elected representatives of power might be interned. The Russian leadership, said the President, declared its firm resolve not to give way to the Committee. Yeltsin also informed the conference about his discussions with the representatives of legally elected authority in various regions of the republic. A special message was sent to the leaders of the countries of the world, calling on them to condemn the coup d'état in the USSR and to regard it as anti-constitutional. The President of Russia also described his conversation with the Ukrainian leader, Kravchuk, who supported the actions of Russia and had informed him that Ukraine intended to take similar measures.

At the end of the press conference Ivan Silaev said, 'Our strength is not in arms but in our open and honest words with which we appeal to the citizens of Russia. We are unarmed, and our hopes rest on the support of the people.'

My communications with the main cities of Russia were very erratic; sometimes we got through, sometimes we were cut off. None the less, we managed to convey our firm resolve to deal with the junta and also to get over the contents of the resolutions we had adopted. The effects of the measures in Moscow and Leningrad were clearly visible. Sobchak had reached an agreement with I. O. Samsonov, the commander of the Leningrad military district, that troops would not be sent into the city and accordingly that a curfew would not be declared. Factories in Leningrad had begun to shut down in response to the appeal, 'To the Citizens of Russia', and their workers were demonstrating against the putschists and demanding a return to the constitutional order. The authorities in Sverdlovsk were also energetic in their actions. But it was Moscow that showed the greatest determination to oust the junta. The city Mayor, Gavriil Popov, and the Vice Mayor, Yuri Luzhkov, played the leading role in putting up the barricades, organising meetings and demonstrations and getting the people out onto the streets.

At 14.00 hours Rutskoi, Silaev, Sergei Shakhrai, myself and a few other people met in the President's office. We adopted four resolutions. The first was that by Presidential decree the Russian State Defence Committee should become the Russian Ministry of Defence. General Konstantin Kobets was appointed Minister and placed in charge of the defence of the White House.

The second resolution was to form a group of members of parliament and government led by the First Deputy Premier Oleg Lobov and the member of the Presidium of the Supreme Soviet Sergei Krasavchenko and to make this group responsible for directing the Russian economy. They were to base their headquarters in Sverdlovsk.

The third resolution was to send immediately to Paris the Minister of Foreign Affairs, Andrei Kozyrev. If the Russian leadership were to be arrested he was authorised to form a Russian government in exile.

The fourth resolution consisted of a decree that Yeltsin had prepared guaranteeing the constitutionality of the transition of power from himself to other persons in high office should the case arise that he was no longer able to fulfil his duties as President.

This and other meetings were continually interrupted by soldiers who were on our side, keeping us informed about the situation. The President spoke to the point. We were all thoroughly determined and did not doubt the outcome of the putsch. Sobchak rang often. He told us that the wave of protest strikes was spreading. There were meetings and demonstrations everywhere in support of the Russian government's position. Similar action was taking place in many large Russian towns.

More and more information was coming in about military units going over to our side. And the barricades outside the White House grew and grew and the number of people defending them increased before our very eyes. The troops expressed the opinion that all that prevented a mass defection of military units to our side was the fear of a court martial: some kind of guarantee was necessary. We quickly began to prepare a Presidential decree.

Decree of the President of the Russian Soviet Federated Socialist Republic

By carrying out a coup d'état and forcibly removing the President of the USSR and Supreme Commander in Chief of the Armed Forces of the USSR from his post,

The Vice President of the USSR – Yanaev, G. I.

The Prime Minister of the USSR – Pavlov, V. S.

The Chair of the KGB of the USSR – Kryuchkov, V. A.

The Minister of Internal Affairs of the USSR – Pugo, B. K.

The Minister of Defence of the USSR – Yazov, D. T.

The Chair of the Peasant Union – Starodubtsev, V. A.

The First Deputy Chair of the State Committee for Defence – Baklanov, O. D.

The Chair of the Association of Industry, Construction and Communications – Tizyakov, A. I.

and their accomplices have committed most serious crimes against the State, in contravention of Article 62 of the Constitution of the USSR, Articles 64, 69, 70 and 72 of the Legal Code of the RSFSR and corresponding Articles of the Criminal Legislation of the USSR and the union republics.

By betraying the people, their country and the Constitution, they have placed themselves outside the law.

On the basis of this I decree that:

Those who work in the Public Prosecutor's departments, in the departments of State Security and Internal Affairs of the USSR and RSFSR and those in the Armed Forces who feel a sense of responsibility for the fate of the people and of the State, and who do not wish to see the advent of dictatorship, civil war and bloodshed, have the right to act in accordance with the Constitution and laws of the USSR and RSFSR. As President of Russia in the name of the people who elected me I guarantee you legal defence and moral support.

The fate of Russia and of the Union is in your hands.

The President of the RSFSR   B. Yeltsin

Moscow, the Kremlin

19 August 1991, 22.39 hrs

No. 63

As we were to discover, this decree particularly aroused the indignation of the putschists. Early on the morning of 20 August a 'warning' was broadcast on television in the name of the SCSE to Yeltsin, Khasbulatov and Silaev, for 'calling upon the people to disobey the legitimate authorities'.

The decree did indeed play a vital role. We received a telephone call from Yevgeni Shaposhnikov, Commander in Chief of the Air Forces (later Minister of Defence of the USSR and now Commander in Chief of the Armed Forces of the CIS), thanking us for it. News of the decree spread quickly to military districts and many units of the Armed Forces, including those blockading the White House. The first military unit to

148

come over to our side was the tank company under Major Yevdokimov, consisting of ten vehicles. His vehicles took up battle positions, turning their turrets to face our opponents who were preparing to storm the Parliament.

As we looked out of the window at the crowd gathered there, someone suggested that it would be a good idea for someone to talk to the people. Yeltsin resolutely strode out of the office, accompanied by guards, deputies and journalists. He went briskly through the crowd until he reached one of the tanks, climbed up on to it and began to deliver a speech through a loudspeaker that someone handed to him. Another two or three people climbed up next to him, I recognised Vyacheslav Bragin, our deputy. I caught a few odd phrases: 'A group of traitors has overthrown President Gorbachev . . . Now they want to deliver a death blow to democracy in Russia . . . This will not happen . . . I call you to the banner of freedom.' Yeltsin concluded his short speech with a call to the people to rise in defence of the legally elected authorities and to ignore the orders of the junta. There was bewilderment on the faces of some of the tank officers. They affirmed that they would not fire on the people.

Among the soldiers there were many from Central Asia. The explosions of popular unrest in the republics of Central Asia and Transcaucasia, caused by conflicts between the nationalities, were 'pacified' by soldiers from Russia, Ukraine and Belorussia, and so their presence was a sinister reminder of the consistent nature of means employed by totalitarianism to enforce its will, even as it suffered its death throes.

Yeltsin spoke for fifteen minutes and then made his way back to the building through the exultant crowd. Two hours later I also went outside, but I did not climb up onto a tank as this would now have appeared farcical. I thought it would have meant something else entirely if I, as the leader of the Russian parliament, had copied the President's action, and I would have had no respect for myself. Immediately I was surrounded by a crowd of people, with journalists wielding dictaphones and clicking cameras. They suggested that I climb up on to the top of a staircase and gave me a megaphone. As far as I remembered, I had never been so nervous in all my life. I saw thousands of people in front of me. They seemed to soak up every word I said. The street was filled with defenders – and with silence. Faces were unusually suspicious. I talked about the junta who had carried out the coup d'état, about the betrayal by the people whom the President had trusted, about the cynicism which they had absorbed in the corridors of bureaucratic power. I finished my speech with the words, 'Long live free Russia!' which were greeted with thunderous applause and shouts of approval.

The White House gradually went over to a state of siege. The overwhelming majority of the Armed Forces was still on the side of the putschists, although tanks and armoured vehicles under Major

Yevdokimov and the Ryazan paratroopers had come over to the Russian banner.

An anxious night began. It was the first night after the putsch. The Russian Minister for Internal affairs, Victor Barannikov, had brought into the building the entire 'Russian Armed Forces', which comprised around 300 officers and sergeants of Interior Ministry forces and militia, well prepared and equipped to suit the occasion. Deputies and officials were armed. Together with the guards and Alexander Rutskoi's detachment there were about 1,000 fit men. In charge overall was General Konstantin Kobets. Rutskoi was exceptionally energetic – he was everywhere and was a universal source of inspiration. News reached us about attempts to get some kind of people (obviously KGB) into the building through underground corridors. There was a rush to find maps of underground installations, cellars, corridors and passages. Nothing was found. We tried to block them all off. We hammered in posts, we filled the entranceways with concrete. And the barricades around the White House continued to grow.

The fate of the journalists was complicated on this, the first day. Unfortunately, I have to admit that we did not really have time for them, although we had realised from the first that this particular body of people might well become our main buttress in the struggle that had begun. On the morning of 19 August it was extremely difficult for them to get into the White House. Only when the attention of the police was distracted by the sporty appearance of lads carrying neat bags over their shoulders (these were the members of the private detective agency, 'Aleks', who had volunteered to help us) did the journalists manage to slip inside. Valentin Sergeev, Silaev's plenipotentiary, turned his small office into a press centre. He helped the journalists in every way he could. A group of journalists spent two days in this room, passing on information to all newspapers imaginable and unimaginable, to magazines, via the radio television. Several journalists also lived and worked in my small press room around the clock. As a rule they interviewed me between 3 and 4 a.m. Particularly persistent, in the best sense of the word, was the television journalist for CNN from Norway, and Veronika from the paper *Kommersant*. Throughout those days and nights there were more than twenty foreign journalists in the building, who kept the world constantly informed about events in Moscow.

In the hall in front of the door with the sign 'President of the RSFSR' sat a group of four strong lads with a field radio. From behind the door opposite, which did not have a number, there came the slamming of bolts and the sound of a voice, 'Only two cartridges each, and that's your lot', and then people came out with submachine guns.

Towards evening the radio room was set up. Bella Kurkova told me about this and invited me to open transmission with a speech. I immediately agreed and we headed off to somewhere in the cellars. Lopatin, General Kobets' deputy, was called along to help. We spent a long time moving through the underground passages, treading in all kinds of holes, on cables and in puddles. Eventually we arrived. Lyubimov and Politkovskii were already there. Kurkova had told them that the free radio of the Russian parliament was about to commence operation.

Late in the evening we were informed that the underground floors of the White House, where there is a secret entrance to the Metro, had been mined. We were told that the Taman and Kantemir divisions were heading for Moscow. The press centre buzzed continuously with the ringing of telephones. The happiest event of the day was the news that part of the Taman division had joined the defenders of the White House.

We needed mass support so that we could get through the night and broaden our contact with the Russian hinterland, with the union republics and with the leaders of Western countries. We had to teach everyone on hand the basic rules of defence.

In these circumstances the President and I thought out a plan: I was to call Anatoli Lukyanov and ask him for a meeting tomorrow morning. In the conversation I expressed a certain degree of readiness to talk with him in person, and I alluded to the possibility of some kind of compromise. This conversation took place at around 8 or 9 p.m.; and I said that I, together with Silaev and Rutskoi, would like to meet with him and talk it over.

'Why only with me, why not with somebody else from the leadership as well?', Lukyanov asked.

'No, Anatoli Ivanovich, we only want to meet with you, because it seems to us that you are not involved in the coup. At the moment only you represent the highest source of power in the country. We would like to discuss some questions with you, the resolution of which could lead to the situation being brought under control,' I said. After a minute's silence Lukyanov agreed to meet us at his office at 10 a.m. on the morning of 20 August.

By the evening of the 19th, news had begun to reach us about uncertainty and quarrels amongst the leaders of the coup. Yanaev and Yazov had begun to waver, whereas Kryuchkov and several others were more decisive, and spoke in favour of an immediate offensive. In these conditions it appeared to me that the hint of a possible compromise heightened the doubts of those who were already in two minds, and increased our hopes of earning that 'one more night', during which we would be able to strengthen our position somewhat. We needed that time like we needed the very air itself. It is even possible that this ploy influenced the fact that troops were not sent in on that first tragic night. It is possible, but then, on the evening of the 19th, a curfew was declared.

The night passed uneasily, a constant stream of deputies, government and parliamentary officials, servicemen, journalists (both Soviet and foreign) came to see me. Academician Georgi Arbatov, the head of the Academy of Science's Institute of the USA and Canada, phoned from Helsinki and told us about his work on interpreting the events in the USSR and the views expressed in political circles in Scandinavia (and not only in Scandinavia) about the Russian leadership.

The phone calls from other countries were a great source of strength to us. The first to call was John Major on the afternoon of the 19th, then the Presidents of Hungary and Bulgaria called, President Bush called on several occasions, and the Presidents of Italy, Argentina and many others as well. They were sympathetic, and asked what had happened to Gorbachev.

I would like to recall one episode from the events of this first day, about which we first learnt on 22 August. It so happened that at 6.00 p.m. on 19 August, Prime Minister Pavlov was holding an extended meeting of the Cabinet of Ministers, attended by around sixty Ministers and other leaders. One topic was discussed, the need to support the coup conspirators. Pavlov was insistent about this. Everyone came out in favour of it except two ministers, Vorontsov and Gubenko, who protested. The tragedy is that these two opponents did not come and tell us about the Union government's stance. We really needed this information. If, on the evening of the 19th, we had known about the position of the Union government we would have been able to make a more realistic evaluation of the situation, and would have had a better idea of the immense scale of the conspiracy. And then, some of our actions taken on the evening and night of 19–20 August would have been more decisive.

8

DAY TWO
20 August 1991

THE ULTIMATUM

There were barricades and small fires across the square. Early in the morning of the 20th, at around 6.00 a.m., we gathered in Yeltsin's office: Silaev, Rutskoi, Gennadi Burbulis and myself. We discussed the contents of the proposals which we were going to put to Lukyanov at the meeting which had been arranged for 10.00 a.m. We composed a document, similar in character to the ultimatum given to the junta.

At 9.30 a.m. we left the White House, Rutskoi and myself in one car, Silaev in another. A solid wall of people surrounded the building, we slowly passed through them. On seeing who it was they greeted us, many shouting: 'Don't go, they'll arrest and kill you.'

We entered the Kremlin without incident, stopping at the Palace of Congresses. We were met and taken upstairs to Lukyanov's office. He met us warmly. We sat down behind a long table. The host asked for cups of coffee to be brought for everyone. He immediately set about trying to convince us of his non-participation in the emergency State Committee, and of the fact that he had received a telegram summoning him back from his holiday on the 18th, and so on. I told him that it was because of this that we had decided to meet with him alone, and with no one else.

Silaev took out our document from a file and passed it to Lukyanov. The Chairman of the Supreme Soviet of the USSR read it closely. Our demands can be summed up as follows:

First, to arrange at some point within twenty-four hours of the document being handed over, a meeting between Yeltsin, Khasbulatov and President Gorbachev. Yanaev would also be asked to this meeting.

Second, if President Gorbachev really was ill then, within the next three days, he should receive a medical examination witnessed by specialists from the World Health Organisation. We thought that if the Union

153

authorities proved unable to provide us with the funding for such a check-up, we might even pay for it ourselves in foreign currency.

Third, the results of the medical examination should be published. If the results showed Gorbachev to be in good health he should immediately be reinstated and resume his presidential duties.

Fourth, to remove immediately all the restrictions imposed on the mass media in Russia, especially since such restrictions had not been imposed in other republics. 'You know only too well, Anatoli Ivanovich', I said, 'that our recently established television channel and our newspapers have been closed down, and only the central party newspapers are still in circulation.'

Fifth, to lift the state of emergency throughout the RSFSR. 'All the more so since the emergency session of the Supreme Soviet of the RSFSR will be commencing its work, and the deputies have to be given safe passage to Moscow.'

Sixth, to reinstate immediately all types of communication in order that the Russian leadership may function normally. 'You know that communications have been severed. Not to mention bugging, to which we are now accustomed.'

Last, to announce the dissolution of the illegally formed State Committee for the State of Emergency in the USSR and to rescind all of its resolutions and decrees.

'Is this an ultimatum?' asked Lukyanov, having familiarised himself with the text.

'No, of course not,' I replied. 'It is a basis for talks.' (We needed to gain time in order to allow the deputies to gather for the session of the Supreme Soviet.)

In my conversation with Lukyanov I reminded him that in his television speech on 19 August he said that it was rumoured that Gorbachev was fully aware of all the events and even that he approved of them. We expressed our doubt about what he said. Lukyanov attempted to link the coup d'état with the policies of the Russian authorities, as though it were they who had created the situation, which could only be resolved by declaring a state of emergency. He even tried to blame Yeltsin for Gorbachev's illness, as if, after a heated discussion which Yeltsin had imposed on Gorbachev, the latter had fallen ill.

We emphasised that the state of emergency, which had been declared by an unconstitutional, illegal committee, should be immediately rescinded. And consequently, all the actions of this committee, being illegal, were also subject to be abrogated. From this it followed that the members of the junta had committed heinous crimes against the state, were responsible for the betrayal of the motherland and the Constitution, and thus they would obviously be liable to criminal proceedings. If our demands were implemented we would attempt in the shortest possible time to put an end to the demonstrations, strikes and other forms of mass protest by the people. In the course of that very day we would endeavour to initiate cooperation with the armed forces so as to commence their withdrawal. Lukyanov repeated somewhat confusedly. 'But this is an ultimatum! It won't do!' Then, having calmed down a bit, he asked his secretary to duplicate the texts and to send them to Yanaev. A thought struck me: would they let us out of here?

We talked for a long time, Silaev calmly, Rutskoi forever getting excited, so that several times I had to restrain him and bring the discussion back to the topic of our demands. Lukyanov is a cunning man and a wily politician, he was aware of our refusal to compromise, and thus adopted a new tactic and began to justify himself. He again tried to convince us of his non-participation in the activities of the Emergency State Committee, and promised to allow the Russian deputies to attend the emergency session of the Supreme Soviet without hindrance, and also to try convince the coup conspirators to withdraw their troops positioned around the White House. (Those troops which had earlier surrounded the White House, having become aware of the situation, and having talked with the people, had begun to show their loyalty to us and had therefore been withdrawn and replaced by new divisions, mainly from the KGB and the OMON special purpose troops. We received reliable information about a planned assault on the White House, set for the night of 20–21 August.)

We left Lukyanov's office with the feeling that we were going to be arrested. We got into the cars. We set off. We still had not been arrested. We passed through the Kremlin gates, and then breathed a sigh of relief. We had to stop at the beginning of Kalinin Prospect and get out of the car as it could not get through the thick crowd. Thus it was that we walked up to our building amid cheers and greetings by people, who were genuinely gladdened by the fact that we had not been arrested. We actually had not been arrested because tens of thousands of people knew that we had gone to the Kremlin. The coup conspirators had simply taken fright, and decided not to arrest us.

On the night of the 20th, I had another two short conversations with Lukyanov. I telephoned him from Yeltsin's reception room and asked: 'Well, Anatoli Ivanovich, will we be attacked today?' After a pause he replied: 'I don't know, I'll have a talk with Yazov, Pugo and Kryuchkov and let you know in fifteen to twenty minutes.' He put down the receiver. Twenty, thirty, fifty minutes passed. I called again. I was quickly put through to him. 'Well then, Anatoli Ivanovich, have you found anything out; should we expect an attack on the parliament building?' 'Ruslan Imranovich, I've talked with Yazov and Pugo, and they both deny that there are any preparations being made for an assault. I couldn't find Kryuchkov, but I'll have a look for him,' he replied.

'So, will there be an attack on parliament or not?' I asked.

'I don't know, Ruslan Imranovich, I don't know. I've told you all that I know. I'm having no part in all of this.'

It became clear that we should expect an attack to be made.

I would like to emphasise one important point. Even as early as the 19th it was obvious that in the worsening situation, the army had to be brought under control. On the 19th, military leaders proposed that in the event of the country's President, who is in charge of the armed forces, being dismissed, it would be completely natural for the President of the RSFSR to carry out such duties within the boundaries of the RSFSR. This plan was drawn up by the military leaders on the night of the 19th. They decided to await the outcome of the conversation with Lukyanov. But when we became fully aware of the fact that we had been deceived (at 17.00 hours), and that there was a division of troops heading straight for the White House, the respective decrees by the President and the Presidium, and parliament's resolution were promulgated. They had a tremendous impact, giving rise to a large number of military divisions refusing to obey the coup conspirators.

Decree of the President of the Russian Soviet Federated Socialist Republic

On the Control of the USSR's Armed Forces within the boundaries of the RSFSR under the conditions of the state of emergency.

As a result of the attempted coup d'état which took place on the night of 18–19 August 1991 the President of the USSR, the Supreme Commander in Chief of the Armed Forces of the USSR, has been deposed. The Vice President of the USSR, the Minister of Defence, the First Deputy Chairman of the Ministry of Defence and other members of the Ministry of Defence have embarked on an unlawful path of forcible change of the Constitution, and in so doing have acted outside of the law, and thus cannot carry out the duty of running the Armed Forces of the USSR or of the defence of the territorial integrity and sovereignty of the Republics of the USSR as a whole.

Taking into account the need for providing security under the conditions of the lack of constitutional control of the Armed Forces within the boundaries in the RSFSR, I decree that:

1 Until such time as the activities of the USSR's constitutional bodies, and of the institutions of state power and running of the USSR are fully restored, the command of the Soviet Armed Forces

in the RSFSR from 17.00 hours Moscow time on 20 August 1991 will now come under my control.

2 All military units and sub-units of the Soviet Armed Forces, together with the troops of the KGB, which are stationed in the RSFSR, will until I notify otherwise, remain at their posts. Unit and sub-units which have already been moved will return to their previous deployment.

3 In connection with the involvement of the Minister of Defence D.T. Yazov in the coup d'etat, all orders and other commands issued by him from 18 August 1991 are hereby countermanded. Future orders and other commands signed by D. T. Yazov and V. A. Kryuchkov are not to be executed.

4 The Commander of the Moscow Military Command, Colonel General N. V. Kalinin, will return the units of the Moscow Military District to their permanent posts.

5 Senior commanders, officers and other members of the Soviet Armed Forces in the RSFSR, who are loyal to the Constitution of USSR and to the military oath which they have sworn to our multinational motherland, will come under the command of the President of the RSFSR and will carry out their military duties in accordance with the Constitution and laws of the USSR.

6 My authority as Commander in Chief of the Soviet Armed Forces within the boundaries of the RSFSR will cease when the President of the USSR, the Supreme Commander in Chief of the Soviet Armed Forces, returns to carry out his duties, or if a new structure of ruling bodies of the Soviet Armed Forces is formed, in accordance with the Constitution and laws of the USSR.

7 The Vice President of the RSFSR, A. V. Rutskoi, will draw up proposals for the creation of a national guard for the RSFSR.

8 The Council of Ministers of the RSFSR will take on the payment, both monetary and in kind, of the Soviet Armed Forces stationed in the RSFSR.

9 The present Decree will come into effect from the moment it is signed.

The President of the RSFSR   B. Yeltsin
Moscow, the Kremlin
20 August 1991
No. 64

This document gave commanding officers a free hand to reject legally all orders issued by Yazov and his deputies. Many military commanders in the heart of Russia took advantage of it and announced that they were transferring their allegiance to Yeltsin. Even several submarines raised the Russian tricolour.

The President's decree about the provision of economic sovereignty for the RSFSR proved to be an important event on this day. It had been approved by Gorbachev, and was to have been signed after the Union Treaty had been signed on 20 August, but fate ordained otherwise. I cannot emphasise enough the importance of this document; it contains everything that we had been fighting for since we came to power over a year earlier. An analogous resolution had been adopted in August 1990 by the Presidium of the Russian Supreme Soviet when B. N. Yeltsin was on a long visit to the Russian Far East. At that time, Gorbachev, Pavlov and Gerashchenko had prepared a whole package of draft Presidential decrees directed against our domestic policies, including the liquidation of the Central Bank of Russia. In response to this we took an extremely important decision. However, in the course of talks between Yeltsin and Gorbachev this resolution was revoked. In the new circumstances we decided to return to this document.

Decree of the President of the Russian Soviet Federated Socialist Republic

On providing the economic basis for the sovereignty of the RSFSR.

In the interests of the multinational population of the Russian Federation, governed by the decisions of the Congresses of People's Deputies, of the Supreme Soviet of the RSFSR and by the laws of the RSFSR on the provision of an economic basis for the sovereignty of the Republic, I decree:

1 That the Council of Ministers of the RSFSR
   - shall, before 1 January 1992, take over the jurisdiction on behalf of the state authorities of the RSFSR and the republics within the RSFSR, enterprises and organisations situated within the Russian Federation which are subordinate to the Union, and which belong to the Republics located within the framework of the RSFSR, with the exclusion of those whose management is, according to the legislation of the RSFSR, transferred to the corresponding agencies of the USSR. The appointed businesses and organisations are compelled in 1991 to fulfil unconditionally all state orders and contractual obligations;
   - shall, in the interests of raising the population's living standards, devise and present to the President of the RSFSR before 1 January 1992, proposals for augmenting the utilisation of powers possessed by companies in the defence sector of industry in the RSFSR;
   - shall, before 1 January 1992, implement the necessary

measures for working out and introducing a unified system of economic and statistical indicators of the fiscal-budgetary system, of managers' account-keeping and the categorisation of products, which meet the requirements of international law.

2 Companies and organisations located or carrying out operations within the RSFSR (including those subordinate to the Union), should be controlled by the legislation of the RSFSR, and should implement the laws and other acts made by bodies of the USSR in the manner established by the RSFSR Law on 'The jurisdiction of acts passed by USSR bodies in the RSFSR'.

3 The Council of Ministers together with the Central Bank of the RSFSR shall before 1 October 1991, put forward proposals to the President of the RSFSR regarding:
- the establishing of gold reserves, and of diamond and hard-currency funds in the RSFSR;
- the determining of the share owed by the RSFSR in the liquidation of the USSR's foreign debts, and also the share to be received by the RSFSR on division of the debts owed by foreign countries of the USSR;
- the imposing of taxes on the hard currency incomes of companies, organisations and citizens;
- the improvement of the credit and accounting mechanisms and the amelioration of finances, in the light of the envisaged possibility of joint action with other union republics.

4 The Council of Ministers of the RSFSR is to advance proposals for the suspension of the enactment in the RSFSR of the Decree issued by the President of the USSR on 2 November 1990 on the 'Special procedures for the use of hard currency reserves in 1991'.

5 To establish that within the RSFSR (including the continental shelf) mineral prospecting and extraction, commercial fishing, the harvesting of the oceans' flora and fauna, shall only be carried out with special authorisation (by licence). All companies, organisations and citizens engaging in these practices are to obtain the relevant licence before 1 July 1992.

The Council of Ministers shall, before 1 January 1992, put forward proposals for administering the licensing of the aforementioned activities, along with the attraction of foreign investment and the granting of concessions to foreign legally incorporated bodies for mineral prospecting and extraction within the boundaries of the RSFSR (including the continental shelf).

6 The Council of Ministers of the RSFSR shall:

159

- before 1 October 1991 establish a system of union republic trade bodies for the RSFSR;
- reach an agreement with the Cabinet of Ministers of the USSR on the joint establishment of customs duties for import-export operations taking place within the RSFSR.

Decisions by Union bodies concerning the organisation of the import and export of goods, and also the fixing of trade duties, taken without the consent of the ruling bodies of the RSFSR, will not be implemented within the boundaries of the RSFSR.

7 The Council of Ministers of the RSFSR and the executive bodies of republics in the RSFSR shall, by 1 January 1992, register all the economic objects who will come under the jurisdiction of the authorities of the RSFSR and its republics by the terms of this decree.

8 The State Tax Inspectorate, together with the Finance Ministry of the RSFSR shall, before 1 November 1991, prepare and implement proposals for a system of audit by tax departments of commercial operations and the issuing of certificates (licences) which authorise the realisation of such operations.

9 The Council of Ministers of the RSFSR shall, during its implementation of this decree, cooperate with the other union republics and republics within the RSFSR on issues affecting their mutual interests.

10 A committee for the defence of the RSFSR's economic interests will be formed under the Presidency of the RSFSR in order to control the maintenance of such interests.

11 The Council of Ministers of the RSFSR will take on the duty of checking that this decree is implemented.

12 The Council of Ministers of the RSFSR will regularly inform the President of the RSFSR about the progress of this Decree's implementation.

13 This Decree will come into immediate effect from the moment of its signing.

The President of the RSFSR   B. Yeltsin
Moscow, The Kremlin
20 August 1991
No. 66

To return to the evening of 20 August. At about 8 p.m. I was sitting in Yeltsin's office, opposite him at his great desk. The telephone suddenly rang and Yeltsin pressed a button. Silaev's voice was heard: 'I've let the government employees go, and I'm off home myself. Goodbye, Boris Nikolaevich.' I saw Yeltsin go pale. He said: 'Now, now, Ivan Stepanovich, Ruslan Imranovich and I are here together, working out the details of the defence. Why not join us?'

Silaev answered, 'Ruslan Imranovich, goodbye, Boris Nikolaevich, goodbye. It'll all be up with us tonight. I have it on good authority. Let them take the buildings. Goodbye.'

That was all. White-faced, Yeltsin looked anxiously at me without speaking.

I said, 'Today at Lukyanov's Ivan Stepanovich fought bravely. He's just lost his nerve, don't be angry with him.'

Yeltsin responded, 'I'm not angry, that's not the point.' He was silent. Then again: 'Surely they aren't coming to kill us and our supporters?' Leaving Yeltsin in a disturbed condition, I returned to my office. Soon Popov rang and asked what was to become of him and Luzhkov, as they had no one to defend them, and they would probably be among the first to be taken. I suggested they go to the White House on foot: no chance of getting through by car as the streets were choked with military hardware. Popov with Luzhkov and his wife arrived two hours later, all wet. They gave a detailed report of the situation in the streets around the White House and in the centre of Moscow and conveyed information received from reliable sources: the attack was apparently planned for about midnight, or possibly in the small hours. My bodyguard looked in, also the deputies A. Aslakhanov and Yu. Rudkin armed with submachine guns. They recommended crossing to the President's section of the White House since the wing where my office was situated was the most vulnerable part, and the attackers would try to seize it first of all. I went on sitting in my chair, smoking my pipe, and then coolly remarked that I did not see the need to leave my office: if they took my wing of the building they would take the other too; what difference would it make where I was?

At that moment the deputy head of Yeltsin's guard came running in and said we were to go down to the basement. I left Popov with Luzhkov and his wife in the care of the guard and quickly went to see the President to find out what was up, there being no reply on the intercom. When I entered the office, Yeltsin, the head of the guard Korzhakov, the head of the President's secretariat, Oleg Petrov, and his assistants Lev Sukhanov and Ilyushin were going out of the back door. Seeing me, Yeltsin said that we had to make a decision, since there were only a few minutes left before the attack. I could not make out what was going on until we had gone down in the lift to the garage, where Yeltsin's ZIL limousine was standing. They told us in a businesslike tone that as soon as the automatic doors of the White House opened, the armour-plated ZIL could dash through the light barricades and force its way into the yard of the American Embassy.

'What is to be done?' the President asked me, obviously finding it painful to have to decide such a thing. I said that I thought the President's life was too valuable to risk. 'I reckon you'll be doing the right thing if you go to the American Embassy,' I said. 'I ought to stay with the deputies.'

The President said 'No, I shan't leave here.' He caught me up, and we returned to the fifth floor to our respective offices. A couple of hours later I realised that my 'guests' Popov, Luzhkov and his wife were no longer with me. Sergei Filatov informed me that they were in the basement. We went downstairs, and threaded our way through dimly lit corridors for about a kilometre. We came to an enormous steel door. It was opened for us and we went through into quite a big hall into which emerged two more corridors with similar doors. Seeing the President's guard, I asked: 'Where?' 'There' they said, and pointed to one of the doors. I went closer and read the inscription: 'Chair of the Supreme Soviet of the RSFSR.' Opposite was another for the deputy chair. 'Mine,' I thought, and entered. Inside Popov with Luzhkov and his wife were having a cup of tea.

After a little while I left the basement, feeling that I was in a burial vault, airless and lifeless, and I returned to my office, constantly coming across people with submachine guns by staircases and at turns in the corridors.

9

DAY THREE
21 August 1991

A TRAGIC NIGHT

At about 8 p.m., extremely tired, literally worn out, I got the deputies together and told them that the most critical moment had arrived. 'The Taman division, which was defending the White House, has deserted us by order of the Defence Ministry. We have also been told that special detachments of the KGB are going to attack us by parachuting onto the roof from a helicopter.'

By midnight you could hardly breathe owing to the smoke from the fires, even in the building. The tension and the fear made it worse, but one just had to overcome them. Suddenly all the lights went out. We heard the footsteps of guards and men from 'Aleks' in the corridor. We decided to move all the women out. They did not want to obey the order, and hid. The female journalist never did go.

Over the radio were broadcast constant instructions from Rutskoi and Kobets: 'Be calm and vigilant. Don't panic. Those who are standing near the building, move away 50 metres. If the tanks come, let them pass.' 'All those in the building take up position in twos at the windows.' 'Don't let anyone in. Be wary of provocation. KGB detachments will try to enter the building by pretending to be our defenders.' 'If someone tries to break in through a window or door, shoot without warning.'

00.06 The first bursts of submachine gun fire were heard near the American Embassy. The internal radio of the White House reported that tanks and armoured personnel carriers (APCs) were closing in on the parliament building from all sides.

00.10 Submachine guns fired tracer bullets over the tanks from the White House. The lights went out in the building. Photographers were forbidden to use flash.

00.21 News came in that a barge carrying troops with some kind of cylinder was moving along the Moscow River. A possible gas attack or a smoke-screen. Handkerchieves and gauze bandages were quickly soaked in puddles. It later became known it was Mikhail Malei, a Deputy Prime Minister, sending a squadron on the barge to our aid. Radio Liberty, quoting Lukyanov, announced that President Gorbachev was involved in the conspiracy.

00.30 In the region of the Garden Ring a column of APCs, having broken through the barricades, was now entering the tunnel under Kalinin Prospect. They came up against a roadblock formed from trolley-buses. The leading APC opened fire with its machine guns. Tracer bullets were fired into the air.

The nightmare was beginning. A youth jumped onto the APC and attempted to climb through the open hatchway. Later it became known that they had shot him at point-blank range. Witnesses saw his limp body hanging from the hatch. A man tried to get him off, but at that moment the APC went into reverse and he fell under the caterpillar tracks. Molotov cocktails were flying through the air. The APC burst into flames like a haystack. The soldiers inside clambered out and scattered. Another two APCs coming out of the tunnel attempted to break through the road blocks. Petrol bombs were thrown at them too. One of them began to spin round and round on the spot: a third man had been crushed to death under an APC's caterpillar tracks. Blood and human remains were spread on the concrete. Soldiers climbed out of the APCs. Several of them were horrified. An hour later we managed to get them to join us in defending the White House.

01.30 News came in that the Kantemir and Taman army divisions were being pulled out of Moscow due to their 'unreliability'. Only KGB and Spetsnaz forces remained in Moscow.

02.45 Tug boats brought in three old barges with which they blocked the Moscow River opposite the Russian Federation's Supreme Soviet building.

03.05 News arrived that 40 km away on the Minsk Highway a convoy of units of the Vitebsk KGB Paratroop Division were moving towards Moscow.

04.15 GAI (the State Motor-vehicle Inspectorate) informed us that the KGB troops had stopped near to the Mozhaisk Motel.

04.30 It became known that the State Committee for the State of Emergency, under the leadership of Yanaev, was meeting in the Hotel Oktyabrskaya. We received conflicting reports of the outcome of the meeting. The White House radio also reported that Pavel Grachev, the commander of the Paratroop forces, had once again made it clear that he would not give the order to open fire.

I was given a gas mask. At about 1 a.m. there were shots. I went to the window which looked out on the square. 'Keep away,' cried one of the defenders. 'There is a sniper on the roof of the Comecon building. He has your office in his sights.'

Somebody reported that two men had been killed at the American Embassy. There was another burst of shots and a pale blue explosion lit the sky. There were shouts and rumbling in the square.

An hour later the tension had eased somewhat. A report was handed to Yeltsin's assistant Lev Sukhanov by a Western ambassador, informing us that parliament was going to be stormed at 4 a.m. This information was confirmed by other sources.

'The most dangerous time is between 4 and 5 a.m., according to psychologists: one's attention and reactions are dulled. That's when they'll start,' I thought, recalling the words of Alexander Lyubimov.

I thought the moment critical. Just then, Bella Kurkova looked in. I told her I was going to the radio office to relay a broadcast for our defenders. 'And for history,' she quipped wryly. We went downstairs to the basement and along dark corridors to the radio office.

What could I say to the thousands of people eagerly listening to the dead pre-dawn silence of the retreating night? To those tired, half-starved rain-soaked but untameable, fearless people whose only weapons against the tanks and soldiers armed to the teeth were their own bodies?

I began with a description of the heartless criminal clique that had governed us for seven decades. I reminded people of the cruelty, and cynicism, the lack of honour, probity and conscience of all generations of our so-called leaders since the time of Lenin. I mentioned my position on the coup, saying that I had been wrong in denying its possibility. 'Those who carried out the coup were devoid of intellect and common sense. They neither knew nor understood the people, who are ready to accept death but reject the slavery they want to impose on us.' Altogether I spoke for twenty minutes. Afterwards I was told I had spoken at an exceptionally critical moment, when the defenders' morale was at a very low ebb; I had to cheer them up, make them believe in our success, and in democracy.

However, the OMONists and KGB did not resolve to storm the building, and the army did not move either.

Difficult times are very revealing, especially about people. I remember one incident. One of the leaders of the defence, either Kobets or Rutskoi, sent me a group of about ten officers whom I did not need as I had enough of my own, so I sent them on to one of Yeltsin's aides. The officers entered his office, and before they could say a word he blurted out, 'It's not me, I'm only a secretary — it's all Yeltsin and Khasbulatov.' The officers promised not to tell about this episode.

THE SESSION OF THE SUPREME SOVIET

By the morning of the 21st the members of the Supreme Soviet and many deputies had arrived for the opening session at 10 a.m. We were relieved to learn that they had been allowed into Moscow without any trouble. True, most of the deputies were in the White House, organising the defence, chatting interminably with the soldiers, giving them our instructions and decrees, explaining the unconstitutional criminal nature of the coup.

Of course, we had to think of our tactics too; it was important to outmanoeuvre the enemy. One tactical success was already ours: we had survived the night. Here is another of our stratagems.

Early on the 21st, when there were only two hours left before the session, Kryuchkov took a desperate step, practically the last chance to save the cause of the SCSE and remove Yeltsin. He phoned Yeltsin and suggested flying him down to Foros with Lukyanov to meet Gorbachev. We decided on a double bluff. And so at 9 a.m. on the 21st Yeltsin rang me up to tell me he was flying straight away to Foros to see Gorbachev. He spoke to me very frankly and persuasively. I dissuaded him just as frankly, saying that perhaps I ought to go instead, since he had no right to leave without parliament's permission. We put this on for Kryuchkov's benefit, of course: we knew he was bugging us. The putschists were planning to shoot down the plane with Yeltsin on board, just as they had planned to destroy the airliner which was to have brought Yeltsin from Alma Ata on 18 August after the signing of the Russo–Kazakhstan pact. We had to lure the conspirators out of Moscow, beyond the protection of built-up areas and countless guards, so as to arrest them without bloodshed. Kryuchkov was hoisted on his own petard. When, after heated debate in parliament, it was decided to send Silaev and Rutskoi to Foros, the conspirators somewhat changed their original plan. No longer hoping to seize Yeltsin, they decided to forestall us and immediately flew off to Foros themselves. In this way we managed to outmanoeuvre the conspirators and arrest them outside Moscow. But that was a little later.

The President and I had decided that the report 'On the political situation in the republic as a result of the unconstitutional coup d'état' would be given by him. However, Yeltsin was extremely tired that morning, and asked me to do it. I quickly jotted down a few ideas for my speech, and exactly at 10 a.m. Yeltsin, myself and Boris Isaev went up to the Presidium. The session was opened by me. Just then a deputy approached the microphone and asked: 'On what grounds has Isaev, a Deputy Chair of the Supreme Soviet, joined the Presidium? Isn't he against the extraordinary session of parliament? He almost supported the junta. The same goes for the Chair of the Chambers, Vladimir Isakov.' Another deputy asked if there was still such a thing as conscience. Isaev and Isakov gave feeble explanations. They said something about having a right to an opinion. The deputies demanded nothing less than their expulsion from the Supreme Soviet. I had a job to calm things down, appealing to them to remember that at any moment the building might be stormed: a ring of tanks was threatening the White House. We had to ignore secondary issues and discuss the main one: evaluate the coup, decide how to overcome the putsch, pass only the essential motions. They calmed down. I offered to speak and went to the rostrum.

Before summarising my speech I will explain my position.

During those difficult days, to be frank, I only considered my duty as head of the Russian parliament, my own honour. I organised people, encouraged them, helped them to orientate themselves. I reckoned I had to unite President and parliament into a strong force of resistance. Now the President has ample armed men and special troops and broad popular support, but then there was only parliament, or rather, a hundred deputies. Yes, indeed, that same parliament which is now no use to the government (at the time Gaidar was one of the editors of *Pravda*), hinders the President, comes out against the 'freedom' of half a dozen venal newspaper editors, and so on. But then – then parliament was needed by everyone, and hated only by the supporters of the putsch.

Yet our parliament is still the same, strong, resolute body, not at all like the old Union parliament. They call us a 'Lukyanov' parliament, simply because it is different: our parliament does not kowtow to the executive, it does not refuse to treat either with the left or the far right, it shows its strength, its political maturity. Unfortunately, we placed too much faith immediately after the suppression of the coup on the President and his team. We squandered valuable time pandering to the *nouveaux riches*, did not form a powerful, efficient government, did not make Gorbachev alter the whole strategy in the reasoning of the Union Treaty by tabling a bill for a Confederation Treaty, which had long been prepared and was accepted by the union republics. Yes, the Russian parliament and I personally made serious mistakes in relying on two Presidents, Gorbachev and Yeltsin. They took the line of least resistance, and failed to save the Union which they could have done by adhering to the principles laid down by the Russian Congress of Deputies and the Supreme Soviet of Russia.

To be truthful, I must say that my opportunities at that time were extremely limited: at the Congress of People's Deputies I had not been elected Chairman of the Supreme Soviet. I still chuckle over the touching unity of the group of top democrats like Shakhrai, Fr Gleb Yakunin, Lev Ponomarev, Sergei Baburin, Nikolai Pavlov, Mikhail Astaf'ev and Ivan Polozkov, who took up the slogan: 'Anyone but Khasbulatov!' This 'unity' is highly revealing. Of course, the whole presidential caucus led by Burbulis, Shakhrai and Poltoranin were against my being elected, except, perhaps, the President himself. The information that the President received and receives has always reached him in a distorted form. So I remained acting Chairman of the Supreme Soviet; perhaps this also entered into the calculations of those who deliberately aimed at the dissolution of the Union: this is possible. That is not all. The resolution of Congress giving the President extraordinary powers and even the right to rule by decree, which runs counter to the Constitution, was foisted on parliament just at that time when its leadership was weak. A powerful distortion in favour of the executive dates from that period. But then, from 19–21 August, we were together and defended the cause of the freedom of democracy and not our own power, so that we behaved towards each other with exacting attention. And now the speech:

In the struggle with dictatorship we must be united.

On the night of 18–19 August 1991 the legally elected President of the country was removed from power. Whatever the reasons, his removal was not justified. We are dealing with a rightist, reactionary, unconstitutional coup.

Besides the removal from power of President Gorbachev, the conspirators had the strategic objective of removing from power Boris Yeltsin, the leader of the Russian state, the seizure and internment of the President of Russia, and progressive members of the Supreme Soviet and of the government of the RSFSR. There is obviously no doubt about this.

These objectives were achieved consistently, rigorously, cynically and with great dispatch. Troops were moved to Moscow: more than five hundred tanks and about ten different divisions, various regiments, including units of Spetsnaz, KGB, OMON, MVD, paratroop units, moreover all of them concentrated on the area round our White House, constantly manoeuvring. The direct objective was the seizure of the Supreme Soviet building, the residence of the President of Russia and his government. It was surrounded by a solid ring of armoured vehicles and troops ready to seize the last bastion of freedom. By capturing it the putschists could gain control of the whole country and unleash a reign of terror on the nation, which had chosen the path of freedom and national renaissance.

It must be noted that in the circumstances the President of Russia, the Presidium of the Supreme Soviet and the government, acted energetically, yet sensibly and calmly. There was no panic here, all our efforts were aimed at resolving the matter peacefully. With this in mind, Lukyanov, the Chairman of the USSR Supreme Soviet and virtually the sole legitimate leader of the country, was presented with a list of rigorous demands by the Russian leadership.

Alarmingly enough, membership of the conspiracy could be traced to the higher echelons of the KGB, and the Communist Party of the Russian Federation. So far the leaders of the Communist Party have kept quiet about it – and not without reason: they are direct participants and the inspiration of the coup.

I suggest passing a law approving the actions of the President of Russia during the coup. The point is that the President passed a whole lot of decrees which nullified the actions of the putschists. Of course the President has a right to pass them, but taking into consideration the situation, it is expedient that the Supreme Soviet should approve them by passing a special law. I have in view here the purely moral aspect, but this aspect would unite us in the struggle against the advance of dictatorship. Our opinions may differ in many respects, but on the cardinal questions of the development of society, in regard to dictatorship and totalitarianism, we must be united.

The discussion was lively; there was unanimous harsh condemnation of the junta. No one dared say a word in favour of the coup. Of course, it had its supporters, but they were afraid to speak. Gorbachev was criticised for his indecisiveness and concessions to the right which gave the reactionaries the idea of a plot. The Russian parliament's condemnation of the putsch before the whole country, the whole world, symbolised the latter's defeat and began a new page in the history of the Soviet Union and Russia. Which path would the republics take? Would Gorbachev really return to power? Had he learned the lesson of his personal tragedy, the tragedy of a great state?

10

23 AUGUST 1991

Gorbachev in parliament

I am often asked about my meeting with Gorbachev after his return. On 23 August at about 11 a.m. his assistant rang me and put me on to him. He said he wished to meet the Russian deputies. We fixed a time, 12 o'clock. At about 11.30 I called on Boris Yeltsin. From his office emerged Vice President Rutskoi, announcing as he went that he was meeting Gorbachev. Ten minutes later in walked the President of the USSR, firmly shook Yeltsin's hand (they had already met since Gorbachev's return from Foros), and even embraced me. Of course I could not forget his malevolence towards me for nearly eighteen months. But I let that pass.

So we moved into the large auditorium filled with deputies. The balconies, it seemed, would collapse beneath their weight. Yeltsin, Silaev, Rutskoi, Gorbachev and I took our places on the Presidium (I sat on Yeltsin's left). The session was chaired by the President of Russia.

Yeltsin congratulated everyone on the victory and announced that that morning he and Gorbachev had been working together, mainly on staff appointments, and then he gave Gorbachev the opportunity to speak. Gorbachev began by saying how much he appreciated the role of the Russian Federation, and especially 'the outstanding part played by its President Boris Nikolaevich Yeltsin and the Russian deputies'. He described how the putschists had demanded his resignation in favour of Yanaev. Moreover, Valeri Boldin (Gorbachev's chief assistant) had told him that the President of Russia and his comrades-in-arms had already been arrested, and he had no support left. They had, of course, been trying to break his morale and make him retire. Gorbachev attempted an analysis of the reasons for the coup and its failure, informed the delegates of certain actual things he had done. He had met the heads of nine republics, appointed new heads of the Ministry of Defence and of the KGB, Yevgeni Shaposhnikov and Vadim Bakatin, respectively, and also transferred units of the KGB to the Defence Ministry. He mentioned his cooperation with Yeltsin in deciding various important questions. The auditorium literally exploded with indignation when Gorbachev spoke of the apparently 'good' position of certain members of the government, to be precise, the deputy Premier Vladimir Shcherbakov.

Here are extracts from the transcript of the session:

Gorbachev: Boris Nikolaevich . . . gave me an account of the session of the Cabinet of Ministers of the USSR, but I didn't read it.

Yeltsin: Read it out, Mikhail Sergeevich.

Gorbachev: That reminds me: Primakov told me that Nikolai Nikolaevich Vorontsov said clearly and precisely that he was against the SCSE.

Yeltsin: Mikhail Sergeevich, read that document out. It is the transcript of the session of the Cabinet of Ministers on 19 August at 18.00 hours. That was the time when the first storming of the White House should have begun.

Gorbachev: I'll do it right away. I'll just finish what I was going to say and then I'll read it out. [Whereupon Gorbachev went on to explain why he had dismissed Alexander Bessmertnykh as Minister of Foreign Affairs, what problems the new Cabinet of Ministers had to solve, whilst all the time from the floor there were cries of 'Read the document'.] I'll read it, I'll read it. There are a few questions, and I'll read it immediately. [But he once more got carried away, seeming not to notice the growing dissatisfaction in the auditorium.] So, we must above all keep on course for change, and a suitable structure of power which can assume responsibility and carry on, this is the best guarantee that the coup won't succeed. Secondly, we must move, and quickly, towards a Union Treaty. . . . We are on the right road. . . . A single group is being formed of Soviet and Russian investigators, and they will conduct the investigation into the coup. (Shouts from the floor.) They will report to us and we will inform both you and the Supreme Soviet of our country how the investigation is progressing. (Shouts from the floor.)

Don't make my task more difficult, my situation is hard enough as it is. Don't make it worse. . . . I think that in adopting such an approach, we must be show maturity and the achievements that we have. . . . The guilty must bear the utmost responsibility. We must avoid a witch hunt, I think you will agree. (Noises, shouts, protests in the auditorium.) If you won't . . . (Noise) . . . Well, I think you understand. . . . For me certain questions are clear, absolutely clear . . . (Noise and shouts). Gently does it, we mustn't be too hasty.

Yeltsin: Quiet, deputies. Quiet. There will be time for questions afterwards.

Gorbachev: The USSR Supreme Soviet will meet on the 26th. The Supreme Soviet of the USSR consists of deputies just like you . . .

(Noise and shouts, general dissatisfaction.) . . . Just now, when Boris Yeltsin was absent, my friends asked me to say that all the republics, in those worrying days having given firm support to Russia, when . . . (Shouts of dissatisfaction.) . . . .

Yeltsin: Please, respected deputies, quiet please. [The noise and shouts in the auditorium went on a long time. From the exclamations the deputies were making it was evident that they were annoyed because Gorbachev had not correctly grasped the situation.]

Gorbachev: I think that Russia, in taking a strong line, and stating what happened in Moscow, where the Supreme Soviets and the Presidiums had taken up their position, carried the day, as Boris Nikolaevich will confirm . . . (Displeasure from the floor, shouts.)

. . . . I said yesterday, and must say to you sincerely: for me it is a most difficult drama! I was brought the ultimatum by the head of the President's Office, Boldin.

From the floor: And who chose him?

Gorbachev: A person I fully trusted, fully. Shenin, a member of the Politburo, Secretary of the Central Committee of the Communist Party . . . (noise) . . . Baklanov, my deputy in the Defence Council, former Secretary of the Central Committee of the CPSU. The fourth one who was with them was Varennikov, an army general. It seems he later went to Ukraine to present an ultimatum to Kravchuk. [Evidently Varennikov had partly got what he wanted from Kravchuk, as the latter did not interfere in the Russian affair and the SCSE did not impose a state of emergency on Ukraine – author.] Now I shall read out the notes Boris Nikolaevich has given me, 'A short account of the session of the Cabinet of Ministers of the USSR 19 August 1991, chaired by Valentin Pavlov'. Pavlov as it were introduced the session.

Pavlov: How are we going to proceed in connection with the state of emergency? Are you prepared to rescue the country from the crisis? All previous resolutions are being disobeyed. Do you agree with supporting the Supreme Soviet on the Union Treaty? (I quote Lukyanov.) How do you envisage managing industries and firms? And in a word, do you support the coup?

Speeches

1 Katushev: 'The staff of the Ministry today at 10 a.m. examined the situation and fully supported the Committee. We sent a directive to all agents abroad to carry out its policy.'

2 Orlov (Finance Ministry): 'Work is being organised along special lines. Together with the banks (Viktor Gerashchenko), I sent the

necessary telegrams to the usual firms, in support of the Committee. Gerashchenko and Moskovskii are actively supporting the coup.'

3 Sychev (Gosstandart): Actively supported the Committee and offered his services in carrying out its policy.

4 Churilov (Neftegazprom – oil and gas industries): 'We all support the coup.'

5 Davletova: Her speech was neither one thing nor the other . . . like the person who wrote it down, no doubt. She asked for help in reviving industry. She cunningly avoided the question of allegiance to the Committee. (Lively reaction from the floor.)

6 Gusev: Actively supported the coup and proclaimed that if the Committee did not win the day it would mean the end. 'We will fight.'

7 Panyukov: Turned this way and that, but supported it. (Noise in the hall.)

8 Stroganov: Actively supported the Committee, reported that the *apparat* was ringing around the engineering factories and advising them to support the Committee.

9 The first Deputy Minister of the Economy: Neither yes nor no. Demanded additional protection for strategic sites.

10 Timoshinshin: For the Committee.

11 Minister of Transport: For.

12 Vorontsov: As a deputy of the Russian Republic, announced that in the morning of the 19th at the meeting of the Presidium of the Supreme Soviet of the Russian Republic, the actions of the Committee were declared unlawful and suggested mediation to establish contacts with the Russian leadership, a view which was rejected.

13 Tizyakov: For the SCSE.

14 Shcherbakov, a Deputy Premier: The national economy will have to function effectively. There will be an embargo; in 'three to four days we will have to resolve all questions and suggestions on the utilisation of the mobilised resources, there will be no imported resources, we will have to seek internal solutions.' Still has not formulated his relationship to the Committee in so far as the Committee changes its mind during the day. 'I am unable to define my position, but I do not have great expectations from those I know well such as Tizyakov and Starodubtsev.'

Gorbachev: This means that at the end of the day Shcherbakov was involved. [He was certainly rather cowardly and did not speak out against the Committee – author.]

Yeltsin: Nor did he condemn it.

Gorbachev: In short we will have to look into it. Next!

15 Maslyukov: 'The published material does not show the way out of the crisis for the country.' He asked five questions. Became involved in a wrangle with Pavlov. He did not clarify his position.

16 Ryab'ev: Expressed himself cautiously but on the whole supported the Committee.

17 Doguzhiev: Went to the podium and actively supported the Committee. (Noise from the floor.)

18 Gubenko: 'Tomorrow I am to meet the intelligentsia. They won't understand the Committee.' (Noise from the floor.) He did not express a clear position. However, it is rumoured that he later resigned.

19 Shchadov: Actively in favour. He demanded the immediate introduction of a state of emergency in Kemerovo. (Laughter in the hall.)

20 Laverov: Twisted this way and that but did not commit himself. (Noise.)

Gorbachev: It is strange that no one from the Ministry of Defence either spoke or participated in the discussion. Pavlov did not force them to do so.

Yeltsin: Mikhail Sergeevich, I can explain. Pavlov had a separate, closed meeting with them, before the Cabinet of Ministers met, and that is why they did not speak at this meeting. [By this stage we knew about this meeting where the ministers persuaded Pavlov openly to formulate the question of trust in the Committee].

Gorbachev: I must say the following: I am still doing a lot of catching up because for four days I had no idea what was going on. This morning Boris Nikolaevich sent the resolutions which you have taken. I have glanced through them and yesterday when I was asked I said: 'The country found itself in such a situation that the Russian leadership saw no other means or methods of action, and nor do I. Everything which the Supreme Soviet of Russia, its Presidium, the President and the government did was dictated by circumstances and was legitimate.' (Tumultuous applause.)

Yeltsin: I request that this should be officially registered by a decree by the country's President. (Laughter.)

Gorbachev: Boris Nikolaevich, we did not agree to reveal all our secrets immediately!

Yeltsin: It is not a secret. It is serious. (Laughter in the hall.)

Gorbachev: Comrades, Boris Nikolaevich and I certainly exchanged opinions on this question when we met today. Why? Because these decrees were dictated by circumstances, by a critical situation; it was necessary to match force with force and by the same token, it is necessary to recognise them. Therefore we agreed that there ought to be a presidential decree to confirm, albeit retrospectively, this strong position from a juridical point of view. (Applause.) It is also a precedent but it is a necessary one.

Yeltsin: A whole package of documents has been specially prepared, Mikhail Sergeevich, 'Decrees and resolutions adopted in the besieged House of Soviets'. (Applause.) Here it is. We are entrusting them to you.

Gorbachev: Now I will read the questions which the Russian deputies are putting to me, though perhaps we have already answered some of them. Here is one about the Supreme Soviet of the USSR. I have already given my point of view. (Noise. Voices.) Probably, I will have to answer.

Yeltsin: Let us begin with the questions sent up earlier.

Gorbachev: Here is a proposal by Stepanshin, Kobets and Lopatin concerning the KGB and the armed forces. I have already mentioned, incidentally, that we have relieved Moiseev of his position as Chief of the General Staff and appointed Lobov. We intend to promote Grachev, the commander of the airborne troops as First Deputy to Shaposhnikov.

Yeltsin: Yevgeni Ivanovich Shaposhnikov has been appointed Minister and Grachev the First Deputy Minister of Defence. Grachev who defended us is also the Chairman of the Russian Committee for Defence. See what we have done. I fill in what you, Mikhail Sergeevich, sometimes forget to say!

Gorbachev: We have certainly passed many resolutions. I will not be announcing all of them. All those whom we have appointed will soon be making new proposals. Therefore a personnel shake-up is in hand. Do not worry! Are we agreed?

Yeltsin: I have given the country's President a declaration conferring the title of General of the Army on Colonel-General Konstantin Ivanovich Kobets. (Applause.) The President agreed. I signed the declaration conferring the rank of Major General on Colonel Rutskoi. The President of the country also agreed. (Applause.)

Gorbachev: Comrades, there will be many such questions, I would think, of a practical nature. I will try to answer briefly. Question: 'Evidently not all members of the SCSE ought to bear equal responsibility for the coup. So far as we know, Starodubtsev was informed of his inclusion on the committee at 10 a.m. on the 19th. Did you get Starodubtsev's letter with his explanation and how are you going to treat him?'

I have not received anything, am not aware of anything. (Noise, voices, cries.)

Yeltsin: Attention, please!

Novikov: I have the following question, Mikhail Sergeevich. You regularly managed to confirm your adherence to socialism. At the same time you announced that you were preparing to undertake the improvement of the Communist Party. My question is this: do you not consider that socialism should be banished from the territory of the Soviet Union? This is the first thing.

Secondly, do you not agree with the caucus of non-party deputies of the RSFSR that the Communist Party of the Soviet Union should be disbanded as a criminal organisation? (Applause.)

Gorbachev: Well, the question is frankly put. I will answer with the utmost candour. If you give the Supreme Soviet and the government of the Russian Federation and all the supreme soviets and governments the task of banishing socialism from the territory of the Soviet Union we will not be able to resolve this problem. It is a new type of crusade, a latter-day religious war. Socialism as I understand it consists of certain convictions of people not only in our country but around the world, and not merely today but in other periods of history and we have proclaimed freedom of conscience, pluralism of opinions. (Noise in the hall.) No, you will hear me out. You yourselves want me to answer openly. I believe I am answering the question in the spirit in which it was put. (Noise in the hall, heckling.) Well then don't ask me questions to which I ought to reply with a speech. No one has the right to raise the issue of banishing socialism from the territory of the Soviet Union – it is just the latest utopian nonsense and, moreover, it is a veritable witch hunt. A person has the right to his opinions, to choose a movement, a party or to remain unaffiliated, that is the first thing.

Secondly, when you say ban the party as a criminal organisation, I cannot agree because in this party there are people, there are tendencies, there are groups who have taken a criminal path, interfere with us and even became participants in such a crime, of course they should bear the responsibility, some politically, some in a court of law, but I will never agree that we ought to suppress communists – workers, peasants – this is what I was talking about. (Noise in the hall.)

To forbid the party as a criminal organisation. I answer: there are people who have assumed leadership of the party and country, and in the Secretariat of the Central Committee of the Communist Party who lacked the courage – and there the struggle went on for three days – to come to the defence of their General Secretary and secure a meeting with him. There are party committees who decided to do everything to help the so-called Committee, these people ought to answer for it – each according to his deserts. However, I will never agree to branding millions of workers and peasants as criminals. (Noise in the hall.) The more so, as the Programme of the Communist Party which is under discussion puts forwards ideas which even you would find hard to better. (Noise in the hall.) If this

Programme were to be adopted, then those who supported it would be democrats who would be together with you. (Noise in the hall.)

Yeltsin: Second microphone please.

Zadonskii: Honoured President. Please formulate your position with regard to the opinion of a group of Russian deputies who consider that urgent measures should be taken to eradicate the fertile environment for coups to take place leading to the situation which occurred. These measures should consist of the following: the immediate removal of parallel government of the country by party structures, for which purpose for the period of establishing democracy, disband the central ruling structures of the Communist Party Central Committee and the Russian Communist Party including the Politburo, regional territorial party committees, the political organisations in the KGB, MVD, in the army and in the navy. Nationalise the property of the Communist Party publicly, under the control of deputies and public commissions. Disband the KGB, creating new security organs recruited through the unification of corresponding organisations of the republics. Border guards should be pleased under the direct command of the President.

Gorbachev: Beginning with the last question. By appointing comrade Vadim Bakatin Chairman of the Committee for State Security we achieved the second point. We are now awaiting ideas for the reorganisation of the KGB. As far as the other questions are concerned, they all merit immediate attention. Incidentally thoughts covering the points you raised were discussed at the meeting with leaders of all the republics. We will examine these questions urgently and work out ways and means. But again everything must be done according to the law. (Applause.)

Yeltsin: Third microphone.

Academician Ryzhov, Deputy of the Supreme Soviet: Mikhail Sergeevich, I would like your opinion on a very important question. As you have informed us, you have made very good appointments to important governmental positions. But the nomination for the post of Prime Minister is of crucial significance, and, at the same time, has broad social significance. I think, and probably my colleagues will support me, that this post should be given to a representative of Russia. And I consider that there is a very good candidate in Russia, highly competent professionally, Ivan Silaev. (Stormy applause.) If, of course, he agrees. I would like to know what you think about this.

Gorbachev: I don't understand what is under discussion, the Prime Minister of the Soviet Union or Russia? (Noise in the hall.)

Academician Ryzhov: The Prime Minister should be a representative of Russia, specifically comrade Silaev.

Yeltsin: Mikhail Sergeevich, the first part of the question: do you think the question has been fairly put by the Russian deputies, that the Prime Minister ought to be from Russia, that we should nominate our candidate for this position?

Gorbachev: Boris Nikolaevich knows my position. When in December we formed the organs of power I said that the President and Prime Minister should represent Russia. As regards the Vice President, I hold the view he should be a representative of the republics, preferably from Central Asia. (Noise, animation in the hall.) Wait, wait. I am telling you what we discussed at the Federation Council. My view remains the same.

The second part of the question is a different matter. Due to the fact that the situation in the Cabinet of Ministers of the USSR is especially acute, and I see you share this view, we agreed that in the course of the next two or at most three days that all leaders should think it over in order to work out a unified approach. Comrades from the republics expressed the view that a government coalition should first of all consider the representation of the republics.

From the floor: A wise person will have to be appointed.

Gorbachev: This is an absolutely correct assumption.

Yeltsin: Fourth microphone.

Deputy (did not introduce himself): Mikhail Sergeevich, to a certain extent I am also a political worker. I am a teacher and taught our contemporary young people who stood in defence around this White House. You have just spoken about a certain anti-communist hysteria. I am well aware as a political activist and teacher, that anti-communism arises in response to communism, as anti-fascism in answer to fascism. Therefore, such an organisation as the Communist Party was created from the very beginning on criminal principles and is a party of high treason. This being so, what prevents you as President from issuing a decree sealing up all buildings belonging to that organisation. According to my sources, the Central Committee of the Communist Party is withdrawing vast sums from its accounts, including hard currency, and I think that this should be stopped immediately. Thank you.

Gorbachev: In principle I have answered that question. Practical questions stemming from it will be resolved in the near future. Therefore I will not develop my argument on this issue. As regards the information which has been received about certain activities taking place in the building of the Central Committee of the Communist Party, I have agreed that measures should be taken to put a stop to them.

Yeltsin: Measures have been taken. The building of the Central Committee of the Communist Party has been sealed. (Applause.) Fifth microphone.

Gorbachev: But do not give way to emotion. Now of all times it is necessary to remain clear-headed.

Arutyunov: Mikhail Sergeevich, this my question. There was a prevailing opinion among the defenders of the Russian White House that, allegedly, you knew about everything which had happened beforehand. This point of view is supported by an interview which Lukyanov gave on the 19th where he announced that he had conferred with you and agreed upon the personal composition of this group of conspirators. I would like to know your position on this.

Gorbachev: I think that many figures will of course now try to extricate themselves, justify themselves. Groups which suffer defeat invent anything they please. It is the crudest fabrication, an attempt at mud-slinging to compromise me because they did not succeed in breaking the President through blackmail. They did not manage to get anything out of me, no document, no announcement nor any speech of support. After hearing on the radio that I was allegedly incapable of thinking or functioning, I understood that in the hours ahead everything would be done to reduce my condition to a state corresponding with that announced by the conspirators. Therefore in Foros we took all possible measures: refused the food they delivered to us, made do with what food we had in the house. Strengthened the security, arranged circles of defence, brought everybody together and began to live according to a siege psychology.

Therefore I think all this is being done now to discredit me because they failed to break my morale. Now they have released a new false version of events. The President is in league with the conspirators!

From the floor: You are saying that Lukyanov is lying?

Gorbachev: In the first place I have not yet heard nor seen this announcement. If he says this, he is a criminal. (Applause.) I have not spoken to Lukyanov nor any of the members of that junta.

Arutyunov: Second question. Mikhail Sergeevich, you will remember that at the Fourth Congress [in May 1991] our present Vice President Rutskoi approached you. He wanted to invite you to the Congress. You did not receive him. He waited for you for three hours. He said that we did not need you but you needed us. And you see current events have proved that your only support is the Russian parliament. Do you understand this? [Incidentally, Yeltsin sent me to invite Gorbachev after Gorbachev had refused Rutskoi, and also unfortunately to no avail. Gorbachev did not come to our Congress – author.]

Gorbachev: I think that we need each other as adherents of democratic reform, and to allow divergence and division would be to go off course. I have already announced this publicly, it is not

179

news, but I wish to confirm after everything which you and I, myself, have been through that nothing on earth will divert me from this course. When I was told that some kind of mission had arrived about which nobody informed me, I decided to pick up a telephone and find out what kind of a mission it was, and when I realised that everything was cut off, I realised that it was going to be a matter of life or death. After I told my family, they said that we would live as we had lived together, or, if needs be, die together. This was the position of my family which remained the same till the end, although things are not completely back to normal now in my family. So we need one another.

Yeltsin: First microphone.

Gorelov: Mikhail Sergeevich, at your press conference yesterday, you paid much attention (in my, perhaps, purely personal opinion) to how you were treated in the Crimea, to how your granddaughter behaved, but we heard nothing about the course of actual further actions. Apart from announcements about a staff reshuffle we have heard nothing at all, unfortunately, about what is to happen, for example, to Russian property. Well, it would probably take a long time to answer this. You have said it would be necessary to deliver an entire speech, therefore I have some personal questions for you.

Gorbachev: Just a moment, you are again switching over to personal issues and you will say that I have not answered the question. Firstly, I cannot agree with you, I said that the whole affair consisted of the fact that we were approaching that stage of realising a direct transformation to a new form of life: the signing of the Union Treaty, the implementation of anti-crisis measures, urgent matters of rationing and fuel, affairs such as the stabilisation of finances. All this has to be done. In order to accomplish all these things we need a major realignment of forces, new responsible legislative and executive authorities which would enjoy the people's confidence and resolve all these problems. We have to continue what we were doing, we have approached the phase of realisation of concrete tasks in all directions of democratic transformation. So I cannot agree with you.

Yeltsin: One moment. The topic, Mikhail Sergeevich, was property. I would like to remind you that we had reached agreement before all these events that if you would not take the decision to assign property on Russian territory to the jurisdiction of Russia, the President of Russia would do so by decree. I signed this decree on the 20th of this month. All property and valuables on the territory of the Russian Federation, apart from that handed over to the Union, belongs to the people of Russia, is Russian property. And you said today that you would sign a document upholding all my decrees issued at that period. (Applause.)

Gorbachev: I do not think that you have chased me into a trap. I confirm once more that the Supreme Soviet of the Russian Federation, the President and the government in this extreme situation acted as the circumstances prompted, and that they took such decisions as dictated by the situation, and they all have legal force and should be confirmed down to the last one by the President of the country.

Everything concerning the question of the achievement of the Union Treaty, Boris Nikolaevich, is as we discussed. And I confirm that after signing the Union Treaty, the decree of the President about property should be accepted, relating to all republics, and the implementation should begin. One thing is clear, there will be such a decree immediately after the signing of the Treaty, and it is being drawn up.

Yeltsin: For some light relief, comrades. Allow me to sign a decree suspending the activities of the Russian Communist Party. (Tumultuous applause growing to an ovation. Shouts of 'Bravo'! Yeltsin signs the decree.)

The decree has been signed. (Cries of 'hurrah'. Ovation.)

Gorbachev: I do not know what is written there and what it is called. If it is as Boris Nikolaevich says, then the Supreme Soviet of Russia, which has done so much and has so much to do, now in this instance should scarcely support President Boris Nikolaevich whom I respect and . . . (cries from the floor). Wait a minute. The whole Russian Communist Party did not participate in the coup, nor did they support it. (Cries from the hall.) Therefore if it is established that the Russian Committee of the Communist Party and some committees in the regions sided with this Committee, then I would support such a decree. I can tell you outright that banning the Communist Party would be a mistake on the part of such a democratic Supreme Soviet and the President of Russia. Therefore, is this decree correctly named?

Yeltsin: Mikhail Sergeevich, it is not about banning, but about suspending the activities of the Russian Communist Party until judicial organs have cleared up its participation in all these events. It is completely legal.

Gorbachev: That is another matter. (Tumultuous applause.)

Yeltsin: The more so as the Russian Communisty Party has not yet registered with the Ministry of Justice.

Gorbachev: Be democrats to the last. To the last. And then everyone will be behind you – genuine democrats and people with common sense.

Yeltsin: Second microphone.

Petrenko: Esteemed Mikhail Sergeevich. I would like to ask you the following question. Please tell us that you have sufficient resolution (only honestly, directly) now to evaluate all the personnel, all the individuals, who headed the state committees (apart from the ministries; we have already heard the answer to that question).

And the second question concerns the events which took place. You are well aware that being silent in this situation is worse than being a traitor. Everything should be called by its proper name.

And now, bound up with suspending the activities of the Communist Party of Russia is a parallel second question. Can you evaluate the secretaries of the regions, municipal committees of the party, regional parties, etc. right up to the Central Committee of the party? What action will be taken? You said just now that not everybody behaved identically. I am not referring to the rank-and-file of the party, I am speaking about the apparatus of the party leadership, which quite frankly did not support you, or the Russian parliament in the given circumstance and went along with the putschists. What kind of action are you going to take? And my request. Now people expect only decisive steps from you. I am asking you simply, as a woman. Be decisive at this difficult moment.

From the floor: Well said! (Applause.)

Gorbachev: Comrades! Where the most decisive measures are called for and they are justified by the situation, and the situation which we have experienced is just such a one, the hardest lessons are to be drawn. For my part, the most decisive measures will be taken on the basis of all your advice. I am prepared for this morally and politically. I shall, however, always insist that if we tear society apart we shall be unable to unite the democratic forces and movements that lie within any healthy society, and therein lies the route to violence in our society. We must avoid it now, and the people won't accept it either. You noticed the way in which a section of society reacted, with calls to restore order: 'Give us a Brezhnev, a Stalin, so long as there's order.' It is for this reason that we have to demonstrate our ability to solve problems and show that we can solve them within the rule of law and democracy. I will insist on this kind of action, but not to the detriment of a resolute and firm approach.

Yeltsin: I can confirm that during a one-and-a-half-hour conversation alone with Mr Gorbachev today he assured me quite firmly that the appropriate measure will be applied according to the law, resolutely and sharply and with no effort spared, to all those who are involved directly or indirectly in this coup. (Cries of 'Bravo!'. Applause).

[To be frank, I felt sorry for Gorbachev. So I whispered to Yeltsin: 'Time we ended this.' 'Why?' asked Yeltsin. 'I can't help feeling sorry for him,' I replied. Yeltsin smiled and nodded agreement. Then he turned to the deputies.]

Respected people's deputies! For an hour and a half the President has been at the podium (cries of 'not enough!'), and now . . . the thing is that there is a meeting of the 'nine' leaders of the union republics at 6 o'clock. And both the President and I will have to continue there the discussion of questions of principle: the economy, dismissals and appointments and so on. (Noise in the auditorium.) For this reason I would like to ask your permission to close this meeting, to thank President Gorbachev for agreeing to meet with you, and to thank you for the firmness and decisive action which defeated the putschists.

The coup d'état was defeated. Goodbye, and thank you.

A number of impressions were left by Mikhail Gorbachev's speech and his answers to the questions. Evidently, he still had not got over the shock or come to terms with the situation, nor had he managed to digest the torrent of information and disinformation with which he had been confronted.

Overall, his answers were weak. Gorbachev often jumped from one subject to another, mixing personal and family sufferings with highly complicated political events. Moreover, it was evident that President Gorbachev had convinced himself that the Russian deputies would welcome him as a hero. This opinion was unfounded: having spent two days and three sleepless nights braving mortal danger, having thrown themselves at the lines of tanks at the approaches to the White House, and having talked themselves hoarse discussing and arguing with the paratroopers persuading them to reject their evil intentions, to refuse the planned massacre of thousands of people, the deputies felt that Gorbachev too bore a good deal of blame. They recalled the miscalculations he had made in his appointments, his constant criticism of left-wing forces which he dismissed as 'destructive', his continual leaning towards an alliance with the reactionaries – with reactionary generals and followers of Kryuchkov, with the upper echelons of the military–industrial complex, with the right-wing Peasants' Union led by Starodubtsev, and the reactionary Central Committees of the CPSU and the Communist Party of Russia, and his support for regional and republican party 'bosses', together with all our provincial vendées who openly fought the Russian leadership. Of course, it was up to the President at the very least to make his position clear on a number of questions.

Firstly, he was expected to thank the Russian deputies and acknowledge the crucial role of the people of Moscow, and also the people of Leningrad. Secondly, to recognise his own personal responsibility for government appointments. Thirdly, to declare his firm intention to strengthen the democratic process and economic reforms, and acknowledge the necessity of restoring the principle of private property. He said all these things in very general terms, but in a somewhat flowery and diffuse manner. For this reason his speech was constantly interrupted by shouts from the deputies, who behaved fairly unceremoniously. Generally speaking the President wilted, and to some extent became confused. President Yeltsin too was fairly rough on him, making a number of demands and getting Gorbachev to agree. Frankly, I felt sorry for Gorbachev.

After the meeting had closed the two Presidents and I went into Yeltsin's office. We talked for a couple of hours. The President of the USSR was very emotional: he recalled how he heard my voice for the first time on the BBC, where I described the members of the Committee as state criminals and read out the 'Appeal to the Citizens of Russia'.

'I said to Raisa Maximovna,' said the President, 'that if Russia rose up in defence of the Constitution, then we would not need to wait long before regaining our freedom.'

'What was Raisa Maximovna's reply?' I asked quickly.

'She said that she would never have thought that we would be saved by Yeltsin and his associates.'

It was nearly time for the session of the Russian Supreme Soviet's Presidium, so I bade the Presidents farewell and left the office.

And so, the coup d'état in the Soviet Union was suppressed. It had, however, effectively dealt the USSR a mortal blow: thereafter began the headlong collapse of a great empire.

11

THE ORIGINS OF THE CONSPIRACY

QUESTIONS, QUESTIONS

At his press conference on 22 August after returning from his 'Crimean imprisonment', Gorbachev indicated the time when the coup had begun: 17.40 on 18 August. It was at that moment that the conspirators confronted him. What was going on meanwhile in the offices of the Kremlin is not yet known. The task of seizing the White House building of the Russian Federation was only entrusted to the KGB's 'Alpha' Group at 19.30 hours on 19 August. We understand from other sources that we were supposed to be 'taken' at 6 p.m., when Pavlov was leading the session of the Cabinet and practically all the ministers approved the actions of the Committee. However, we need to consider the following questions: why did the putsch ringleaders 'having announced the overthrow', wait nearly twenty-four hours? Why did they not take any practical steps before the leadership of the Russian Federation, early in the morning of 19 August, officially declared the members of the SCSE to be criminals? Why did Yanaev after this limit himself to issuing a warning to Yeltsin, Khasbulatov and Silaev?

Doubts have even been raised about the refusal of the special units to storm the White House, picketed by thousands of demonstrators, on the evening of 19 August, even though it was both logical and understandable. One further fundamental question remains: why was this not done (following the 'normal' logic of the conspirators), by 12 noon or 2 p.m. on 19 August, when barricades had not yet been erected?

There is a further question. Why, having cut all the USSR President's lines of communication, did the conspirators leave a partially working link (which included the governmental link) in the dachas of the Russian leadership and in the White House? These questions are being asked by many political commentators and journalists. Clearly, they do not accept that the conspirators had not foreseen a strong reaction to the coup from the Russian leadership. They had not considered the possibility of thousands of Russians rushing to the aid of parliament and President, nor of barricades or of the disaffection in the army, the reactions of international public opinion and so on.

The overthrow had been expected in the depths of autumn, to take advantage of food shortages. Now many conspirators or the tacit supporters of the coup talk angrily of precipitate action of the conspirators, referring to the members of the Committee as provocateurs. They ought to have waited for food shortages to bite (and, of course, to have prepared the ground for them to occur). Hunger would have led to bloodshed, tanks, indiscriminate arrests and deportations – all this no doubt was dreamed up in Sergei Kurginyan's 'laboratory' – in any case this scenario had been worked out and presented as early as September 1990 to Nikolai Ryzhkov, the then Soviet Premier.

On giving his late-night interview at Vnukovo on his return from Foros on 21 August, President Gorbachev, stunned by events, first gave the name of Boldin as 'emissary of the so-called SCSE', which had come to the Crimea with an ultimatum. General Varennikov, the commander in chief of the land forces, and the KGB General Plekhanov, the head of government security, behaved particularly aggressively towards the President. This was no accident. Flatterers and toadies always surround the throne of Tsars and the tribunes of dictators. It is from their number that conspirators, squabblers and traitors emerge.

The conspirators were counting on a straightforward scenario of seizing the White House and arresting the leaders of Russia, but became confused when this scenario collapsed almost instantly. From the very start the conspirators' plans went wrong. President Gorbachev was only isolated in Foros, but not arrested. Yeltsin and Khasbulatov declared war on Yanaev and did so firmly and implacably.

Even the part of the overthrow which involved the arrest of difficult people's deputies was unsuccessful. Although the leader of the KGB for Moscow and the Moscow region, Lieutenant-General Vitali Prilukov, at a meeting of district KGB leaders spoke of the arrest of Yeltsin, Khasbulatov and Silaev, this was most probably done to boost morale: the KGB group assigned to seize them arrived in fact twenty minutes late. The President of Russia and the leader of the parliament were on their way to the White House at great speed at the very moment when the KGB burst into their dacha, but not before they had signed and distributed their appeal 'To the Citizens of Russia'.

The only thing that the putsch organisers achieved (and even then with only partial success) was that they managed to suspend the activities of the democratic mass media, by closing down newspapers which were inconvenient to the reactionary regime and taking control of radio and television.

However, at the same time the consequences were catastrophic. The general economic loss was estimated at around 35 billion roubles, while politically the coup had put an end to the existence of the Soviet state in the form and on the principles by which it had existed for nearly seventy-four years.

I should say a few words about bringing in the armed forces. Most of the soldiers and even the officers at first did not know why they had been sent here. After all, when the news of the coup d'état was published, they were already marching into the city. The population managed to establish contact with the troops and thereafter it would have been ridiculous to suppose that the soldiers of the Taman and Kantemir Divisions would fire at the people. And there were, of course, quite a few Muscovites in these divisions too.

The soldiers of most of the units, including those loyal to the KGB, had no practical combat experience. And it would have been inconceivable that the conspirators would have refrained from ordering the storming the White House on that first night had the Ryazan Regiment of the Tula Airborne Division not crossed over to support the legitimate Russian government – the soldiers of this unit had fought in various regions of this country. We have already discussed the position of the leader of the paratroop forces, Pavel Grachev: he manoeuvred and deceived the Committee, remaining true to the pledge he had made to Yeltsin, and did not send in the paratroopers to storm the White House.

The real threat in this situation came from the special units of the KGB and MVD which tried to infiltrate the parliament building, but were exposed in time. The three companies which managed to cross the cordon were ample to storm the White House. They needed only to break into the building itself, the rest would have been a simple matter of technology. However, the timely appearance of armed defenders of the parliament thwarted their attack.

It is not entirely clear why specialist KGB groups, which had been trained for precisely such situations, were not brought into action. Most probably they took fright at the sight of the fury and determination of the defenders, who were ready to tear to pieces anyone connected with the KGB or its organisation. General Shaposhnikov, the Commander of the Air Force, refused to transfer these units by helicopter, and thus undermined the whole plan to storm the White House. However, one cannot rule out the possibility that they refused to obey a criminal order, even though it is more likely that the putsch organisers simply got scared of taking responsibility for the inevitable bloodshed, including the slaughter of women and children, of which there were many and who would not have been spared in such a scenario.

The rain which had often poured down over Moscow was cursed by many during those days and nights, even by the conspirators. In such adverse weather conditions it was impossible to use nerve gas. However, as became known, a special section was opened in the Sklifosovskii clinic, equipped to deal with gas victims. An order for 250,000 pairs of handcuffs was also hurriedly completed.

Those who thought up the coup reckoned that the tanks and the curfew would deal with a 'bunch of extremists', but the basic, or main part of the population ('real Soviet people') would support a return to the old regime. But the numbers were wildly out. According to a survey on 20 August, not more than 18 per cent of Russian citizens thought that the economic situation would improve if the Committee came to power. On the second day of the uprising, in a Moscow occupied by troops, 1,792 persons were questioned. Three-quarters of them reckoned that mass repressions were about to begin. But to the question: 'Do you think the action of the SCSE is legally justified?', only 13 per cent answered 'yes' and 73 per cent said 'no'. By 24 August only 7 per cent regretted the ending of the state of emergency. The people clearly did not support the putschists.

THE ROLE OF THE MILITARY

The military brought troops into Moscow and prepared to storm the Russian parliament. Apparently they were preparing to 'take steps' in the Baltic and Moldova, and leaned on the leaders of Ukraine and Kazakhstan.

But there were other officers who were not definitely on our side who quietly sabotaged the advance of the SCSE. These included Yevgeni Shaposhnikov and Pavel Grachev. Pavel Grachev commanded the paratroopers, and had served in Afghanistan. During the attempted coup Grachev took a firm line against the actions of the SCSE. Here is a transcript of his conversation with reporters.

'Pavel Sergeevich, when did you learn that lawful authority was passing to the so-called SCSE?'

'The idea that Gorbachev had fallen ill and was handing over the leadership of the country to Vice President Yanaev and that a state of emergency would be declared had been stated on August 18.'

'By whom?'

'By Yazov, Minister of Defence. Early on the morning of 19 August Boris Nikolaevich Yeltsin rang me up and asked what was happening. I told him all I knew, Gorbachev had fallen ill and his duties were taken over by Yanaev. Yeltsin said shortly "It's a put-up job." He asked if I would send my men to defend the White House, and I said I would. Soon after I sent General Lebed' to the White House.'

'How were the preparations for storming the White House proceeding, and what role were the paratroops to play?'

'On 20 August, between 2 and 3 p.m., there was a meeting in the office of General Achalov, the Deputy Minister of Defence for Emergencies. Present were Generals Varennikov, Kalinin, Karpukhin and many civilians whom I didn't know. The mood was tense. . . . They said that the government of Russia had come out against the SCSE, talks with it had broken down . . . it was necessary to ensure that the Committee was recognised. A task was set: to blockade the parliament building without letting Khasbulatov and his colleagues enter. I was told that the paratroops had been deployed in the region of the American Embassy, the MVD were on Kutuzovskii Prospect, and the special unit "Alpha" were on the Embankment. The plan was as follows: troops of the MVD clear people from round the parliament and "Alpha" go through the gap and storm the building.'

'How did the commander of "Alpha", General Karpukhin, behave during the meeting?'

'I didn't notice any enthusiasm on his part. He was rather passive and subdued. In the small hours of the morning he rang me – there were still two hours left before the attack – and said "I've rung my boss and nobody answers." "Where are you?" I asked. "Two kilometres from the Russian parliament." I knew we were being bugged, as he did, too, of course. He paused, and I didn't hurry him. Then he continued: "I shan't take part in the attack, I'm withdrawing them from Moscow, and I shan't take another step against the Russian parliament and the Russian President."'

'What time was the attack planned for?'

'We were to move out at midnight on the 20th. The attack was to be at 3 a.m. Nothing unusual. Long before the attack all the members of the SCSE had "gone to sleep"; nobody gave us any orders. At midnight we didn't move our paratroops up. An hour went by, nobody rang. My deputies joked gloomily that *they* were obviously fast asleep whilst we were once more being used as cannon fodder. *They* hoped *we* would begin the bloodbath. Not if we could help it!

'I rang General Gromov. I had kept in contact with him before and knew he found the putschists antipathetic. I told him about my conversation with Karpukhin. I asked what the MVD were doing. He answered briefly: "They're staying put. And they won't move."

'After that I realised that the Committee had had it.'

'The defenders of the White House have been complaining about the paras, who left their posts in spite of being asked to stay on for a while near the White House.'

'If you've noticed, the paras were on manoeuvres all the time during those days. My conversation with Yeltsin – as I said already

– was no doubt bugged. My deputy, General Lebed', was also under suspicion. Therefore all our movements must have looked to an outsider like a game of chess. For instance, Yazov ordered the Belgorod Division to be moved to Moscow. I consulted with Shaposhnikov and he advised me to drag my feet. We made out we were not giving the order to take off because of the weather. It appears that Shaposhnikov already had a link with Khasbulatov. But there was more pressure from the Minister. I ordered the landing of troops, chaotically, on two aerodromes at ten-minute intervals. After that they were ages being rounded up. Then I gave the order to one of the regiments to march along the ring road and not to show themselves.

'An hour later the Divisional Commander rang me to say that some people's deputies had arrived and wanted to know what they should do. I said: "Calm them down. Tell them we're not entering Moscow."'

'Pavel Sergeevich, how was it that the Special Airborne Vitebsk Division was transferred to the KGB?'

'That division plus two motorised rifle divisions and one motorised rifle brigade was handed over to the KGB. It was justified at the time on the grounds of fears of breaches of the border, international conflicts. The officers were indignant about that decision, and spread the slogan "Paras will never sell themselves to the KGB". More than 150 officers refused to serve in the KGB and were transferred to other units. There was a lot of pressure put on people, they let them keep their name, increased their pay, gave them other perks – and incidentally that division didn't favour the Committee.

'General Konstantin Kobets played an active role. He had recently become head of the Russian Defence Committee, moreover his transfer to the government of Russia had displeased Yazov, Varennikov and Moiseev.'

'According to Yazov's deputy, troops were brought into the capital because the leaders of Moscow Military District had on their own initiative passed a resolution to organise manoeuvres in Moscow.'

'But there were no manoeuvres planned at that time by the Moscow Military District. The troops were called out on a red alert.'

'Not for training?'

'No, no, a red alert. Full equipment, live ammunition, not blanks, as people were told at the time.'

'So, what orders were they given?'

'They had to blockade all vital buildings, government buildings, that is, the Russian parliament and the Moscow Soviet. Secondly, to prepare the way for ending all lawful authorities not subservient to the Committee and its defenders.'

'Did the officers who brought their troops into the capital know the aims of these "manoeuvres"?'

'Of course not. They were given the objective of moving to a definite position. They really thought, when they went to carry out the order, that something serious was going on. But when on the way they met crowds of people who explained what had happened in Russia, when the tanks and armoured personnel carriers were met by people's deputies, and Boris Yeltsin and I spoke to the people from the top of a tank, the officers and other ranks began to understand why they had been brought in, and several units went over to the side of the Russian authorities.'

'Was there any plan for the defence of the Russian parliament?'

'Yes, in my safe on the morning of the 19th there was a prepared plan of opposition to the putschists. As soon as I learned about the putsch, and contacted Yeltsin, I received clear indications. It was called plan "X". We began erecting barricades. By sectors, outside and inside the building.

'I began appointing our officers to be in charge. In the HQ of the defence there were only nine generals. We had worked out previously which factories would supply reinforced concrete slabs, metal, etc. We thought how to cut cables, barricade the bridge to prevent tanks from crossing it. According to information reaching HQ from people's deputies and others, there were barricades already set up on roads used by the troops, utilising bulldozers, watercarriers, any machinery that was to hand.

'When barricades appeared on the streets in places that prevented military hardware getting through, the troops began to retreat. All in all, it was chaos; discipline went by the board.

'Under the leadership of the Deputy Prime Minister Mikhail Malei, fifteen cutters and a barge were brought in to blockade the Moscow River.'

'At the moment of the coup, did you have any military units under your command?'

'No, we had no troops. We were helped out by voluntary para-troop units, the "Afghantsy", the security unit "Kolokol", young private detectives from "Aleks" and a few others. There were approximately 150 professional officers in the building, about 300 special-purpose troops (OMON) of Viktor Barannikov, and about 300 armed deputies. There were about as many reliable trusted men, recent Afghan veterans, the President's body-guards and a few others. Altogether about 1,000 men.

'I told the officers in charge of units which had entered the capital "I realise that you have to obey orders – but obey them with a ten to fifteen minute delay. So that we have time". After all, they had tanks and I had snow-ploughs, lorries, etc.

'On the night of 20–1 August everyone expected that a detachment of KGB paratroopers would land on the roof of the White House.

'This was our main task, not to let the advance detachment of the 103rd Airborne Division of the KGB to break through, and so not to allow them to create the conditions for "Alpha" to storm the building.

'And secondly, not to allow firing to start. Once they had opened fire we wouldn't last long. Shaposhnikov was a great help: he hadn't given them any helicopters.

'And since the advance detachment had not made a breach, "Alpha" couldn't storm the building: it just wasn't able to overcome that mass of people. It wasn't just a crowd: people were divided into sections, platoons, companies, and every unit knew its task. We even managed to train them to let "Alpha" through, then crowd them with our bodies and disarm them.'

'Why in your opinion did the putschists not take extreme steps, why did they not above all arrest Yeltsin and Khasbulatov? People say that the Committee was mixed up in something even bigger, not everything is clear.'

'For those who defended the White House for three days and three nights, the coup was pure enough, a terrifying affair. On the other hand, the coup was carried out by men who were unsure of themselves, so it is not surprising that they made mistakes: they didn't know what the Russian leaders might do.

'What were they relying on? On brute strength. Although they were taking a chance, they made their plans on a simplified basis. Tanks would arrive and surround the White House. They would put in two or three companies and Yeltsin, Khasbulatov and Silaev would come out waving a white flag and let themselves be led away in handcuffs. But this was obviously where they misjudged people. I still cannot understand Yazov's point of view. Yanaev was a KGB agent all his life. I spoke to him on the telephone at 10.30 on the morning of the 19th. He rang me and said that we had to submit to the Committee, and if I didn't I and my family would be interned. By the next day a decision had been made to prefer criminal charges against Yeltsin, Khasbulatov and myself, but during that telephone call on the 19th I replied that I had already taken my decision the previous day when I had arrived at the Russian parliament.'

'Rumour has it that behind the Committee of the eight there are others, including Varennikov.'

'Yes, Varennikov played an important part in the coup. He signed the "Address to the People", a reactionary declaration calling for a state of emergency. Before the putsch, incidentally, he was in the

Crimea, in the same delegation which "persuaded" (or rather, black-mailed) Gorbachev to hand in his resignation. He was aware of everything that was happening. The Commander in Chief of the Navy, Chernavin, was also called out there. But he, to his credit, proved to be a real admiral and did not take part in the deal.'

'*Do you think it is possible that the plan to seize power was formed a long time ago by the infamous "eight"?*'

'I think that this "work" began from the moment when Valentin Pavlov spoke at the July session of the Supreme Soviet and requested additional powers. Then Kryuchkov and Yazov also came forward. It became clear to me that the first stage of the military coup was already being planned. I have no information on this: the office of the public prosecutor will go into it. But logic would suggest the following version of events. They tried to repeat the silent revolution of 1964, which deposed Khrushchev, in August 1991. But our country today is not the same: people will no longer be blindly led.'

THE MILITARY–INDUSTRIAL COMPLEX

We have noted that during the meeting of the USSR Cabinet the ministers from the military–industrial complex kept silent because they had already held a separate meeting with Pavlov. These ministers in turn carried out intensive discussions with directors of the military–industrial complex. Already in the first half of August Arkady Volskii, the head of the Union of Industrialists, met with Pavlov and arms manufacturers on several occasions. It is clear that if the generals of the military–industrial complex, both those in and out of uniform, did not actually take part in the conspiracy, then they sympathised with the putschists, and, wanting to strengthen their own shaky position, they longed to keep democracy in check. Baklanov and Tizyakov represented the military–industrial defence complex on the SCSE.

The gigantic military–industrial complex is one of the main reasons for the lamentable condition of our economy. By spending vast sums on its formation and development, the ruling circles distorted the structure of our entire economy. This was the course of action taken by Ryzhkov, and Pavlov also acted in this way.

Now we understand the real reason why heavy engineering was designated a priority at the beginning of perestroika: in order to divert yet more resources to the military–industrial complex to assist its restructuring. The plan fell through because the economy entered into a period of crisis and then of slump. And then just before the coup, Pavlov put forward proposals for a second initiative, yet another attempt to give priority to the development of heavy industry with exactly the same goals as before, the militarisation of the country. The Ministry of Defence, the military–

industrial complex and the State Planning Committee (Gosplan) worked out a programme for the conversion of the defence industry up to 1995. What sort of conversion was this?

By the end of the designated period of 'defence conversion' the production of radios for domestic use was to increase by 20 per cent, that of tape recorders by 4 per cent, and that of colour televisions by 60 per cent. The production of other, smaller items, was also to be increased. In order to provide this small increase in the number of goods available, the captains of industry demanded an additional sum in excess of 40 billion roubles at the value of three years ago, which in today's terms would be at least ten times as much. Thirty billion would have gone on the creation of new sites and only 10 billion on retooling the defence factories, that is, on converting them. In this way the defence industry would have been preserved while at the same time civilian factories would be built, which would, however, have been subordinated to the defence industry. The authors of Pavlov's programmes suggested nearly doubling the supply of metals and other resources for civilian industries, but had no intention of diverting resources from defence industries. On the contrary, by 1995 the supply of materials to the defence sector was to have increased by 7–8 per cent! In addition to colossal capital investment they reckoned on receiving an extra 36 billion roubles for scientific research and construction work in the civilian sector.

Pavlov constantly reiterated the idea that it was necessary to spend vast sums on the restructuring of industry, but that there was no money in the Treasury, so it had to be found outside of the military–industrial complex and could possibly be borrowed from abroad. 'But,' said Pavlov, 'simply to curtail the defence complex would be to drive the country into an impasse from which it would never again emerge.' The seed of rationality in this idea is, of course, that there is no point in trying to reform the military–industrial complex in the short term by weakening it by a lack of funds. But in Pavlov's interpretation the question was really to do with keeping spending on the military–industrial complex at its traditional and senselessly high level.

Conversion is a complicated matter. For example, we poured huge resources into the construction of a gigantic car factory in Elabug, building the entire site from scratch. Would it not have been much cheaper to convert one of the 'tank towns' for this purpose, since these already have factories and excellent staff and living quarters? We have begun to buy passenger planes from abroad, but this hard currency would have been much more profitably spent on the conversion of the defence aircraft industry. Many of the engines are the same for civilian as for military aircraft, thus within a short period of time we would have been selling passenger airliners instead of buying them. The reduction in military orders should be accompanied by competitive conditions and support for the development of civilian industries, and then mastering civilian production will become a matter of life and death for every enterprise, and the workers will not be doomed to mass unemployment.

The putschists did not want to solve the central issues confronting the country by a real reduction in military spending, carefully considered economic reforms and democratisation. They wanted to draw the country into a new spiral of the arms race, to warn of the danger of an attack on the Soviet Union by a foreign enemy and to militarise society. The people would have been muzzled under the pretext of a likely war. But this does not mean that our path will be an easy one, that we know the answers to the questions with which life confronts us, that the reforms ahead of us will be easy. God grant that we will not make the same mistakes as Gorbachev, Ryzhkov, Pavlov and the putschists. Perhaps we will make worse mistakes. The most important task facing us now is economic reform with a social orientation, a variation of Ludwig Erhard's social market economy.

THE DIRTY WORK OF KRYUCHKOV'S KGB

The dark and tragic role of the security organisations in Russia's history since October 1917 is well known. Mass executions, persecution of dissidents, eviction of entire populations from their birthplace, hatred of the intelligentsia. The constant bugging of millions of people, the flagrant infringement of people's privacy, open mockery of human rights and total control.

From the very beginning no one doubted that the KGB was the guiding force in the organisation of the putsch. To these ends, according to specialists, its officials actively worked on the committee's operating staff. Yeltsin and I were placed under enormous pressure from the KGB from the very first moment that we started work at the head of Russia in 1990.

In 1990 an Information Analysis Administration (IAA) was set up within the KGB. Valeri Lebedev became its first head. All documents which entered the central apparatus from the localities passed through the IAA, and all the most important documents passed from the central KGB apparatus to the state and party organisations. It was this administration which had its finger on the pulse of everything that was going on. It was thus able to mould the views of the country's leaders and, most importantly, those of the Central Committee apparatus, sending them information and their recommendations; this same administration received directives from them in return on what the KGB should do and how, all based on the information and analysis given to them by the IAA.

The IAA's duties also included analysing information on internal affairs received from the presidential apparatus of the USSR where the successor to Lebedev, Yuri Kobyakov, worked.

The President of the USSR received almost all his analytical information on internal affairs from the KGB because there was no other institution which could study such a large volume of political processes and public opinion. Information came daily from the KGB. It contained evaluations of events, political views and moods. It is obvious what kind of evaluation the KGB officials, who had been 'weaned' on the fight against heterodoxy and dissidents, gave the President. It was not by chance that Gorbachev used KGB terminology in his speeches: 'extremists', 'antisocial elements', 'nationalists'. Russia's Public Prosecutor told me that in the office of the head of the presidential apparatus, Boldin, was an enormous safe filled entirely with recordings of conversations between two men, Yeltsin and Khasbulatov, from June 1990 to June 1991. Later records, from June to mid-August, had disappeared. It was Kryuchkov personally who daily handed Gorbachev the envelopes with the summary of our telephone conversations, and not only telephone conversations. Everything that we said in our offices and in our apartments was recorded.

On the morning of 19 August the directors of the IAA gathered their employees together and solemnly announced that the dream which had been so long cherished by the administration had finally been realised – socialist principles had triumphed.

A by no means insignificant role in the preparations for the coup was played by the Administration for the Defence of the Soviet Constitutional Order (the 'Third' Administration). This administration was formed two years ago, after the reorganisation of the Fifth Administration. The changes at that time only slightly affected the structure of this administration and its name, and the general orientation of work remained the same. Almost all aspects of internal affairs were under its jurisdiction, joint enterprises (apart from those created by the Soviet Communist Party Central Committee), all kinds of cultural and charitable foundations (apart from those created by the party apparatus), organised crime, mass riots and, naturally, interethnic relations. Of course, there were agents in every branch of the mass media, including radio and television and also in the localities. Thanks to agents in the printing and information agencies and social organisations, the Third Administration could not only study, but also influence the country's political processes.

To quote one example, on the eve of the RSFSR Congress of People's Deputies in March 1991 Alexander Rudkin, who headed the interethnic relations section, submitted a proposal for consideration by the KGB's leaders: organise a letter of protest from the Russian-speaking population of the Baltic republics to the Russian parliament. The aim was to discredit the RSFSR parliament. It was said that the Russians in the Baltics were being discriminated against whilst Moscow calmly looked on and did nothing. And even that Yeltsin, Khasbulatov, and their activities were still being tolerated. The KGB leaders apparently gave the go-ahead to Rudkin's proposal. It was then, at the time of the Third Congress of People's Deputies, that special groups were organised within the Third Administration. In general everything which took place in Moscow at this time was reminiscent of the situation at the time of the coup. This appears to have been the second warning of an impending putsch. The KGB was already then calmly anticipating the deployment of troops onto the streets of the capital. On the whole, it was young men who had worked in KGB for up to a year and a half and the most loyal and trustworthy officials who were selected for the Third Administration's specially appointed groups.

On the eve of 19 August the order was given to detail the operational group which was to be used in an emergency. This was headed by Alexander Moroz, one of the Administration's deputy leaders. At the same time as this group an analogous sub-unit was also being set up within the Third Main Administration, responsible for military counter-intelligence and liaison with the militia. This was, in effect, a strike group. All officials were issued with a travel pass with no marked destination. In the evening they were loaded onto a bus and driven away. Some of them found themselves in Vilnius and Riga: it had also naturally been planned to stage a coup in the Baltic republics, but the men were not used since the 'cause' had collapsed in Moscow. One other strike group, led by G. Dobrovol'skii, closed printing offices and radio stations. Apart from the Third Administration, the KGB's Second Main Administration, counter-intelligence, took similar actions.

In general, considering the part played by the KGB in the movement to stage a coup d'état, one gains the impression that it was not only political goals which motivated its generals at the time of the coup and during preparations for the storming of the Russian White House, but also personal ones. The main bulk of those officials who were involved in state security began their KGB careers in the Fifth Administration, that is to say, they cut their teeth in the struggle against the dissidents. What were their feelings about Yeltsin, Khasbulatov, Silaev and their associates? Quite naturally, only hatred.

At this time the Third Main Administration was monitoring troop morale and observing everything that happened to them, right up to the time they were moved out. The 'special departments' of military counter-intelligence were obliged to hand all information concerning army deployments to the Third Administration, they could influence this and stop or order the movement of troops. On 19–21 August the troops were sent to the 'front line' certainly with the consent of the Third Administration; it could not have happened in any other way.

Apart from the 'specials' (*osobisty*) who were monitoring the troops, the KGB traditionally had its own units. In the past these were Spetsnaz, signals, engineering and frontier troops. Recently, in accordance with the Law on the KGB, the state security organs were also allowed to have military units. Apart from this, in March 1991 two additional Spetsnaz divisions were transferred from the army to Kryuchkov's jurisdiction. The reason for this became clear on 19 August. It was difficult to calculate exactly how many troops were under the KGB's control because there were so many of them. It is also difficult to say where the 'Dzerzhinskii Division' was deployed, about which so many questions were asked at the time of the coup and especially before the storming of the White House.

On the night of 21–2 August yet another KGB military unit was talked about, the regiment which was permanently stationed in the Tepli Stan district in the south of Moscow. A group of Russian deputies went down there and discovered that the regiment was ready for action but that the order to move to the centre had not been received. When on 21 August the President of the RSFSR issued a decree on the transfer of all military units on Federation territory to Russian jurisdiction, the Third Administration was united in its view that if deputies came to close the premises or to confiscate the archives, then its employees would take up arms.

On the afternoon of 23 August the order was given to prepare to burn the KGB's Information Analysis Administration documents. But at 18.00 hours the signal to retreat was given. However, all the important documents had already been destroyed on 21 August between 15.00 and 19.00 hours.

Special mention must be made of the KGB's Moscow and Moscow Regional Administration and of the Russian KGB. On 19 August at 10 a.m. a meeting of the heads of the Moscow and Moscow region district and urban KGB apparatus was held in which the deputy committee chairman V. Prilukov, who was, incidentally, an RSFSR people's deputy, gave instructions on how to behave and announced that all KGB officials who disagreed with the actions of the SCSE would be persecuted. Prilukov ordered 'the intensification of work to counteract diversive and subversive enemy activity relating to industrial, transport and communications objectives and concerns vital to the community, warnings of unusual occurrences, sabotage, wrecking and anti-social manifestations'. Temporary operations and investigation groups and the action groups 'Volna' were placed on action stations from 19 August waiting for special instructions from the centre. When all this subsequently came to light I remember my conversation with General Prilukov, and how he heatedly defended his loyalty to the Russian authorities and promised to provide the Supreme Soviet with essential information relating to events and occurrences taking place in the Moscow region and in the Russian Federation. He was, of course, a man who had been corrupted by the KGB system, it had destroyed his human qualities.

Order No. 0036 issued by the KGB Chairman on 19 March 1991 also testifies to the fact that KGB leaders had long been preparing the coup. The order transferred the Moscow and Moscow regional KGB to the subordination of the central KGB apparatus and its release from an albeit limited subordination to the Moscow authorities.

Our Russian KGB was only formed at the beginning of 1991 and by August still had not properly started work. Its leaders could not get a list of staff members from Kryuchkov for the Russian KGB, even though he had personally promised this to Yeltsin. The Chairman of the Russian KGB was assigned only twenty posts, including typists, secretaries and office managers.

All requests made by officials of the central KGB apparatus, who could not bear the idea of more pressure being inflicted on them by the Union KGB leaders and who wanted to enter the Russian KGB, remained unanswered or they were asked to wait. The Russian KGB was inactive for six months. And who knows whether this might also have been a reason why the coup became possible?

12

THE FATE OF FREEDOM

ON THE VERGE OF RUIN

The fate of freedom is hanging by a thread and it is hardly right to say that the conspirators were foolish, that they were unable to organise the putsch properly, that there were not enough 'Soviet Pinochets'. No, our Pinochets acted in accordance with all the rules, but from the point of view of certain modern gloom and doom political scientists, the supporters of democracy led by Yeltsin acted incorrectly. Gorbachev should have agreed to his resignation, they gave him no alternative; Khrushchev in similar circumstances signed, but Gorbachev broke the rules, refusing to sign anything, and what is more, sent General Varennikov to a place that he is still embarrassed to disclose. According to the rules, Yeltsin should have negotiated and looked for a compromise. There were, after all, supporters of this line within our ranks too. But he encroached on the powers of the 'new authorities', and was not afraid to place himself outside the 'new law'. It is just not done. At the time of a putsch people should stay at home and not show themselves as shooting will start at any moment and, moreover, political rallies have been forbidden. But what did they do? It is, after all, completely senseless to go unarmed against tanks!

No, these people are out of their minds. They do not recognise the new laws, not even those of a coup. Yanaev, Pavlov, Kryuchkov and other Central Committee officials of the CPSU and of the Russian Communist Party have good reason to resent the people, Yeltsin and the Russian parliament. Where else can you see MPs take up machine guns and pistols and, like Oleg Rumyantsev, stop columns of tanks by throwing themselves under them? The putschists did not consider all this, but they were not complete fools, although I would not go as far as to call them clever. The stupidity of the conspirators did not triumph, stupidity can be easily concealed by spiteful determination and cruelty; great intelligence is not needed to launch a coup. The short-lived regime failed not because of stupidity but because of the resoluteness of the people and their representatives.

Yeltsin said to the parents of those who died: 'Forgive me, your President, for being unable to defend and protect your children.' These words will never be forgotten. We are all guilty in the eyes of the dead and their parents. But who knows how many people would have died or been tortured in the camps if it had not been for Yeltsin, elected three times by the people – in the elections to the Supreme Soviet, in the presidential elections and in the bloody elections surrounding the White House; if it had not been for his steadfastly resolute comrades-in-arms who inspired confidence in victory. President Yeltsin seemed on top of it all, not one incorrect word or gesture throughout those three tragic days. And yet it was only recently that publicists and sociologists were trying to convince us that Yeltsin was nothing, a mere populist, that he was against the state and against a united Soviet Union. Yeltsin came down decisively on the side of the Constitution. The Communist Party leadership came out against the Constitution. And that is why this same Communist Party as an institution is a danger to the people. But not only because its leaders came out on the side of the putschists (this was to be expected), but because, as was later revealed, it retained enormous and monopolistic power. It was not the putschists, for example, who instructed TASS, but the Secretaries of the Central Committee. Party officialdom became an organisation with massive, world-wide, power, a criminal syndicate. No ideals remained. Cynicism is the basic characteristic of Communist Party workers. I hope that the investigation being carried out will reveal many unexpected and, perhaps, terrible, but extremely loathsome and sordid facts.

THE BANKRUPTCY OF THE DOOMED

A previous attempt at a military coup was launched seventy-four years ago by General Kornilov. Since then there has been nothing like it, until 18–19 August 1991.

It is a startling fact that the preparations for the putsch were made insolently, almost overtly. Premier Pavlov openly sabotaged economic stabilisation and made the people furious with his finance, credit and price manipulations. They were in the papers every day, all the facts were well known, but neither the Supreme Soviet of the USSR, nor its President, reacted accordingly. Our severest evaluations of the government's activities, even from the tribunal of the Supreme Soviet of the RSFSR, only irritated Gorbachev. The *apparatchiks'* coup completed within the Russian Communist Party at the very time of its creation, generated the shock troops of anti-Gorbachev reaction even within the heart of the presidential camp. Attempts to respond to this by democratic means by party members and press criticism were fruitless.

From December 1990 propaganda was persistently pumped out, and from January 1991 in Lithuania and Latvia the plan of 'extraordinary measures' was tested by the creation of the 'National Salvation Committees', prototypes of the SCSE. The call for all problems to be resolved by a state of emergency became louder and louder in plenums of the CPSU Central Committee and the Central Committee of the Russian Communist Party. Somebody was firmly barring people from the democratic wing from speaking. In fact, we know who this 'somebody' was; notes containing requests to speak fell first and foremost into Boldin's hands. And in early summer 1991 Yuri Prokof'ev, the First Secretary of the Moscow Party Organisation, organised special groups to work on the 'scientific' ideology of 'emergency measures', and the fruits of this work were published in *Moskovskaya Pravda* thus preparing people for the coup. Democracy saw everything, shouted about everything, but did nothing. And could do nothing. It is true that some progress had been made in comparison with the decade of silence when society did not have the power to make its own voice heard: but now a system of 'democratic babbling' has been set in motion. But there is no mechanism of democratic action. The pyramid of power controlled by the state party was a terrible thing, with bureaucrats everywhere, observing every move made and every breath taken by a citizen. This leviathan structure was incapable of controlling social development in the people's interests, it governed only in its own interests. But one way or another it managed to govern. Having broken the hundred thousand or so links of this mechanism's chain, from the Central Committee to the district committee, from the factory to the collective farm, what did we put in its place?

As more and more functions were piled onto President Gorbachev, the more insistently we endeavoured to influence him on every question. At first we loved him impetuously because he was so unlike Stalin, and then we began increasingly to resent the fact that he did not act as decisively as Stalin. So we tell him how to act very decisively on such and such a matter, and he does not act decisively. We put papers on his table in which everything is set down precisely, what to do in order to ensure general happiness in the quickest way possible, but he does not act. When he became President as well as General Secretary so many functions descended upon him that it was already obvious that he was physically incapable of absorbing all the information which was coming in. A situation was arising in which his assistants could, by their own choice, regulate the flow of information and, if they wished, the flow of disinformation, and this is what Boldin did. In this case the trouble was not that the President was relying on the wrong person but that he was obliged to rely on someone: that he could not manage to go thoroughly into every question himself.

Why then did the President not abandon party affairs, with which he obviously could not cope? It is difficult to say. Possibly he considered that, finding himself at the peak of the pyramid of party power, he could control the activities of hundreds of thousands of party officials. We had one popular little theory, according to which it is impossible to move directly from a totalitarian to a democratic system, in the transitional period there should purportedly be an enlightened authoritarian regime. Well, if this 'theory' is correct, we have already lived through this interval and consequently must have a future 'democratic paradise' awaiting us. This loathsome putsch, which ended six astonishing years, did not only represent a personal failure on Gorbachev's part. It was also the collapse of the comfortable model of power cooked up by Kremlin theorists in which the good President looks after everyone and everything. It should be clear to everyone: there is no road to democracy via autocracy. The way to democracy is via democracy, via the power of the people.

It is impossible for one person to look after everything, it is easy to lock one person up in Foros. We would all feel more at ease in our country if we were sure that every lieutenant himself knows for sure that he would not drive a tank into a town even under orders from a marshal. Where every factory manager and worker knows for sure that losses will not be tolerated, where neither the State Bank nor the Ministry of Finance will cover them: there will be bankruptcy. Where every editor knows for sure that he dares not conceal any socially significant information from the reader, no higher-ups will come to their help. The whole social system needs to be reorganised so that every single one of its elements will work correctly on their own.

But no, it was all illogical, unreasonable and irrational. And then came 19 August. The roll call of the 'new soviet leadership' is now well known. It is now known who took it upon himself to turn the country back towards Stalinism with the arrest (or murder?) of its rightful President and parliamentary leaders and with the banning of all newspapers apart from those which practised servility. (Soon the so-called 'independent' papers will start on this road, having pushed the party newspapers aside.)

These thoughts accompanied all my actions during those fleeting, tragic seventy-two hours. I remember another thought which sprang to my mind towards the middle of 19 August: who controls the nuclear weapons? It would be madness, after all, if this gang were to begin making plans on the basis of nuclear blackmail. Three men were able to use the nuclear weapons: Gorbachev, Yazov and Marshal Moiseev. And this despite all the agreements with the USA and their own Supreme Soviet, whom the President, as Supreme Commander, should keep informed of any decision taken, to inflict, say a retaliatory nuclear attack.

Why 'despite'? Well, because, from a purely technical point of view, it is impossible to inform members of the Supreme Soviet in a few minutes.

The flight time of a missile launched from the Barents Sea or the Sea of Norway is 7–9 minutes and 12–15 minutes from continental USA. All that the three men invested with such incomparable power and responsibility would have time to do is to exchange a few words with each other. The telephone link which they have at their disposal allows a connection to be made within a second, no matter where they are.

At one point during negotiations with the Americans, an agreement was reached that both sides would inform each other of a missile launch (in the Pacific Ocean, for example), and, above all, of any unauthorised launch. Such a thing can happen after all, and the two sides should not be allowed to exchange nuclear missiles as a result of a monstrous error on someone's part. A special centre for the reduction of nuclear threat has been set up in the USSR, under the direction of Lieutenant-General M. The centre has a special monitoring system at its disposal with the capacity to track every missile launched by the Americans. And the USA naturally has an analogous system.

During the coup a crisis situation arose in the control of strategic nuclear weapons. The 'special communications sytem of guaranteed stability' was taken from the President and sent to the USSR's Ministry of Defence in Moscow. One of its elements is the 'black case' carried behind Gorbachev, about which everything, it appears, was known. The officers who both carry and guard the case threw away the cypher. This meant that not a single putschist apart from Yazov could gain access to the strategic nuclear weapons control system. It is not enough to know the cypher, there is also a code and this is entrusted to only three people.

The President was under arrest in Foros and deprived of communications. Yazov was also deprived of the link on 21 August on the day when he was arrested. Rushing cap in hand to Gorbachev, he left his minders in Vnukova Airport 2, which he had no right to do.

I remember Yeltsin blanching when he shared his anxieties with me on the night of the 20th. 'Don't speak to anybody about this,' he said. 'We are better off trying to get even with this gang.' It was at this time that Bush phoned.

CONCLUSION

I do not wish to write a long conclusion. That is a job for the future. It is possible that some day I will get down to it and write something substantial. The coup was crushed, but the anxiety remains with me. In this whirlwind of political insurrection, have we not forgotten our motherland's biggest problem; how to survive the transitional period towards a market economy? We have shown that we are resolute, but a special resolve is called for here: to adopt painful economic measures which cannot, of course, be postponed, but they need to be implemented

competently, governed by people's real situation, absorbing the experience of the Western European countries, the new German *Länder* and the
world-wide experience of a competitive economy. The harsh reflections of
millions of Russian people must be taken into account. A well-qualified
government is needed. We need to develop with the Union, not destroy it,
and transform ourselves into a Confederation as I suggested in my draft
as far back as August 1990.

The consent of the people is required and an understanding of the fact
that only united, on the basis of a consensus, can we possibly hope to
escape from the crisis. A united society in August 1991 wiped the conspirators out just like an explosion. But I cannot see that consensus has been
achieved in our Russian society. This thought constantly worries me and
makes me anxious. Very anxious indeed.

Part III
POWER

13

ON POWER

THOUGHTS OF THE SPEAKER

I possibly give here a rather subjective view of power and its impact on contemporary society in Russia at an acute turning point in its history. My interpretation will deal with basic theoretical problems: power as political domination, power as a system of state organisation and the emergence of statehood after the fall of empire.

What is the reason for the present severe weakening of state power? How can parliament, the President and the government work together? What are the disagreements between the legislature and the executive? Can one find ways of bringing them together? How can one cement relations between the centre and local authorities? These problems are a constant worry to me.

The Speaker constantly has to think about problems of power. His job is to achieve understanding and a proper relationship between political and economic power, between actual and nominal, illusory power.

Power is that authoritative force which has the actual possibility of governing people's actions and subordinating random aspirations to common interests; by persuasion, compulsion and compromise resolving individual, collective and social conflicts, devising policies which people can accept voluntarily however different their interests. The need to organise human society poses a problem of will and authority, law and enforcement. During a transitional period the aspirations of society are catered for by the formation of a strong government. But does this mean doing away with parliament and representative government? Some people say 'Yes, it does!' In fact, however, such an unequivocal 'yes' creates the conditions for a new totalitarian regime.

But what is strong government? Government capable of repressive action towards society? Such a tendency towards the use of force is endemic in power as such. But power as enforcement must be countered by the right of the people to a change of government.

It may seem paradoxical, but I believe that when the government creates the conditions for its own defeat it is morally stable. In fact it must always be willing to yield. It must create all the necessary conditions for its own departure, and it is precisely such conditions that allow it to achieve stability. This aim is achieved first and foremost by the existence of an opposition. But even an opposition is subject to demands made on it by the government. A strong government may be sustained by its authority, which depends on its doctrine, programmes and proclaimed goals, ensuring the support of the people. Today the government sometimes seems to be floating, since it is not sustained by a clear-cut programme or the broad support of society.

The heart of the problem 'government and society' lies in the undeveloped nature of our country's political institutions, the embryonic state of factions in parliament, the weakness of its political parties and the absence of structured public opinion.

There are many examples ready to hand. Take the 28 per cent value added tax. The argument of the government that the tax represents income sounded at first more convincing than the arguments of MPs. The latter failed to raise the alarm and point out that a moderate tax stimulates production and thus brings in more money. Missing this important point is costing the economy dear. Industry is grinding to a halt.

The establishment of the Russian state system calls for the renewal of legislative, executive and judicial hierarchies. The Federal Treaty provides for the restructuring of the Federation and the regions as subjects of the Federation. This is not merely a process of the separation of powers, but also a process of self-limitation of the parties involved, giving priority to the individual.

This process must incorporate world parliamentary experience, naturally making allowances for the regional traditions of this country. The situation demands new approaches and solutions. There is a definite basis for them in our laws and in the radical changes to our working Constitution. Also, in particular, in the Federal Treaty which affirms the central idea: the rebirth of Russia can only come about in unity with the provinces.

I am alarmed by the universal tendency of acts of parliament, when passed, to disappear into limbo. There is a complete lack of serious effort by the executive to see that measures which have become law are implemented.

Of all the aspects of government, the most important is that of government and the individual, the delegation of power 'from the bottom up' and the adoption of the principle of the priority of those who do the delegating. The power of the vote is personified: it is personal and collective. Whether a country is democratic or not depends on the condition of society. Today, when an impoverished people does not receive its share of property despite all the assurances of both former and present-day authorities, confrontation gives rise to conflicts and exacerbates them. Hence the importance of turning to the individual, of working out an effective social policy and applying the ideas of a social market economy. What stance should the government adopt? The increased differentiation in society is alarming, the phenomenon of inequality is becoming a motive force in the development of the economy, to the dismay of the masses. Is this not paradoxical?

A government that preserves the freedom of the individual and upholds law and order allows normal legislation to proceed for the stabilisation of society. As Speaker, I can see a problem in combining parliamentary power with work for the electorate: members' surgeries, meetings with voters when touring the constituencies, letters from the electors, all imply a solution to problems that runs counter to the powerful traditions of Communist Party rule which are firmly entrenched throughout the executive and in the behaviour of some MPs.

People fight for power, they sneak up on it, strike deals, conspire, arrange coups, start and wage civil wars for it. But there is also another way: the traditional legitimate and civilised way, via elections; and this is how the separation of powers came about, which has proved to be the greatest achievement of the theory of public law.

Thoughts about government and politics and one's own standpoint always turn out in the end to hinge on the citizen, the individual, providing opportunities to express their individuality, affording them legal protection and participation in political life and the structures of government. The democratisation of government on our planet is clearly evident. The epoch of genuine monarchy is virtually over, the rule of totalitarian and neo-totalitarian regimes is on the wane, and powerful empires have disintegrated. Parts of former empires, after achieving independence, live considerably better than we do. It is strange that the country which was victorious in World War II came last in economic development. For seventy years this country compounded the errors of the Bolsheviks and their dictatorship. Having gained their freedom from autocracy in 1917, the people became a hostage to Bolshevik claims to absolute power.

There is another problem: the system brought various people to power in Russia – Lenin, Stalin, Khrushchev, Brezhnev, Andropov, Chernenko, Gorbachev. Times are different now, and yet the greatest inadequacy of the Russian government remains the lack of professionalism of its politicians. The moment is a long way off when someone will say: 'Here it is, our first professional parliament, our first professional government!'

At a moment of extraordinary crisis in society the government is more difficult to restrain: what is needed is action, and there is no time for theory, apparently. The theory is there all right, but there is no time for it. Yet however busy parliament is, its chambers, commissions and committees cannot move without theoretical elaborations, an understanding of totalitarian, authoritarian and democratic government. One cannot do without an understanding of different levels of government and of political regimes. The questions keep on coming: should we still think in terms of class? Should the new 'class of entrepreneurs' have a place in the system? What does 'middle class' mean? Which approach should the government choose, the class approach or a national approach? Or some other? The exacerbation of social and ethnic conflicts cannot but cause heated arguments in parliament. Resolutions are ever harder to pass, but they are vitally necessary. The majority understand this and so parliament constantly gets the necessary measures passed and discusses the most tragic aspects of our life. A tendency towards structural centralism has been noted: the logic of common sense is stronger than ideological convictions.

Centralism in politics is akin to Leonardo da Vinci's 'golden mean', a principle that forms the basis of many of the world's artistic masterpieces. The golden mean is somewhat off-centre, but then so are the solutions to political problems. In this I find the beauty and attraction of politics, which amounts to the expression and formulation of the will of the people.

Parliament needs to consolidate its forces and heighten the weight of those orientated to the centre. In the West the centre is one or more parties between the conservative right and the liberal, workers' or socialist left. It is certainly the job of the Speaker to associate himself with the centre, and he encourages others to do the same. In our parliament there is no official centre, but one is taking shape.

Our transitional period is one in which people are particularly suspicious of the government. Of course, the transitional state is nothing more than propping up the sick organism of society. In assessing current events one has constantly to weigh the arguments, and analysis shows that orientation to the centre is the only thing that saves the day. We see here a balance of government functions, a road to stability.

The disintegration of the USSR and the difficulties of the Commonwealth of Independent States (CIS) gives added significance to the question: what are we going to build in the Russian Federation? Parliament has answered this question by passing laws ensuring the democratic development of our country, the implementation of economic reforms and a Federal Treaty. The latter lays down governmental organisational structures for the Russian Federation and outlines a programme of action, the relations between the Federation and the subjects of federation, the government and the economy, showing a way towards solving the universal problem of the individual in society.

Nevertheless, the path is difficult and the results are more modest than optimistic. Recently, swingeing taxes of the banks have nearly halted industry in our country. The Russian cause is coming to a standstill. The irresponsibility of one government after another, of minister after minister is a fact. Governments change, but the people's situation deteriorates.

The government must not beg credits from the West or squeeze taxes out of businesses and the populace, but establish for the individual, the factory and the region legally secure favourable conditions for industry and investment. Two powerful institutions, parliament and federalism, support this idea. Tax cuts which were passed in July 1992 and other measures adopted to get industry moving will hopefully awaken the forces which are at present crushed under the weight of government policy and held back by the incompetence of the administration.

Two generations of Russians are used to being dependent on the government, have lost their initiative, the sense of running their own lives. The individual, the worker, the head of the family and other members of it, found themselves divorced from property ownership, retaining a minimum of personal property, so that all their offspring were forced to hire themselves out to the state. This led to permanent enslavement by the state. Economically, the individual was divorced from power. The ideas of parliament and federalism encapsulate the protection of the personal freedoms of the individual, the constitutional nature and legality of our daily life.

Alarm, and constant alarm at that, is caused by the appearance of a considerable number of systems of administration, which are not subordinated to the united federal centre, and capable of implementing their own policy, in some instances in a mutually exclusive way, violently opposed to each other and to the government. This leads to the disintegration of administration and the paralysis of federal and regional government. The transfer of the functions of higher government departments to lower bodies which have not the requisite informational and organisational resources, or indeed the authority, leads to a general weakening of the system of government as a whole. These questions require thorough analysis both in the government and in parliament.

Russia's loss of prestige in world politics is alarming, not only as a result of the disintegration of the USSR, but also the inadequate exploitation of the whole potential of Russia which determines her true influence on foreign policy. Only reliance on the state itself will allow Russia to play an active part in world political leadership and avoid the possibility of her exclusion from forming and making decisions which affect the future of the world.

Russia is in a favourable position compared with many other states, since she has her own raw materials, manpower and intellectual resources, which far exceed the potential of the greatest powers. In addition, an important factor allowing a nation to occupy a leading position in the world, historically contributing to the development of society, is that of nationality, which has all the advantages of the American version, in the sense that it includes a variety of nationalities living on the one territory of the federal state.

This very circumstance, together with economic, political and other factors, prevents nations from splitting up completely. Intuitively, each nation knows that it will only lose by seceding. This is reflected in Russia's nationality policy. There is every reason to believe that the complete disintegration of Russia and the CIS will not happen under any circumstances. It is possible that disaggregation will continue up to a certain level, defined by particular conditions of development of one nation or another for historical reasons. However, it is quite possible that in the near future, given a carefully considered policy, Russia may become a centre of integration for all nations, above all her nearest neighbours. We must be prepared for that eventuality.

There is a special role for the country's leaders and their ability to ensure the security and welfare of their own peoples within the framework of a united multi-ethnic federal state. It is important, contrary to traditions of historical rivalry, to establish for the sake of security a federation of forces not on an aggressive military basis, but adopting a strategy of non-violence to secure peace. This is a much more complicated task, since it involves above all the ability to foresee threats and avert them. Such an approach radically changes the position of the government itself and the state, and puts a different gloss on the role of force in international relations.

Such political and diplomatic innovations may in a short time raise the authority of our country and her leaders in international relations, and will permit the maximum realisation of our potential.

Such a tendency in home and foreign policy will stabilise society in the face of present tasks, will allow it to consolidate and seek opportunities to solve our own conflicts and those of our near neighbours. It will help to give a second wind to recovery processes in society. Such activity and the fulfilment of these aims is an organic part of the concept of the 'Russian idea' and the 'Russian character' of our peoples.

14

THE SEPARATION OF POWERS
AND RUSSIA'S CRISIS

THE SEPARATION OF POWERS

The rational organisation of state power is undoubtedly the most important condition for overcoming Russia's multiple crises, economic, financial, social, political, cultural and moral. However, such a rational organisation of state power is a complicated business. It is impossible in the short term. It requires an improvement in the social climate and a broader base of support for reforms.

The theory of the separation of powers is derived from the ancient world. Aristotle, Marsiglio of Padua and other scholars formulated the political and legal idea according to which state power is understood as the sum of various governmental, legal, executive and judicial functions, implemented by state departments independently of each other. The separation of power means keeping power in check.

In the seventeenth and eighteenth centuries teaching on the separation of power, connected with the theory of natural rights, was reflected in the American Declaration of Independence and the French Declaration of the Rights of Man and the Citizen. Rousseau, Voltaire and Diderot and other Enlightenment thinkers made a notable contribution to this concept. The doctrine of the separation of powers formed the basis of the state systems of democratically orientated countries in Europe and America. Since then, the principle of the separation of powers of the state has been accepted as a fundamental cornerstone of the constitutions of nearly all states.

The Marxist-Leninist theory of unity of power consistently denied the principle of separation of powers, since it runs counter to the class nature of the state. This caused an impasse in countries that adopted Marxism, quite apart from the role of personalities. Today we see that the Bolsheviks missed out on cybernetics, information theory, sociology and political science. Marxism, rejecting the ancient theory of the separation of powers, failed to understand that a system of checks and balances gave civilised countries and peoples a reasonably high standard of living, and gave individuals freedom, personal dignity and the quest for happiness.

It is astonishing how the 'abolition' of the CPSU instantaneously led to the drastic weakening of Marxist-Leninist ideology in society; whatever people say, this is a determining factor in the present argument. But this also created a vacuum in civil society, and, moreover, in the social sciences. There is, however, a positive result: we have begun to recover our historical memory and our national culture. It is these very processes that help to 'understand Russia with the mind', despite what the poet Tyutchev affirms.

The theory of the separation of powers cannot automatically be adopted by the Russian Federation. It is an integral part of the development of civilisation, but we are not yet used to the concept of civilisation as a level or stage of social development, of material and spiritual culture, of new rights of citizenship, in short, the highest achievement of culture, everything on earth, everything progressive designed by humanity. We can only revive the social sciences by the study of various sciences at the points where they overlap. The law of separation applies to law and philosophy, law and economics, law and sociology. It is here that we can strengthen the theory of the separation of powers.

We see our country parting with the Bolshevik school of humanities, based on half-truths and the shuffling of facts to fit the goal. People have more and more begun to orientate themselves on common sense: economics has seen the return of names such as M. I. Tugan-Baranovskii, N. D. Kondrateev and A. V. Chayanov, whilst the literature itself appears more pragmatic. History has seen the return of V. Klyuchevskii and N. Kostomarov, and sociology the revival of P. Sorokin. Our people can now see the great richness of Russian philosophy in the works of P. Chaadaev, V. Solovev, N. Fedorov, N. Berdyaev and P. Florensky, and it is against this background that law is becoming more open in accordance with the theory of the separation of powers.

Great achievements have been made by civilised countries and their state institutions, based on the horizontal and vertical devolution of power, but Russia has been left behind. A comparison with the living standards and power structures which developed within the theory of absolute power bears this out. The separation of powers and its practical implementation allow general and specific elements of institutional and governmental activity to develop both horizontally and vertically.

The Leninist-Bolshevik slogan of 'no compromise!' is being transcended, although not without difficulty. Compromise is now beginning to permeate the aristocratic thinking of the higher bureaucracy, and enters into everyday life along with the theory of separation of powers itself. At the same time, fewer and fewer people remain who are prepared to assume the responsibilities of power and involve themselves in the business of running the state. Like latter-day courtiers, literally a handful of individuals wield effective influence over domestic, foreign and defence policy, while striving to avoid public scrutiny. The bankruptcy of the neo-totalitarian political regime became evident when the people realised that there was in fact no one to fight. There is no common enemy, although it has become increasingly evident that the old class stratification does not correspond to the reality of an impoverished mass and a tiny proportion of well-off people. Gorbachev's reforms only exacerbated poverty and weakened the state. The notion of nation-states in such circumstances could not fail to be shaped by the conditions of life today, a point which should not be overlooked in practical politics. But at the same time a positive tendency also develops, which translates into our psychology in the form of the English notion of 'my home is my castle'. Individual freedom and self-interest harnessed to the wider national interest can lead society out of the crisis.

This process requires a different approach. Government needs to act in two directions, taking the individual and the state as starting points and protecting simultaneously the interests of both. The primitive glorification of the role of the state should be replaced by the conception of government based on a framework of constitutional law, devolution at the theoretical and practical level. The principle of diktat must give way to one of constructive cooperation. Government should see its role as rather like that of a gardener cultivating a fruit tree, taking into account the characteristics of the local climate, soil, the species, the likelihood of pests and drought, frosts and other variables. Government, however, must be allowed to govern, striving resolutely to ensure the efficient functioning of the state itself.

DICTATORSHIP AND DEMOCRACY

The Leninist theory of absolute power derives from the Marxist concept of the 'dictatorship of the proletariat'. This concept and the conditions for its realisation were in reality already anachronistic by the time of the Paris Commune of 1871. The experience of Russia has in fact shown, firstly, that the concept has been used to arrest the natural historical development of society and impose revolutionary upheaval by the usurping of state power, and secondly, that this led inexorably to a movement away from the dictatorship of the proletariat and towards that of the Communist Party oligarchy, and thence to the dictatorship of the individual, the cult of the leader and consequently to the creation of idols and idolaters. It is this very idolatry, firmly implanted even in the consciousness of our parliamentarians, which is preventing us from consolidating parliamentary democracy and representative government of any kind.

Direct contact between the population and the president, parliamentary and government leaders, is a manifestation of democracy. I would add that frequent meetings with the people, the creation of an atmosphere of direct dialogue with individuals, and the immediate accountability of political leaders represent the very machinery of democracy. Strong government can only exist in circumstances where leaders maintain direct contact: when these contacts weaken, democracy is immediately extinguished.

Contemporary history presents two kinds of dictatorship: dictatorship of the bourgeoisie and dictatorship of the proletariat. Dictatorship of the bourgeoisie in its most extreme form gave rise to the regimes of Hitler, Mussolini and Franco, while dictatorship of the proletariat produced the regimes of Lenin, Stalin, Mao Zedong and Pol Pot. When we think about dictatorship, we recognise that both kinds of regime have extremely negative features, denying the very bases of civilised behaviour and deep-rooted national values while nurturing base subconscious instincts and raising them to the level of moral values. For these reasons, both varieties of dictatorship represent the rejection of natural societal development, and the short-term nature of their existence is evident.

ECONOMIC AND POLITICAL POWER

The severing of traditional economic links and the collapse of production, thoughtlessly set in motion by the experiments of 1985–6, have proceeded apace. All relations which had been sustained by force are falling apart, never to be revived. What are being revived, and will continue to be revived, are mutually accepted and beneficial relations which better serve the interests of all sides. The picture is altered by the provisions set out in the CIS documents and in the Federal Treaty, allowing former republics and parties to the Russian Federation to deal with their own particular problems. No one is calling for economic isolation. The transition from the planned economy to the free market represents a complete turnaround and it should surprise no one that much has ground to a halt. There is only one way forward: the establishment of a legal framework providing the conditions for industry to thrive and creating normal working conditions for those who produce and trade goods.

The weakest link is social policy: greater effectiveness in this area requires greater political centralisation and a stronger middle class to provide the basis for reform. Such an approach lays the foundation for social stability. In the post-revolutionary years the Bolsheviks supported the process of equalisation through distribution. We are faced with the task of equalisation through production, which is a harder and more tortuous path, but it is in this revolution that a new conception of government actually emerges. For a new market economy, society needs a new form of political organisation. But as before, political power remains the key to the economy. To achieve equalisation through redistribution, all that is required is the machinery of repression. To raise the living standards of the population, power is required to protect private, collective, state and foreign property.

History has taught us that a concentration of ownership in state hands creates a powerful economic basis for totalitarianism. Only property represents real power: power over production. The question of property is one aspect of the central problem, the problem of genuine power, since this stems from power over production, and control of production, distribution and redistribution. The failure to address the questions of property inhabits the democratic process itself, whereas to reinforce private and collective property, and that which is held by corporations, is to strengthen democracy and thus to put into practice the theory of the separation of powers.

The most important task today is to prevent the lumpenisation of the less prosperous and the dispossessed, to prevent their turning into opponents of reform. From the standpoint of creating a state apparatus, however, the intelligentsia requires special attention. A significant section of this group could now become the yeast, the engine and the barometer of society, by which ongoing changes can be evalued and their effects forecast.

It is becoming clear that the creation of a new state system is vital not just for our own future, but also for that of our children and grandchildren. Destructive processes have affected the structures of power: the break-up of the USSR could not fail to affect the governance of Russia. In the October Revolution of 1917 power had to be taken and won, and a monolithic party structure created. A very different process is being seen today: power needs to be created, rather than 'separated', to create state government for Russia, guided by the theory of the separation of powers, with the various branches of government mutually accountable.

We are witnessing the total destruction of the planned economy. The inefficient areas of the economy are showing signs of atrophy, while the enterprise which society needs can be seen in city market stalls. Monopolistic criminal market forces have emerged, and the separation of producers from property. A small group of speculators are working in concert to make fortunes. Illegally gained capital has been legalised and constitutes redistributed rather than created wealth. The speculator, knowing the corridors of power, has become a key figure in the economy. Astronomical bank lending rates can only be supported by a system of redistribution. Since competition cannot flourish in present conditions, we are moving away from the market rather than towards it. The law of value, discovered by Adam Smith, cannot work. Conditions are leading us not to a market system, but to the possible introduction of 'war communism'. This results from actions taken by those who were not professionally competent to make them.

219

Parliamentary government must offer legislative support to professionals of all kinds, peasant farmers to engineers, specialists and managers, and to our own entrepreneurs and those from abroad: everyone, in fact, engaged in productive employment. This support should sustain that 'middle force' on which the formation of a democratic constitutional state for the Russian Federation needs to be founded.

The paradoxes of government can be seen in any state. The Russian paradox is distinguished by a discredited and chaotic 'separation' of political and economic power, at a time when the most energetic and able specialists, business people and politicians are being driven away. A superficially reasonable view is taking hold, namely that to stamp out the corrupt bourgeoisie, strict financial, administrative and criminal legislation must be observed, preventing citizens involved in state and political activity from taking part in commercial activity.

One cannot disagree that such activities should be prohibited, nor that legislation relating to such people should be tightened. But 'prohibition' entails isolating the most active people in the economy and thus severing the process of economic and political government. Success must be built upon trust. If political power continues to distrust economic power, or makes ill-informed decisions which divorce it both from contemporary experience and from economic power structures, then the country will once more achieve nothing. This point needs to be carefully considered: who benefits when the most experienced of our new business people are driven out of politics? And who has wielded power up to now? The emerging business sector has not managed to become established, but throughout the country investment has been thwarted, creating the conditions for large-scale speculation while squeezing the lifeblood from industry and business.

If economic power were at the helm, with patriotically inclined business circles holding the reins of power in Russia, an unthinking reliance on Western hard currency for economic survival would not be tolerated, particularly at a time when the country is addressing a most serious problem, that of monopoly. Money and bank interest rates now work for monopolists and middlemen: money does not work for industry or the workforce. Labour is one of the few commodities whose cost has fallen sharply. The effects of monopolies are seen in the price of salt, bread, vodka and children's footwear, and take their toll upon the living conditions of officers' families, and the parents of soldiers, affecting not just their stomachs, but also their thinking.

Parliament needs to think fundamentally about the relationship between the economic and political domains. One thing is clear: the word 'prohibit' serves the interests of those who require a weakening of the power of economic forces at the helm of government. The policies which brought industry to its knees, and left it waiting for government to ease its tax burden or for parliament to force the executive to pay attention to its problems, defy economic common sense. Business stagnates rather than grows, and economic policy has practically cut off the money supply to industry. As for the tax on imported consumer goods, we did not produce them ourselves yet we practically forbid anyone from importing them. Meanwhile anyone can export whatever they like, including gold and diamonds.

The incompetence of this country's politicians is frightening. Parliament fiercely opposed the introduction of a 28 per cent value added tax, but gave in to huge pressure from the executive, which blackmailed the legislators just as it had done at the Sixth Russian Congress of People's Deputies in April 1992. With a 5 per cent tax, production will be reduced; make it 28 per cent and entrepreneurs will go under or be reduced to barter; make it 50 per cent and all industrial activity will cease. It is high time that those who make and force through such recommendations were called to account. Parliament should be reducing tax rates forthwith.

A whole range of issues, from price-setting to the tax system and the eventual establishment of federal and regional budgets in Russia, today remain unclear. This is also a problem of the separation of powers, involving the role of each governing institution in monitoring business activity. The absence of genuine power in governing authorities engenders disillusion among civil servants, unable to derive satisfaction from their practically fruitless bureaucratic activity. The more able leave to work in business, while the less talented are lured into corruption. Corruption rules the roost in our motherland.

Who benefits from this? We need to separate powers, and by strengthening legislative, executive and legal authority create the conditions for a genuinely independent press and establish a formal legal basis for the scrutiny of those involved in both political and industrial or business activity, so that such people may be allowed and even encouraged to enter the political arena, instead of being driven away from it as at present. We need to think about how, in this transitional period, the government can change the prevailing political wind to fill the sails of industry.

THE CIS: THE COLLAPSE OF A GREAT EMPIRE AND POST-UNION COOPERATION

We cannot yet comprehend the full significance of the collapse of the Union. Have the results been largely positive or negative? Did it result from a natural historical process, or from the malevolent will of political leaders with messianic ambitions?

Can we, however, answer the specific question of who is to blame for the break-up of the Soviet Union? Perhaps the correct view is that of our famous Russian historian, Yuri Polyakov, the former director of the

Institute of Soviet History of the USSR Academy of Sciences, who dared even in the early 1970s to state that the October Revolution and the principles behind the creation of the Soviet state represented a deviation from the process of historical development. Perhaps Zbigniew Brzezinski was right, too, in writing, also in the early 1970s, that as soon as the process of democratisation began in the Soviet Union, then the Soviet state, founded as it was on shaky foundations, would be doomed to oblivion as latent interethnic tensions were released. Many understood that our bureaucratic system of administration could not survive in its existing form, necessitating major changes in April 1985. How and in what form these changes were realised, however, is another question. If one talks of our historical responsibility, then perhaps we too are guilty. It is entirely possible that each of us, and the leaders of the Supreme Soviet, are to blame. Nor would I deny my own share of responsibility.

I should, however, like to stress that our Declaration of the State Sovereignty of Russia on 12 June 1990, in particular Point 5, and also the decree of Congress restricting the functions of Union government organisations on the territory of the RSFSR, in no way signifies – and I can state this categorically – that we 'laid the foundations' for the collapse of the Soviet Union. Look at what actually remained under Soviet control: practically all the basic functions which make a state a state, in this case a single federal state. That is the combined armed forces, common rail network, airlines, defence and military–industrial complex, communications and many other areas. The Declaration does not, in essence, deal with sovereignty at all, but only with decentralisation of the excessively centralised Union state. If we had worked together with the Soviet leadership to complete our work within the framework of that Declaration and the above-mentioned decree, then I believe the unfortunate consequences which we are now witnessing could have been avoided. At issue was the need to decentralise, and it must be stressed, to decentralise in a sensible manner.

In my view, the Union Treaty was one of the main factors which ruled out a gradual transformation of our Union society into one of a qualitatively different kind. From the constitutional standpoint, there was no point in discussing a new Union Treaty at all. The first Union Treaty (1922) was to all intents and purposes incorporated into the three subsequent constitutions (1924, 1936, 1977) and had thus lost its substantive significance. In the heated discussions about the Union Treaty, it was given a completely new sense: it was now a question of creating an entirely new state structure of some kind, made up of ostensibly independent states. The heated arguments about a new Union Treaty weakened and shook the Soviet state to its foundations.

We were among the first to sanction a delegation to sign the Union agreement, although we were aware of the dangers that lay in so doing.

And in spite of all the contradictions between the different political views of our Supreme Soviet deputies, we ratified the agreement. Unfortunately, this process was interrupted. And it is entirely possible that the events of August 1991 had their own logic and objective character. We are unlikely in the foreseeable future, or even in years to come, to discover the full truth behind those events. It may be that this is known only to Gorbachev, and perhaps one other person. But it is also true that the events of August 1991 scared the former Soviet republics to death. As soon as the Soviet state had been mortally wounded, undermining the prestige of its state institutions, the highest organs of power and the holders of that power themselves, then the momentum of centrifugal forces increased dramatically.

Here too, in truth, historians will probably be interested in just one question: that of the period of inactivity of what was already a Russian state and its leaders from August until the Fifth Congress resumed its work in October 1991. The extraordinary passivity of the state during this period remains a mystery to me. I would even say that the preparations for the Fifth Congress saved us from the final collapse – or at least, saved the Russian Federation. The executive was roused from its hibernation and somehow we began to act.

In this period nearly all the Soviet Republics embarked on the path of independent development. For this reason the Minsk Agreements of 8 December 1991 on the creation of the Commonwealth of Independent States, for all their internal contradictions, were perhaps, given the legal and constitutional impasse, the logical conclusion of a *fait accompli* – the fall of a great empire. The CIS so far has been a weak and sickly child. But if we want to maintain the hope of unity in the future, let us say, in the form of a confederacy of some kind, then we must encourage the creation and hastening of this process within the framework of the Commonwealth of Independent States.

The process by which the countries of the CIS are becoming states is complicated and riddled with contradictions. In the economy destructive processes of severing economic ties have gained ascendancy over constructive ones. The regulatory role of the Russian government in economic management has been abandoned in favour of a rush towards the free market, in which the psychology of the population is not taken into account. A quick and easy transition from a planned economy to a market economy is not possible. The country has abandoned the five-year plans, and now needs to pay more attention to the regulatory role of the state in order to make the transition more comprehensible to the people. We need plans and programmes, of the kind which can be found in all more or less prosperous countries.

The balance of interests of the union republics, planned and maintained by the leadership of the former USSR, has been destroyed. The balance of interests of the CIS countries is being tested to the full by their economic and political instability and by the development of their attitudes towards each other under conditions of social and socio-political disintegration in the member states. Today the balance of interests of Russia itself is in question. The Russian Federation and the regions of Russia are dependent on the state-building processes in the countries of the Commonwealth. The situation in these countries varies, but our attitude towards them should be based on equality of rights, traditional cooperation, the state interests of Russia and the necessity of defending our compatriots, the Russian-speaking population, in these countries.

The new Commonwealth is already bound by a multitude of treaties and agreements, including those made at parliamentary level. Groups have even been formed for the joint examination of questions whose solution would considerably neutralise points of tension and conflict.

The principle of interest always comes to the fore and defines programmes of activity. In whose interest is the concept of the separation of powers? In the interest of those who are drawn towards various forms of property, seeing in the solution of the property question the solution of all remaining questions. The main function of the separation of powers is to act as a mechanism upholding the interests of the creators of property. There is more justice in the balanced treatment of political and economic interests than there is in the totalitarian solution of problems.

The concept of the separation of powers is especially important in solving interethnic conflicts. By their very nature conflicts between the nationalities act on a variety of levels; therefore such conflicts would be more easily settled were they to fall within the competence of and be studied in greater depth by all the branches of power: legislative, executive and judicial – and the press. Problems which one side lets slip from its purview would be detected by the others.

It is impossible to create a new power structure based on the former USSR, as it was then or as it stands now. Russia was the first to move from Tsarist autocracy to become a planned, totalitarian state, and the first to revert from a planned to a market economy, losing much in the process and as yet gaining nothing. For this reason restoring the faith of the people in power is one of the most gruelling tasks facing the reformers. Another of the main problems facing parliament is the elaboration of effective forms, channels, and mechanisms of interaction between the legislative and executive branches of government.

This will effectively mean that bodies responsible for legislative and executive decisions will no longer be duplicated, and the absolute power of decrees, taken by one organ of power that is virtually autocratic, will cease to exist. It is for this reason that there is a growing demand for a clear demarcation of the functions of all institutions of power, for a sharper definition of the functions of parliament, the President and the government based on checks and balances, on the principle of interdependence and mutual limitation, on the renunciation of the 'tug-of-war' principle.

Today the authority of all components of state power is falling: the authority of power itself has declined accompanied by legal nihilism, the denial of generally recognised rights and laws, the non-fulfilment of laws by both the centre and the localities, and the failure of parliament even to obey its own 'internal' laws and regulations, the constant interminable debates on issues of secondary importance which greatly reduces the standing of parliament in the eyes of the electorate. There is also a tendency for the socio-economic and political systems of power to be weakened. In Russia there is a clear inadequacy of state power, as well as colossal difficulties in local government and a lack of professionalism in governing bodies in general, many of which are almost unfit to serve.

15

POWER AND RUSSIA

THE SEARCH FOR COMMON SENSE

During the long years of Bolshevik power the dominant principle was the subordination of the individual to society. This gave privileges to the group of people clustered around the apparatus of government. Local authorities were monstrously dependent on the centre and on attitudes in the capital. The development of the country's economy, the fate of the people, everything was decided subjectively. The theory of the separation of powers is based on a search for good sense, and for forms of government based on an objective legal foundation and the rule of law.

The fundamental principle of democracy, that only law can act in defence of power, has become the reference point of parliamentary activity. Throughout its history Russia has never known such an intense period of legislative activity as now. In its fourth session the Supreme Soviet passed 131 laws, 27 at the first reading, and 153 resolutions on special questions. In its first four convocations the Supreme Soviet passed over 800 normative acts, including nearly 200 laws. The present Constitution alone underwent more than 250 changes and additions, and as a result of this it took on a radically different character. Parliament sees its role as securing legitimate government by means of legislation. The needs, wishes and aspirations of society must be discussed and 'embodied in law'.

Parliament has passed both good laws and laws which were poorly considered and badly worked out, especially in the early days. Today we are witnessing the consequences of these laws, and the press and even parliament itself are dealing with them. However, we have been slow to learn from the contradictory processes of the period of transition and have not really considered sufficiently the attitude of the generation which underwent perestroika and which did not respect law and order. It is particularly important to re-educate people to accept legality as a way of life. However the thesis, 'legality as a way of life', does not guarantee that legislative power can introduce and reinforce that tradition. Here it is important to view the position differently: how to strengthen those features which appear as norms of life by means of law. This is particularly important in conditions of developing market relations.

The rule of law is also an important condition for the separation of powers, with clearly marked criteria limiting each branch of power. The rule of law facilitates the welfare of the people. When the branches of power are independent, the authority of the law gives a much greater guarantee of justice than does personal rule. The implementation of the principle of the rule of law affirms equal opportunities for each citizen, equality defended by law the observation of which is regulated by an independent judiciary and by the fourth power, the press. This is how society may be taught to respect the law.

I am also worried by the time it is taking to adopt the Constitution. The situation is too unsettled and a lot depends on the Constitution. The objective course taken by events, first laws, then the Federal Treaty, and only then the Constitution, hindered the process and dragged it out. It would have been much more fruitful to have been able to pass laws within the framework of a valid Constitution.

Now more than ever good sense is important. For good political sense one must be a politician; for good economic sense one must be an economist; and for good legal sense one must be a lawyer. Of course, in our politics it is important to orientate oneself on the centre. This is where the good political sense of government is to be found, now and always. In order to unite society we must determine the centre of the formation of interests for both the individual and for the country; we must regulate these interests and support the centre; we must increase the part played by centrally orientated people in society, in electoral campaigns, at Congresses, in parliament, in the President's office and in the government. It is very important to rally blocs of both the right and the left around the centre, creating a balance of power, equilibrium in society and a clearly defined procedure for the support of the government, and the patriotic unity of the people.

The success of the politics of reform depends on the 'grass roots', on the 'provinces'. It is the grassroots and the regions that determine the 'centre' and fill the competent institutions with common sense and efficiency. The majority of the population live in the provinces; in the provinces there are more centrally orientated people.

A strong Russia with its unique republics, regions and districts would ensure that every citizen of Russia respected their own worth in their native land. The multinational character of power aims to provide peace for all people, to remove the after-effects of the neo-totalitarian regime and the tensions created by it. The transition from a totalitarian monolithic power to the democratic separation of powers is accompanied by crises in the sphere of relations between the nationalities. Under the pressure of the avalanche of new information bombarding the individual from the pages of newspapers and from the television screen not only the private individual but also society as a whole has begun the as yet unfinished process of re-evaluation of the ideology of existence. A return to the mainstream of world civilisation demands that we re-evaluate and re-think our position in society. This is where we need a well-designed programme of activity lasting three to four years, a programme which would follow on logically from the Federal Treaty. The Treaty has provided the outlines and direction for such a programme.

The strategy and tactics for defining the place of the national republics in the constitutional-democratic model of the Federation and the creation of a coherent single state is an extremely difficult task, aggravated by the not especially competent theorising of a whole group of social and political figures about the division of Russia into dozens of parts, and by their 'reflections' on difficult questions. But this is the only way of creating a Russia where the private person will enjoy genuine individuality and the possibility not only of feeling free but of actually being free and knowing that they are defended by an effective mechanism of state power, based on the theory of the separation of powers.

When considering the theory of the separation of powers we should remember that for seventy years Russia was isolated from world civilisation, with which she had been linked before the revolution by capital, technology, tradition and the common fate of Europe. It should not be forgotten that as early as the twelfth and thirteenth centuries, long before the time of Peter the Great, Russia was closely linked to Europe and to the West economically, politically and culturally, and without losing any of her national identity. It was with great difficulty that Russia established a body of legislative acts, summarised in the *Digest of Laws of the Russian Empire* in six volumes, a great achievement of legal culture and a great work of Russian lawyers. Knowledge of its laws demonstrates just how thorough was the work of the Russian juridical system. Despite its heavy bureaucratisation executive power was highly effective, and there is much in the experience of pre-revolutionary officialdom that is useful to study even today. After the famous reforms of 1864 judicial power consisted of courts and the Bar, based on an organic unity of the experience of civilisation and Russian traditions, a tradition which has left its legacy in legal history.

The great Russian scholars of the nineteenth century were attracted to Marxism, but they rethought his body of knowledge and turned away from his dogmatic teaching. The ability to re-evaluate is perhaps the most valuable attribute of a scholar or politician. M. I. Tugan-Baranovski and Nikolai Berdyaev, Sergei Bulgakov and Peter Struve were all quick to see that Marxism would be disastrous for Russia. In discussing the theory of the separation of powers we cannot ignore the warnings given by opponents of Marxism. This is important for an understanding of the current situation at a time when we are embarking upon a new phase of civilisation after a break of seventy-four years. At a time when Russian culture abroad continued the great traditions of the golden and silver ages of literature, Russia itself turned off the path of civilisation. Today Russian good sense is alive and well in the provinces and is being reinforced by the return of freedom of conscience, historical memory and national culture, the conditions necessary for the rebirth of Russia.

PARLIAMENTARIANISM, PARLIAMENT AND DEMOCRACY

Parliamentarianism is a system of state organisation in which parliament plays a prominent role not only as a legislative body but also as the supreme body supervising executive power. Parliamentarianism does not exist in all constitutional countries.

The history of the development of parliament in the world is both instructive and interesting. Parliament has become the main focus of political life in most countries of Europe and America. In many states a number of local and historical factors led to the establishment of a parliament to settle contentious issues. The British parliament, about which anyone interested in the problem of power should know, is not circumscribed by any constitution and enjoys absolute power of a kind unknown in the parliaments of other European countries. Parliament, or more precisely, the crown in parliament, can not only change the ordinary laws of the state but can also, in the words of Blackstone, 'change the entire state structure and create a new one; it can even completely reform itself; it can do anything within the bounds of the possible, and whatever is done by parliament cannot be undone by any power on Earth'. According to the well-known aphorism, the only thing it cannot do is to 'make women out of men, and vice-versa'. Parliament concerns itself in the most trifling local interests, and in turn the growth of local government limits the sphere of activity of parliament.

The problem of the Russian parliament is central to the country's future. That is why we need a law concerning parliament. We need laws clearly defining the limits of parliamentary activity, the rights and responsibilities of deputies, commissions and factions, and the privileges which those elected by the people are entitled to enjoy. The electorate should know that its defenders are themselves protected from material adversity and also what kind of income they are receiving. Parliamentary power must be strong, durable and protected.

The functions of parliament have been finely tuned over the centuries.

The interests of most social strata are represented in parliament, and in this sense parliament is a genuinely representative body. In parliament various social conflicts between groups, classes or nationalities which have arisen as a result of the clash of interests of various social tendencies are resolved, and in this sense parliament is a public and open forum for settling conflicts.

In the organisation of state power parliament acts as a counterbalance to the executive power and this function is realised in three separate aspects: public supervision of state expenditure; the establishment of a framework for government legislative activity and the public supervision of the legality of governmental actions; public supervision of the members of the government, that is, of government appointments.

By its very nature parliament stimulates the development of a multi-party system, and in so doing appears to create its own instability, but this is not actually the case. The multiparty system is a defence mechanism against authoritarianism, a threat which as a rule comes from executive power. Parliament is the target of the struggle between various organised political groups and the arena where the battle for votes is turned into the battle to realise political programmes, but on a democratic basis.

If the political system and political life are unstable and there is a general crisis of power, then parliament acts as a stabilising factor, softening the changes to the political course followed by the government. Furthermore, it is not only to the President, and not even to the President, but to parliament that ordinary impoverished Russian people turn. This is a fact and, like it or not, it cannot be ignored. At critical moments parliament assumes responsibility for the strategic political decisions that have to be taken. It is up to parliament to resolve tensions in economic, ethnic, military and other spheres which accompany the growth of a new system of government and administration.

In keeping with the constitutions of democratic countries, parliament represents all the various nationalities and is the supreme legislative body of the state. The role and place of parliament in the system of supreme state organs cannot be defined without an understanding of the fundamental nature of parliamentarianism as a socio-political phenomenon.

Parliamentarianism represents a special system of relationships and management of society by the state in which the legislative and executive are separated and parliament occupies a very privileged position. Essentially, the separation of powers means that members of parliament first pass the laws and then have the right to monitor their implementation, while the government and other executive bodies try to put them into practice. This is democracy in action. In a democratic state the refusal of the government or of a member of the government to obey parliament's orders results not only in the dismissal of the persons in question but also in their political demise, and perhaps even in criminal proceedings.

Parliament and parliamentarianism are very similar concepts in as much as parliament, invested with the appropriate powers, is the basis of parliamentarianism. But at the same time parliamentarianism reflects the highest, although not always most apparent, quality of parliament. Parliamentarianism cannot exist outside of parliament, but the presence of a supreme representative body in the country does not automatically mean that one can talk of parliamentarianism. A classic example is the seventy-year period during which we had a parliament of sorts – a representative organ of power – but subject to the dictates of the Communist Party and its functionaries. It was no accident that in the years 1986–9 the slogan 'all power to the soviets' rang from the lips of people who have become famous but who now favour the removal of any kind of representative power. Even at that time I was putting forward the idea of the municipalisation of the soviets, suggesting they be reordered in accordance with age-old experience, traditions and rationalism, but not that they be either extolled or denigrated. The concept of the 'soviet' (meaning a council), is not an ideological concept: it is neutral and merely reflects popular tradition.

Throughout the whole of its existence the place of parliament in the system of civil society and in the structure of supreme state institutions has repeatedly changed. In the period when the feudal orders were destroyed and new structures established, based on the rights of the individual, parliament occupied the central place in the system of state organisation. In later years, because of the complexities of state management and the increasing number of legislative acts, parliament had to delegate part of its absolute power to government institutions, on the one hand, and on the other to restructure its own activity so that much of its work took place in committees and commissions, giving rise to the thesis of the decline of parliamentarianism.

The following feature should also be noted: the relative independence of parliament in relation to the government does not appear to be stable. It increases and decreases and is in the main conditioned by the concrete relationship of political forces in the country in the period in question, and sometimes by the appearance of a strong and gifted and often charismatic leader inclined towards populist slogans and demagogy. European parliaments and parliamentarianism survived the crisis years of the 1920s and 1930s and, having dramatically altered their functions, were able to adapt to the new conditions. If at the present time the idea of a supposedly prominent role for parliament in the system of supreme state organs can only be voiced with certain reservations, to voice the opposite idea, that the role of parliament is irrelevant and that the system of parliamentarianism is withering away, would be merely laughable, not to say dangerous.

We are faced with a much more complex problem – Russia has hardly any experience of parliamentarianism, although one might refer to the various types of parliament that have existed: the Boyar and Zemskii Dumas, the Veche, the State Councils, the Senate and the Constituent Assemblies, right up to the All-Russian Executive Committee, the Congresses of Deputies and finally, after 1936, the Supreme Soviets, and once again after 1989, the reborn Congresses of People's Deputies, an amazing creation, coming to life when Russia is experiencing a 'time of troubles' and which acts as a force for political stability.

Influential political groups are demanding the early cessation of the authority not only of the Congress of People's Deputies but also of the Supreme Soviet as the supreme legislative and representative body. These groups hope to put an end to the Supreme Soviet's term of office with the help of institutions of direct democracy which do not as yet exist, based on the model of the Constituent Assembly and so on. Therefore it is essential to explain the role of parliament in the political system of society and in the entire political process, and on this basis to defend parliament's position as one of the supreme organs of state power. In doing this it is of course necessary to consider two problems: the organisation of the Russian parliament on two levels (Congress and Supreme Soviet); and the position of parliament in a general crisis of state power.

Democracy needs a strong parliament to act as its surest guarantee against anarchy. But legally supported rights of opposition are also essential. All laws dealing with freedom of the press and freedom of conscience contain articles dealing with questions of opposition. Democratic pluralism depends on creating the legal framework for opposition. A legal framework for opposition gives rise to civil peace, while the peace-making activity of parliament depends on the legal right of opposition with its own rights and responsibilities.

Modern parliamentarianism developed in European countries during the period of their transition from a military, barbarous style of direct democracy to the representation of the independent private interests of the various developing social strata and groups who owned property: namely the knights, the merchant guilds, the craft workshops, and various corporations. From this perspective, parliament is a means of institutionalising the process of democracy, of imparting the latest cultural or, as it has now become usual to say, civilised norms. Thus, to quote the famous Russian political figure and eminent lawyer, G. Chicherin: 'Parliamentary rule is indicative of the political maturity of the nation.'

Strictly speaking, parliamentary development is not possible outside the framework and requisite conditions of parliamentarianism as a wider cultural phenomenon, as a system of legal, moral and political norms, traditions, and the 'rules of the game' drawn up either as a result of the practice of administering the formal side of democracy, or as a result of borrowing. Parliament itself is only the institutional head of this system, but without it, as the genuine form of organised state body, then clearly the development of democracy and the imparting to it of this civilised model is impossible. We must make parliament the guarantor of democracy.

PARLIAMENT AND OPPOSITION

The right of the minority to voice its opinion during a parliamentary debate is crucial. The fostering of this right means protecting new ideas, which only under the care of the minority will thrive and then go on to win supporters. That is why parliament is discussing the rights of the opposition, seeing in this the democratic basis to the whole undertaking, the very essence of parliamentarianism.

The authority of the powers of a democratic parliament, specified by law and defining the vital functions of society, is consolidated by taking the aspirations of the majority of the nation into consideration. Parliament loses its authority when either the right or left opposition 'absorbs' the problem into itself.

In Russia there is no 'official' opposition to the power structures because, for the seventy years of Soviet rule, opposition in the country could only exist in two forms, namely dissidence and 'kitchen' discussions. The changes in the country taking place as a result of the events of August 1991 demand that we should reject these two means and replace them with new ones. The question of opposition is the question of the future of Russia. Opposition is potentially both a very constructive and destructive force. It is just as essential here as poison is in medicine. Opposition is a problem of heterodoxy, of the freedom of speech, of pluralism, and of democracy and civilisation. Demonstrations and academic and political debates have a purifying effect on society. If there were no polemics, stagnation would set in. Opposition from the left must be strong, but similarly, opposition from the right should not be weaker. The development of the centre is of no less importance for society than for parliament itself.

Parliamentary opposition and its political extension into society in the form of parties, movements, funds and oppositional press represents a democratic alternative to the government. This is usual in many countries having two-party systems, and the consolidation of democracy in the country is now in evidence. Opposition of the type of the 'Ostankino movement' (when in June 1992 the television centre was besieged by rowdy demonstrators), not having its own outlet in parliament, is a different matter. It must be pointed out that here the government appears committed to firm measures for dealing with the conflict; power is strong when it can protect itself from unconstitutional opposition. Government is compelled to inflict well-timed blows against non-parliamentary opposition.

Politics is effective as long as there is an opposition. Sensible politics allows for the harnessing of the potential of power and economic development. Politics is determined by the norms and rituals of society. The opposition always strives for power, and this is completely natural. An opposition comes to power, but an opposition in a civilised society works constructively with the government which it is trying to replace. For the Russian parliament this is a new process. The aim of the opposition's attack is clear: it is take over the reins of government. The replacement and defeat of the government is a natural process in society, and one which is carried out by two methods: by usurpation or forcible seizure of power; or by the take-over or receipt of power by parliamentary vote.

The experience of foreign countries, with long histories of parliamentary development, can teach us a lot. In Great Britain the 'shadow cabinet' of between one and two dozen members has officially existed since the beginning of the twentieth century. The members of the cabinet in power consult with members of the 'shadow cabinet'. In the USA the President meets, although not very often, with leaders of the minority in the Senate and the House of Representatives. The benefits of such contact with the opposition should not be underestimated; it provides an opportunity to discover, and sometimes even to understand, the stance of the ideological opponent. But in these countries opposition works on the basis of the 'party principle', that is, the leaders of the country belong to one party, and the opposition to another.

In Russia almost all leaders suddenly found themselves to be 'non-party', but in the country there are numerous legal parties, many of whom, having an insignificant number of members, are only involved in political mobilisation, self-advertisement, propaganda and lobbying support in the struggle for the settlement of some political, industrial, economic or social problem.

How does opposition manifest itself today? Apart from the struggle to influence decisions from within, there is also 'internal opposition' within power structures taking the form of a more direct, negative form of lobbying. It is direct because those involved in trying to get resolutions passed apply straightforward pressure. The term 'iron triangle', in the American sense of the word, is applicable to our own situation when the adoption of a decision involves the cooperation of three parties: legislators associated with a given issue; the given department; and lobbyists (in our case, those concerned with one or another outcome of the affair). In other countries laws regulating lobbying have long been in existence. Thus, in the USA for example, in accordance with an Act of 1946, all lobbyists must be registered and give an indication of the organisation they represent. An Act passed in 1987 prohibits people from lobbying for any institution for which they have worked in the past year, since the knowledge of official secrets (in parliament this can mean the knowledge of the procedure of decision-making, or the knowledge of the organisational structure of parliament) can be used to the same group's advantage. No such laws have yet been passed in Russia, thus the lobbyist enjoys greater freedom of action in our country. In the localities lobbying takes the form of the simple bribery of officials, but in the central structures of power it sometimes leads to the passing of an unconstitutional resolution. Such a state of affairs demands the adoption by parliament of appropriate laws concerning lobbying and its regulation.

Lobbying is the term applied to the activities of a pressure group, and a lobbyist is a person who, in the name of another and often for money, tries to influence the legislative process by direct contact with the legislators. Such action includes providing legislators with information, sent to them with the express purpose of inciting action against some decision or other, also propaganda or the threat of denial of support at the elections. According to their interests, groups employ such methods as contacting legislators, but the meaning of the word 'lobbying' applies to these acts as well. The exerting of influence upon legislators is not the only action employed by pressure groups. These groups attempt, by different means, to create a good reputation for themselves. They create and develop programmes of political activity, directed at increasing the political consciousness of society. Pressure groups play an important role in American political life, and legislators make easy targets for the lobbyists because of its distinctive political structure and lack of organisation of the political parties. In our parliamentary system we are beginning to encounter similar phenomena, often negative, but whose study can help politicians in their work.

PARLIAMENT AND THE MARKET ECONOMY

The link between democracy and the market economy has long been studied, but the link between parliament and the economy is in no way weaker. Let me make a comparison. The price of a product on today's market reflects the influence exerted by many factors, the consideration of which in the planning stage is, in essence, not possible. The mechanism which regulates a product's change in price is the stock exchange, in which every single factor which influences a product's price is combined. But the actual determining of prices on the stock exchange has the characteristics of a cruel battle, and if there were no stock exchange the whole economic system would be affected.

Parliament plays exactly the same role in the political system as the stock exchange does in the economic process. Changes affecting a political decision are taken into consideration in parliament. In the main, though, parliament is not in a position to examine every factor which affects a political decision or the devising of state policy. A lack of coordination between the political groups involved will inevitably give rise to chaos and political instability, as well as to possible fundamental changes in the basic course of state development. But as we know only too well, political instability affects the economy, forcing the producer to curtail production, sometimes harshly, mercilessly ruining recently established achievements, and in the long run, engendering the stagnation of the whole economic system. In acting as the vector of decision-making, parliament wards off the blows aimed at the entire political system and thus in effect saves it from collapse.

Furthermore, the comparison of the roles of parliament and the stock exchange in the political and economic systems respectively is not merely a metaphor. The fact is that both parliament and the stock exchange are capable of developing under conditions involving the harmonising of various forms of ownership, and market and state mechanisms. Parliament and the stock exchange simultaneously stabilise, and even in some sense, initiate this development. In a society where such market mechanisms are absent, and where there is no intention of creating the institution of private property, then, through 'representing' the whole of society, the representative body of power is actually not a parliament. Examples of this in our recent past are too obvious to need repeating.

THE PROFESSIONALISM OF PARLIAMENT

In initiating radical reforms it is essential for the structures of power to have a high level of competence and professionalism. Two features are required in the first instance for the establishment of a market economy: private ownership and elections for a professional parliament. The creation of a professional parliament is a painstaking and long-term process which cannot be achieved in one year or in just one election campaign.

By world standards, Russian professionalism is still inadequate. This can be explained by the insignificant proportion of lawyers, political scientists, sociologists and economists in the White House. However, we have seen an increase in the professionalism of our deputies over the past two years. We have never actually asked ourselves what precisely is a professional parliament. Who trains the members of parliament? The people choose them from amongst the most active on the political scene. But for our parliament to reach world standards of professionalism as a legislative body, we should adopt high standards of regulating its activity. The popular election of deputies is one thing, but the systematisation of the professional demands made of parliamentarians, the strict definition of the status of an MP, is another. In all democratic European countries with market economies, parliament creates and sustains the legal and judicial basis of the market, the mechanisms that allow the market to operate. It is easy to understand why the majority of MPs in Western parliaments are professional economists, lawyers and political scientists.

The load on MPs is not spread evenly. The choices of MPs over the last two years is instructive, and we have not yet come to terms with who has gone and who has advanced. The most active have advanced, though in general the work of deputies does not have clear criteria on which it can be evaluated and could well be based on the minimum effort in the complete absence of responsibility.

Today an MP's mandate entitles him or her to quite a large range of legal, and even more hidden, privileges. This is why people want to become deputies. The question of privileges is one of the most contentious. Brought up on egalitarian principles, people argue that deputies should not have the choicest privileges but should serve selflessly. This will have to be regulated by law, before the elections and not after. The electorate should know that their deputies are worthy of support, while deputies should be assured of an adequate standard of living. Otherwise we will be unable to create a professional parliament up to the standards of a civilised country. The business world has attracted energetic and knowledgeable people, and parliament, too, should attract the best of the best, the wisest of professional people, the most honest of the honest.

THE VERTICAL AND HORIZONTAL SEPARATION OF POWER

The vertical separation of power between territories, between the Federation and the subjects of Federation, is one of the real achievements of Russian democracy, our greatest democratic breakthrough. In accordance with the Federal Treaty, signed in Moscow on 31 March 1992 and which became part of the Constitution, power began to be devolved to the republics, autonomous areas and regions of Russia.

The most important question is the degree of autonomy for the basic objects of contemporary democracy and the market economy, enterprises and other grassroots structures. That is, the degree of power that they should have to enable them substantially to improve the lives of the direct producers of material benefits, and for the population, every individual, to be able to develop their individuality and creativity.

In this context it would be useful to look at every subject of the Federation, and especially republics, from below, that is, from the position of the electorate, those who delegate power to their deputies. A local view of the voter and the citizen best indicates the mood of the population, the people living there, their material culture, their working traditions, the languages they speak, their level of education, the national atomsphere, their opinion of the world and the link between the older and younger

237

generations. In a word, all that which the neo-totalitarian, anti-democratic regime simply ignored. We have a real task before us, namely better to understand the independence of a subject of the Federation, as well as the way it manifests itself in accordance with the Federal Treaty.

The forming of a Federation from the top down, and the bottom up, has, in different states in the world, historically brought mixed results for the generation concerned. In executing the humanitarian content of the Federal Treaty, the peace-making function of parliament consists of ensuring the demarcation of plenary powers through the delegation of authority by the subjects of the Federation. Our Federation was formed from the top downwards, and this has left its mark on it. The disintegration of the former Soviet Union, the creation of republics with a new status in the Russian Federation, and the new relations with the autonomous regions and districts, are indicative of Russia's transformation into a federal state. Have we come to terms with this?

The federal model of the state system has the most stable tendency for development in the world. In the creation of the European Community, federal forms of rule are being explored. The goals of federalism are:

- To reconcile unity with variety.
- The protection of the republics, regions and districts from centralist tendencies.
- The democratic participation of the population at local, district, regional, republic and federal levels of power.
- The increased efficiency of the government through regional competition.
- The stimulation of innovative ideas in regional bodies of power.

Federalism is based on the principle of democratic pluralism, bringing together on a common basis central and regional authorities through national and regional forms of political life. The Federal Treaty clearly defines the functions of Russia's Federal bodies of state power, along with those aspects which relate to joint management by the Federal and regional bodies of state power, and, finally, clearly defines the authority of regions and territories. Here, in the light of such a demarcation of power, a new type of legislative process is developing, one never before seen in Russia. It is especially important to draw attention to the new rights enjoyed in these conditions by citizens, and by industrial and non-governmental organisations.

The Russian Federation since March 1992 has begun to create a federal system, a model for a constitutional democratic state. Paramount importance has been assigned to the question of reviewing the criteria for policies along the lines of neo-totalitarianism versus democracy, internationalism versus nationalism, and separatism versus regionalism. The cornerstone is a new system of values based on creating the conditions for the democratic life of the people.

The horizontal separation of power at federal and regional level is represented by legislative, executive and judicial branches of power, as well as by the press. The vertical division of power is represented by village, town, region, district, area, republic and federal levels. The most complex and contentious questions arise at the points where these administrative levels overlap, where the Federal Treaty has demarcated spheres of authority and power between the Russian Federation's bodies of state power and the bodies of power belonging to the republics, areas, districts and the towns of Moscow and St Petersburg, and also the autonomous districts and areas in the framework of the Russian Federation. This is the vertical division. Cases of disagreement also arise horizontally at all levels in the process of decision-making.

The democratic breakthrough represented by the vertical separation of power helps preserve traditional links, including economic, political, cultural, and other relations, and while excluding moves towards separatism enhances national and territorial independence of the subjects of federation. It is worth noting that the official name of Bavaria is 'the Free State of Bavaria', but no one is calling for it to break away from Germany. Federalism is the system of relations within a single state, in which the people of the federation enjoy the legal provisions for creating all the conditions needed for their vital activities.

Power, as the right and opportunity to take an active part in national and regional political life, today takes upon itself the function of rectifying former distortions. In other words, to restore people's confidence and to create the conditions for complete self-expression. And it is here that politics, as the activity of state power and administration, begins to seek the genuine implementation of the Federal Treaty: namely to define clearly the functions of the federal government and regional 'governments' and administrations in legislative and executive decision-making. The constitutions of the Russian republics, and the charters of Russian territorial formations on the basis of the already signed Federal Treaty, provide the opportunity to clarify the relations between themselves and with the federal authorities.

Russia and the subjects of the Federation are now faced with the prospect of transforming themselves into a thriving federal state. And this process of flourishing can only be achieved from below, in the provinces. We should not wait for manna from Heaven in the form of Western aid. We should rebuild provincial life and achieve regional prosperity. To achieve this a U-turn should be demanded from the government: from facing towards Europe to facing towards the provinces. The Federal Treaty was designed to create, within the terms of the Federation, strong legal, economic, financial, monetary and administrative power in the subjects of the federation. Russia will be wealthier, stronger and more confident when large-scale regional programmes are independently established in the republics and regions, districts and free zones. The Federal Treaty should change the way in which the provinces are viewed. The Treaty itself was born on the principle that the revival of the provinces was the revival of Russia.

Parliament knows very well that in this process it is particularly important that the Federal authorities should have a firm control over the local organs. A prosperous Russia can only be established if a concerted effort is made by the authorities at all levels: both vertically and horizontally.

PARLIAMENT IN CIVIL SOCIETY

If parliament is an integral part of the parliamentary system, developing under conditions of the priority of private ownership, then its link with politically organised social interests becomes comprehensible. In principle, of course, any social interest ought to be represented in parliament, although their diversity can give rise to as much chaos as if every interest were to find itself formed as the result of direct cooperation between social and political groups. That is why political parties play such a large role in parliamentarianism.

From this point of view, the current political situation in Russia presents a curious picture. The number of political parties formed according to the traditional pattern, characteristic of continental Europe and pre-revolutionary Russia, is not large, and, with the exception of a tiny number, they do not exert any significant influence. The basic political unit is not the party and not even the party bloc but mass movements, that is, a type of political organisation which is unsuited to demands of stability under conditions of parliamentarianism. This is particularly clearly exemplified by 'Democratic Russia', a movement whose entire purpose lies in uncompromising struggle, and it can hardly become the basis of a stable parliament. With a background of budding left- and right-wing extremist movements, parties of a centralist nature are developing. If they had the wholehearted support of the population, they could be a serious political force on which the parliamentary authorities could lean. The whole point, however, is that centralist parties are, as a rule, parties belonging to the 'middle strata' of the intelligentsia, scientific and technical personnel, teachers, doctors and so on, that is, precisely those who are now being ground between the millstones of economic reform. In this muddle of parties, parliament and Congresses of People's Deputies appear more stable and, consequently, meet the principles of parliamentarianism and the needs of the political system to a greater extent than any other power structure irrespective of what outwardly unpleasant impression is made by scenes of parliamentary controversy.

From the point of view of the role played by parliament in the stabilisation of the political situation, it is clear that care should be taken during the transitional period up to the end of the term of office of the present body of deputies and of the current structure of the Russian parliament. The Congress of People's Deputies is undoubtedly a strange organisation in all senses for parliamentarianism of a classic type. However, in conditions where a stable multiparty system has not yet been formed, the Congress, as a kind of stop-gap between spontaneous and parliamentary democracy, reflects far more the essence of the transitional phase.

PARLIAMENT AND THE GOVERNMENT

The relationship between parliament and the government is a classical theme which, perhaps, would not require further commentary if attempts were not so frequently made to present the government as the one and only body capable of carrying out reforms against the opposition from reactionary MPs. This is the main reason given for the need for authoritarian government in Russia during the transitional period. Examples of the premature dissolution of the authority of deputies under the influence of some external force are not so rare in Russian history.

The key moment which allows for the combined existence of state authorities and the government and parliament within a single system arises mainly from the fact that parliament protects the government from a possible slide into severe, authoritarian methods of rule. Since the work of the government is always or almost always conducted in private or in secret, it is very difficult to control. But a government, over whom all control has been lost, especially in critical socio-political conditions, is capable, as historical experience has demonstrated, of simply becoming a body which represents the interests of a certain socio-political group, and no more. By virtue of the openness of its work parliament is more accessible to the people (because of this, incidentally, it is far more often criticised than the government), and is therefore able to prevent the government from taking extreme measures.

The relationship between the Supreme Soviet and the government in Russia is unique, although comparable with all other post-communist countries. The transitional period is itself a factor. Under present conditions it is very difficult to decide what is correct policy both from an economic point of view and from the point of view of the social position of the people. The government's political direction changes quite often and these changes are associated with government reshuffles and even, and this is not uncommon, changes in its entire composition. Under these conditions parliament again appears as a stabilising force.

On the other hand, a power crisis (which could perhaps more accurately be called a political crisis), brought about by the chaos of making badly thought-out political and socio-economic decisions, considerably weakens the stability of a state system such as this one. The mistrust of authority applies as much to the government as to parliament. Any attempts in connection with this radically to change the established system could lead to its total destruction. And as a result, to a radical change in the political regime. Examples of this have been frequently encountered in world history and in the recent past, in particular in Latin American countries where democratic regimes have been overthrown by military dictatorships, reminiscent in their style and mode of action to Russian party leaders at the time of the birth of Bolshevism.

I would like to emphasise an important factor associated with the public discussion of various possibilities for the 'dissolution' of the Congress of People's Deputies, its 'dismissal', and the 'dispersal' of the Supreme Soviet. If such a task is placed before society within the framework of the Russian Constitution and of law, it can only be implemented in the following ways:

1 The Congress of People's Deputies draws up a new Constitution in which no provision is made for a two-tiered legislative body.
2 The Congress declares itself to be dissolved and transfers its powers to the Supreme Soviet.
3 The Congress declares itself the Supreme Soviet, that is, parliament, working on a permanent basis.
4 An all-Russian referendum is held in accordance with the Law 'On Referendums in the RSFSR'. The Supreme Soviet and the Central Electoral Committee become the organisers of the elections according to the results of the referendum. Talk of the possible 'dispersal' of the Congress through an all-Russian referendum is artificial, and in a legal sense is again linked to a decision of the Congress or the Supreme Soviet, in as much as a simple collection of citizens' signatures is only one prerequisite for the acceptance of the decision, by the Supreme Soviet or by the Congress, to hold the referendum, and even more for its organisation.

There are no other legal methods of liquidating the Congress, unless you count attempts to 'legitimise' a type of coup on the pattern of the State Committtee for the State of Emergency.

Of course, we accept that there are a great number of deficiencies in our Constitution which, although it has been fundamentally changed, none the less requires replacing. That is why the Constitutional Commission is operating under the leadership of the President and also why the adoption of the draft Constitution as the base document by the Sixth Congress of People's Deputies can be considered a major achievement. But it should be stressed that the existing Constitution in no way impedes the implementation of economic and political reforms. All that is required is their professional implementation on the basis of the laws and resolutions passed by the Supreme Soviet.

Mechanisms of authorisation and limitation must work within the framework of the Constitution, laws, parliamentary and presidential authority, the prerogatives of the Constitutional Court and legal organisations, given flexible relations within the structures of power.

The following issues are the most important and those on which serious work should be done, both on a practical and theoretical level:

1 Parliament as an independent political force with its own (commanding) niche in the system of state government.
2 Its special role as a legislative body; in this sense there is no authority superior to it. Its laws are of an imperative nature, binding on every citizen, whether they be President, businessman or man in the street.
3 The nature of the relationship between the legislature and the executive.

On a purely practical level, many problems have already arisen in these areas. A great number of different groups have suddenly appeared who want their own say in the political decision-making process and who try to make the authorities work in their interests. To this end they use loopholes in the legislation. For example, the 'Law on the Presidency', which was later 'incorporated' into the Constitution, made a broad interpretation of presidential rights possible in the parts relating to the organisation of executive power. Being responsible for the formation of the government (that is, in fact, the administration), yet another government was thrust upon the President, the 'shadow cabinet', officially called the Presidential Administration, and in so far as certain personalities failed to exercise control over it a third government emerged, the institution of the State Secretariat and other advisers. Three governments were thus in operation which are able to influence the passing of important decisions concerning personnel, politics and the economy. In such circumstances, the official government, unsanctioned by parliament, becomes the object of manipulation from the 'other two governments', which naturally take a tough and aggressive stand by virtue of the fact that they do not bear, all things considered, any responsibility. The danger presented by the 'other two governments' lies also in the fact that, lacking the opportunity of independently implementing their own ideas (lacking any legal status), they act in the following way in an attempt to increase their real powers.

First, they put heavy pressure on government ministers, getting them to adopt the decisions they need and which benefit them, therefore we often see very marked contradictions, confusion and unconcealed chaos.

Second, powerful pressure is brought to bear on the President from various sides, sometimes openly 'exposing' him, suggesting quite primitive scenarios for the development of national affairs and which are divorced from reality. An example of this was the attempt to persuade the President, on the eve of the Sixth Congress and afterwards, that the

Congress was a reactionary force which it was essential to smash. This viewpoint, and a whole series of ideas of an anti-parliamentary cast, seriously weakened the authority both of the President himself and of parliament, strengthened the influence of destructive forces, weakened the state itself and its influence in the field of international relations.

Third, lobbyist groups are formed among deputies with the aim of destroying the legislature from within. This is done using a variety of methods which verge on the criminal.

Fourth, they are aiming to control the armed forces, the Ministries of Foreign Affairs, Security and Internal Affairs, attempting to involve their leaders in political intrigues and thus distract them from carrying out state duties, from the battle against crime and corruption and so on.

Fifth, they often operate in such a cynical way that they far surpass the activities of the former liberal–neo-totalitarian regimes (those of Brezhnev, Andropov and Gorbachev). Direct instructions are given to 'eavesdrop' and to 'check up', impertinent and badly written letters are circulated all over the world, playing an allegedly admirable role by exposing foreign bank accounts (although they themselves have them too, of course). However, it seems that these deviations from the norm are by no means insuperable; a little time is needed and a bit more common sense from all of us, a desire for unity and the coordination of the activities of every branch of authority. And also goodwill. We only have one short life. The poor and the destitute, the Speaker and the President, all share one fate: the crematorium or two metres of earth. All of us should remember this and not tempt fate, either our own or that of our fellow citizens. We must try to leave a good impression behind since this is forever and the rest is dust.

PRESIDENTIAL AND PARLIAMENTARY FORMS OF GOVERNMENT

The debate over a presidential or a parliamentary republic are deliberately conducted on an extremely low intellectual and cognitive level. Such extraordinarily 'original' approaches as the following are even suggested to the President: why, it is said, does the President in the 'presidential republic' not place the office of the public prosecutor, the courts, the barristers and the press under his command or even 'build democracy into the presidential system'? Goebbels argued that 'The greater the lie, the more people will believe in it', and our latter-day 'courtiers' have learned the lessons of this 'master' very well.

In all this reasoning there is no mention of the fact that the heart of the presidential form of government is the doctrine of the separation of powers, which affirms that the function of the legislature is to make laws and that the function of the executive is to make sure that they are properly implemented. These powers are independent but they creatively interact and cooperate without trying to eliminate each other, which in any case is against the law. If this were to take place in the USA, the president would be dismissed and the congressmen recalled by the voters. The population is well prepared politically and the choice is not limited, there being a large number of politicians. The position, for example, of the American president is strengthened by the fact that he is both head of state and head of government simultaneously. The president secures his post through a national general election and is surrounded by his assistants, who, to all intents and purposes, are his government.

In France, Italy, even Germany and many other countries, the heads of state are also presidents. The presidential form of government operates on the surface, but in fact the parliaments form or set the governments up on the basis of party representation. It is therefore essential to rid ourselves of the confusion which has been thrust upon society by various 'theorists' and 'ideologists' for whom destruction is a way of life and creation is an alien concept; in order to do this we need integrity and an understanding of our historical responsibility towards the motherland. Whatever the outward form adopted by authority, the defining symbol of a democratic state is its representative power, the parliament. It is this which guarantees legislative and control functions in all spheres, and its effectiveness signifies stability within the state. It is only we, with our typically autocratic way of thinking, who on the very second day after attaining a 'semi-democracy' after the coup, directed our gaze towards parliament, which, incidentally, had been democratically and freely elected, thereby preparing the people for the coming of the new Messiah, the dictator. It should be stressed that of the 1,040 deputies of the Russian parliament, 1,004 were selected in a tough battle with their rivals: in 906 cases there were more than three candidates and almost 80 per cent of the deputies had to go through to a second round. The Russian deputies of 1990 should not be confused with the Soviet deputies of 1989. This is done deliberately, of course. Was not Boris Yeltsin himself elected with us back in 1990, and how? Is it worth glossing over all this even if there is a strong desire to sweep it under the carpet? Our consciences will not let us.

Democratic government must therefore be at the heart of the discussion and not only its forms, which represent the ancillary links of the organisation of state power. It provides executive power with stable structures, since the latter does not receive a mandate directly from the people as is the case with presidential executive power. This authority relies on the legislature, elected by a national vote, which can deprive the Cabinet of its support at any time. This is called ministerial responsibility and it serves to keep the executive under strict control and observation. The viability of a parliamentary regime is based on the dual-party principle and not on the form of government. In America the Founding Fathers laid the foundations of joint control of all three branches of power, a principle which has gone 'unnoticed' by some of our so-called reformers who support the strengthening of presidential power. Gorbachev's experience taught them nothing: as soon as the Union parliament was weakened as a result of the 'Gorbachev-Lukyanov' alliance, the authority of power, that is, state power in general, disappeared. Gorbachev had practically no power long before August 1991 although he formally controlled everything: the army, the KGB, the government, the parliament, the banks and so on. But all this already had something of the comic-opera about it, even in a semi-democratic society the authority of the state relies on the Constitution and on the law, which are the embodiment of parliament. If you want terror and dictatorship, then abolish parliament and representative government.

16

FEDERALISM AND DEMOCRACY

RUSSIA AND MODERN FEDERALISM

The shortest route to a constitutional and democratic Russia can be found firstly, in the history of Russia and the critical analysis of the application of the theory of the separation of powers. The theory has proved its worth over two centuries, when the strengthening of state power takes place via the separation of power on both the horizontal and vertical planes, with clear vertical subordination and horizontal interdependence. Secondly, in the theory and practice of federalism.

When analysing the state apparatus it is important to define its specific forms of territorial-political organisation, determined by the principles of the interrelation between central and local organs of state power. The specific form of state organisation in a given country depends on a whole series of social, national, geographical, historical and other factors. In the study of state (constitutional) law today, two basic forms of state apparatus are singled out, unitary and federal. The federal form differs from the unitary in that it is complicated and diverse and in any given situation has unique and specific characteristics.

It is essential to note that the concepts of 'federation' and 'federalism' are not synonymous. A federation is a form of state organisation which presupposes the formation of a single state out of several state organisations which enjoy a definite legal and political autonomy. The concept of 'federalism' is broader and more complex than the concept of 'federation', in that it includes not only the theory of the federal state, but also emphasises the principle of the political organisation which allows for the unification of independent states under a central government while leaving them a definite share of power.

The fundamental problem of any federation is the distribution of competencies between the centre and the federation's subjects. This defines the measure of decentralisation, that is, the degree of relative independence given to its subjects. There are various approaches as to how this separation should be made. Some consider that the federation exists until such a time as there is a clear delimitation of functions and powers; others are of the opinion that the present level of development does not call for a strict division of power between the different levels, circumstances allowing or if the logic of state development demands it (the idea of the 'new federalism' in the USA, for example). In practice, one of the most complex questions remains that of the legal and practical division of authority between the centre and the subjects. The world has gained much positive experience in this area, and also many mistakes, failures and errors, which we are trying to take into account in parliamentary work on this complex subject. Parliament undertook the implementation of the provisions of the Federal Treaty with the authority to revive the Russian constitutional democratic state. The long-term problem of the development of Russia is being realised.

Two tendencies in a federal state interact and oppose one another: centrifugal and centripetal. In an extremely simplified form the problem is that one strives for organisation, order, even despotism, at the same time as the other strives for decentralisation, chaos, and possibly anarchy. The federal state can only develop as a result of interaction between the two forces, as a compromise between two extremes, excessive centralisation and anarchy. Federalism has a unique quality, the ability to adapt to constantly changing social, political and economic conditions of a dynamically developing society. And although at the moment unitarism predominates, a federation is a sufficiently widespread form of state structure not merely because of historical factors but also due to its above mentioned qualities. Federalism is one of the most burning issues of the day, the problem of the quest for the optimum mode of state structure which will allow all regions and peoples in Russia to develop.

Many people argue that it would be in Russia's best interests if she ceased to exist as a single state and turned to a system of closely, or not so closely, linked states or, to be more precise, quasi-states. There are those who, on the other hand, insist on unitarism as Russia's most traditional form of state and to counteract ethnic conflicts. It is clear that the Federal Treaty concluded in March 1992, and subsequently incorporated by the Sixth Congress of People's Deputies into the Constitution of the Russian Federation, unequivocally formulated a third path for the development of Russia, the path of a special type of federalism. In my opinion, federalism is one of the most fruitful ideas in developing Russia's state structure. Here the two aspects of each problem merge, from the point of view of the Federation and from the perspective of the subjects of federation. It is necessary to evaluate the applicability of this idea to Russia, to work out a mechanism for its implementation, bearing in mind the development of the CIS.

FEDERALISM AS A METHOD OF RESOLVING ETHNIC DISPUTES

Federalism is associated with the attempt to resolve ethnic conflicts within the framework of a united state while ensuring the right of nations to self-determination as laid down in international conventions on human rights. Political reality demonstrates that the primitive unilinear interpretation of this right is often of an irrational character and leads to conflicts and ethnic clashes. Therefore the emergence of a federal structure is an attempt to interpret more flexibly national characteristics of development within the framework of a single state system, thereby creating firm guarantees preventing ethnic differences from evolving into full-scale national conflicts. The Indian Federation, for example, is constructed on just such a basis, striving in a flexible way to encompass the distinctive features of the national composition of the country. Canada, Germany and Austria have also assimilated the experience of classical federalism, although not, it is true, on a multiethnic basis.

Even the federalism of the Soviet Union, its formal and 'systemic' features notwithstanding, was based on an attempt to take national peculiarities into account. At the same time, pseudo-scientific classifications such as 'one community – the Soviet people', determined the corresponding national-state structure: the Union, the union republic, the autonomous republic, region or district. Every level of Union federalism had its own corresponding set of attributes of national culture, schools, theatres and so on, while at the same time real autonomy was everywhere fictitious. It was this very brand of federalism which gave rise to the problems which led to the disintegration of the Union, caused a great deal of friction between its constituent republics, and in the post-Union period resulted in a series of disturbing phenomena within Russia itself, which without doubt, were exacerbated by the 'Gorbachev revolution'.

However, the application of federalism to resolve national problems has its limitations. This is primarily due to the fact that it is quite impossible to draw a clear line around territory which is inhabited by representatives of only one nationality. Consequently, the problem of the subjects of the federation becomes difficult to resolve. The attempt to solve the problem by consolidating territory for a particular national group by the use of force not only leads to conflicts with representatives of other ethnic groups living in this area, but indirectly affects the position of their own nationals who live in other towns and villages and have become members of mixed families. As events in Yugoslavia have shown, unresolved, these problems can lead to serious crises, even within a federation. Therefore, in implementing the idea of federalism in Russia it is necessary to take into account the national-state structure but at the same time not to allow one's thinking to be dominated by this single element. This factor can allow the application of the so-called principle of 'unequal federation', elements of which exist in India, and partially in Canada. The principle of 'unequal federation' is expressed in different competencies allocated to each subject of the federation, in the form of delineating functions and in the manner of their consolidation. The implementation of this principle may of course engender instability, but their sensible application can have positive results. However, the effectiveness of social policies and the success of economic reform remain a deciding factor.

FEDERALISM AND THE PROBLEM OF SOVEREIGNTY

Federalism traditionally refers to independent states which implement their sovereignty by handing over part of their rights to the federation. However, as I have endeavoured to demonstrate, this approach also suffers from one-sidedness. The establishment of federal relations in a monolithic state is possible by means of providing regions or republics with supplementary powers. Moreover, the subjects of the federation, receiving independent powers to establish their own law and order in conjunction with federal law and order, and having the right to form their own budgets, at the same time are not really independent states.

It is possible that during the development of the state institutions of the Russian Federation a legal regime will be established which will grant sovereignty to the subjects of the federation, but that this sovereignty will be limited. In particular, this concerns questions of citizenship, the establishment of international legal relations (bearing in mind that the federation in any case assumes the responsibility for the illegal actions of its subjects in international relations), and some other powers. In addition, an important feature of a federation, distinguishing it from a confederation, are limits to the full sovereignty of the subjects of the federation. In assuming the obligations arising from the establishment of a federal structure of government, the subjects of the federation are imperatively bound to renounce, in the interests of creating an atmosphere of trust and legal stability in the state, the right to leave the union. The renunciation of this right to a large extent reflected the understanding of the process of integration by all the subjects of the Russian Federation.

FEDERALISM AND THE DECENTRALISATION OF ADMINISTRATION

Separatism in Russia, taking advantage of centrifugal forces and threatening the realisation of the principles of federalism, has taken not only a national but also a regional character. Regional separatism is clearly behind the idea of creating a Siberian, Far Eastern, or Urals republic, and the difficulties which arose with a number of Russian regions at the time of the signing of the Federal Treaty. National features strengthen separatism but at the present time they are stifled by it. I admit that some easing of the problem of regional separatism at the moment is connected purely with subjective factors: if two or three major national figures were to depart the national political scene, the problem would be quickly exacerbated.

One cannot, however, entirely deny the objective causes of regional separatism. This is what Mikhail Nikolaev, President of the Sakha (Yakut) Republic, to my mind entirely justifiably, writes about the situation:

> The thing that stimulates such centrifugal movements is not so much the latent wish of the Northern territories to leave the Russian Federation as a natural feeling of protest over certain forms of discrimination towards the North. [Moreover,] In relations between Moscow and the Northern marches the motif of centralism is as strong as ever.

When the economic policy of the state is ineffective and lacks coherence, where economic problems are resolved at the expense of wretched local budgets, where state monopoly remains the most serious problem swallowing the resources, for example, of raw material-producing regions, it is naturally the wish of certain regions, capable because of their production structure of competing in the international market, to achieve a degree of independence from the notorious 'dictate of the centre'. The population holds the federal powers responsible for their social misfortunes, seeing in them the root of all evil, and it is possible to understand this in human terms.

Real federalism can certainly assist the stabilisation of regional economic systems. Regions, given a way of effectively influencing the policy of federal bodies, can more effectively oppose economically unjustified policies of the federal administration without having to resort to strikes, which often jeopardise the whole economic system of the country. Simply granting supplementary economic rights to regions without a specific mechanism for realising their rights in conditions of the extreme monopolism of the Russian economy will not give the desired results. And in the conflict between the still weak local economic structures and the military–industrial and mining complexes, monitored by federal organs of administration, victory in the final analysis will go to the latter. It is true that this will be a Pyrrhic victory. But the rights of the regions, guaranteed as rights of the subjects of federation, in the given circumstances could provide the regions with supplementary legal mechanisms for settling disputes with federal organs of power.

From this point of view, federalism in Russia, even if in an indirect manner, can assist the establishment of market relations in the economy.

It is true that certain difficulties also arise here. The demarcation of regions does not take into account the process of forming economic regions or economic integration. The economic infrastructure does not coincide with the administrative territorial boundaries of the country. This is an objective process since the economic system is developing more swiftly than the state and legal system. The old rigid links throughout the former Soviet Union (even in the Baltic States) which are still in existence fall beyond the scope of this analysis.

Similar anomalies between the borders of states and the formation of market regions have become one of the most important problems of development in the economic history of the American federation, and the resolution of this conflict led to the redistribution of rights in favour of the federation (from the states to the federal government). The point is that the regional attempts of local authorities to overcome the crisis independently do not take into account the interests of the territorial integrity of the whole country. Some regions of Russia, bearing in mind the requirements of the international market, could remain destitute with all the consequences this would entail for the population. Strong measures are needed for the support of these regions, which could be found with the use of the famous levelling system of financial equalisation, presupposing the operation of a financial mechanism of redistribution of monetary means for the benefit of regions which have fallen on hard times. Powerful expression is given to this demand in our parliament in the form of 'equalisation of initial opportunities of the regions during the transition to a market economy'. This an absurdity which even the government does not understand. But I despaired then of trying to convince MPs of this.

On the other hand, such an approach assumes the strengthening of federal organs of administration, but demands above all a renunciation of local egoism. Furthermore, environmental factors also demand the establishment of well-funded federal institutions. Finally, one frequently encounters the fact that in some regions measures are adopted to impede the development of free enterprise. Such impediments are brought about by formally legal means, such as rigid local tax systems superimposed on the federal one. This situation will also demand a strengthening of the supervisory functions of federal government. Once again, it is a matter of a highly professional approach, which is obviously lacking.

FEDERALISM, DEMOCRACY AND THE TREATY PROCESS

The opinion is often expressed that in a period of reform, it is necessary to have an authoritarian administration in the country. This implies the establishment of a monolithic state system with highly centralised power. There are certain features which could indeed point that way. However, it is well known that a rigid system ruled from a single centre is fragile, and the example of the USSR has demonstrated the potential for the sudden collapse of such a system. For this reason, however paradoxical it may sound, the flexibility of federalism is more capable of dealing with socio-political and economic difficulties associated with the reform process.

Many contemporary political figures dislike federalism because it does not offer simple political solutions. An authoritarian system is simple: decision followed by implementation. Under federalism, on the other hand, these elementary administrative directives have to be combined with the difficult process of achieving consent. But this makes federalism an important factor in counteracting Russia's slide into authoritarianism.

Legality plays an important part in combining democracy with federalism from within. Federalism is not merely the demarcation of competence between the federation and its subjects but also a formal legal consolidation of this demarcation. At the moment this process has taken on the all-embracing form of treaties. Treaties are not merely being concluded between the federation and its subjects but also, for example, between districts and regions. Meanwhile, a treaty as a formal basis for the demarcation of rights is only one of the forms of establishment of a federal structure, and perhaps not the ideal one by a long chalk. The fact is that a treaty first of all presupposes the primary equality of the parties. If state formations create a federation then they are concluding a treaty, and in the given instance it will be the clearest expression of their political and legal position. However, treaties demarcating competencies between the federation and subjects are agreements of parties not enjoying equal rights. Therefore the form of such an agreement, and here the formal aspect is very important, ought to be something else, not a treaty but the establishment of this demarcation in the law of the federation within the terms of which the federation itself appears in the capacity of the guarantor of its observation.

A second problem arises from this, guaranteeing the obligations the parties have accepted towards each other and especially those taken on by the federation as whole. Within the framework of the treaty the independence of both parties should be taken into account. An arbitrator would have to appear as soon as a dispute arises among the parties about implementing the treaty. However, the treaty between the federation and its subjects turns this argument into an international legal dispute which, for a federation, is legal nonsense. Therefore it is necessary to strengthen ways of confirming the division of powers between the federation and its subjects.

FEDERATION AND THE DEFENCE OF ITS PRINCIPLES

A federation as a legal form of establishing state structure presupposes one path to the solution of all conflicts arising in the federation between its members: the legal path. As arbitrator in such a conflict the supreme legislative authority, parliament, should play the leading role, followed by the Constitutional Court, a court responsible for ensuring the conformity of normative acts with the constitutional system. But a Constitutional Court can only function if a common federal system ensuring legal decisions is operating. In principle, it is difficult to exclude conflicts and competition between executive and legislative organs at the federal level and the corresponding organs on the level of subjects of the federation. But this competition can turn into chaos if there is no mechanism to eliminate violations of the federal system itself. It is also necessary to bear in mind the right of each subject striving towards uniformity, regulation, certainty; therefore under federalism as a legal principle of state structure the decisions of only one body should be guaranteed priority. If the federal parliament is unable to bring pressure to bear on the very mechanism of the construction of the Russian Federation, the ensuing legal chaos will provoke chaos in other areas and as a result the very idea of a federation will come to nothing.

FEDERALISM AS A BASIS OF NATIONAL UNITY

Federalism is the road to national compromise and consequently to unity. Federalism by its very essence gives expression to the fact that there cannot be single decisions disseminated through the whole territory of the country by virtue of the fact that these decisions come into conflict with local peculiarities. Therefore the sphere of agreement between subjects of the federation is reduced, but it cannot be rigidly fixed forever, also being liable to change. But in those areas where an agreement is reached, where a compromise is found between all the participants, this agreement cannot be violated in a unilateral manner. Here a certain moral firmness is required, a devotion to moral principles which will not be violated under the pressure of extreme socio-political and economic situations.

Russia, although a completely sovereign state, is part of a whole which was formerly known as the Soviet Union. All the processes taking place in Russia have a direct influence on the CIS, and vice versa. Therefore, the successful development of the Russian Federation as a federation, on whether or not an optimal form of state structure is found in Russia, will determine the establishment, or on the contrary, the gradual disintegration, of the CIS.

If the principle of human rights remains one of the priorities of development, then the birth of a federation in Russia is directly connected with the question of how the problem of human rights will be resolved not only in Russia but throughout the CIS, beginning with the chief right, the right to life. As Aristotle demonstrated, federal structures are not created for the sake of military security and the economy. NATO can exist alongside states belonging to it. A federation creates somewhat larger opportunities for easing the problem of human rights, and that perhaps is its chief value.

At the same time, one should not perceive a federation as the panacea for all ills. In this it loses out in comparison to other forms of state structure. But a federation is more flexible, more mobile, while at the same time constituting a unified large system, an integral whole. A federation is complex, it has no time for simple solutions and demands serious and thoughtful political and legal work. A federation is the constant search for a political balance between the state and its constituent parts on the basis of legal agreements. Competitive market links only strengthen the very basis of a federation. Attempts to increase the dependence of subjects on central organs of the federation provoke a reaction in response.

If we really wish to preserve our single state we must, as soon as possible, call a halt to dangerous tendencies in the socio-economic development of the federation, overcome points of tension, and impart dynamism to economic reform. And first and foremost, reform the reforms themselves. This task was far from fulfilled by the programme for the extension of economic reforms presented to parliament by the government of Yegor Gaidar at the beginning of July 1992. Parliament itself will have fundamentally to improve it, enlisting the services of all the positive forces in society to work on this programme.

Today the federation has every chance of emerging from a deep and prolonged crisis, to a great extent caused by subjectivism. For this to happen we need the stabilisation of conditions within the country, a centre of consolidation, a centre of confidence in Russia, a centre of attraction, which Russia itself was for many centuries. The confidence of the people will not be restored by inaction, by constantly slanging opponents. The people are tired of our promises and are waiting for the energetic and purposeful action which is needed to regulate the economy.

INTERACTION OF PRESIDENT AND PARLIAMENT

Today, many people, politicians, specialists and economists, are coming to the conclusion that a way out of the crisis is possible by adopting emergency political and economic measures on the basis of coordinated action by the Congress, the Supreme Soviet and executive presidential powers but, and this is especially important, only within the framework of the law. Both the Congress and the Supreme Soviet ought to establish a legal basis for effective activity by the government and the President.

We need to create this real centre of trust for our fellow citizens. The conditions for this can be defined. They are as follows:

Point one We must put a stop to the mutual attacks, senseless waste of time in squabbles, distorting one anothers' shortcomings in full view of the population, our total preoccupation with different problems. For this, we need to put an end to the provocation of both people invested with executive power and supporters of those who are exploiting the people's discontent in a time of crisis.

Secondly, we need compromises by executive power. However, a cruel struggle is being waged between lawful, executive power and unlawful but real power, which has occupied the position of a kind of 'Politburo', within the very structure of executive power.

Thirdly, we need to attract to the process of reform not only careerists but also truly high-class specialists and organisers of production, concerned citizens, scientists, men of culture, collective farm workers, in the accomplishment of far-reaching socio-economic reforms. It seems to me that the recently formed bloc, 'Civic Union', could have a large part to play in this.

Point two The question of coordination between parliament and the President has been around for a long time now. This question is by no means simple when one bears in mind the historical circumstances. The presidency is a totally new and extraordinary institution in the thousand-year history of the Russian state. I have spoken and written about this many times already. I will repeat once more; we do not have traditions or experience. We need to study, accumulate and analyse all of this. The most correct harmonious type of cooperation offers various kinds of partnership relation, where the accent is not on the question 'Who is dominant and who is not?', but where every branch of power is subject to the law and Constitution and precisely fulfils its intended function. Partnership and collaboration, these should be the central concepts in the relations between the two main branches of power at the current moment. It appears that, in the first instance, only an approach such as this guarantees the development and extension of the democratic potential of our state and, secondly, will strengthen the confidence of our deputies and parliament, which is an extremely important state institution acting together with the President as a guarantor of democratic rights, the freedom of citizens and the integrity of the state. From such a position, one cannot but condemn those politicians who wage war with parliament, representative power.

Let us ask ourselves a question: could these relationships be entirely without conflict? The first variant of the answer is 'Yes, they could.' But, in that case, the Russian parliament will cease to be a real legislative and controlling power, will cease to be that supreme power whose fundamental purpose is to draw up laws directed towards the development of active democracy, laws reflecting the interests of the people of the Federation. And, in the end, it means that such a parliament will cease to exist, as has happened with the parliament of the Soviet Union.

The second variant of the answer to this question seems more or less correct: 'There may be contradictions, conflicts and misunderstandings in response to different questions.' Yes, there may be, but this should under no circumstances be regarded as a crisis, a tragedy or an attempt to cause some sort of squabble with the translating of important political questions into a matter of personalities. These clashes between different branches of power have happened for centuries in democratic countries and they can be resolved by reasonable compromise. The Russian Supreme Soviet, as the highest legislative organ, is called to act as a strong and dynamic partner to the President, the presidential power structures and the government. The dynamic of equilibrium between the legislative, executive and the judicial powers has always been the basis for the successful functioning of both the political and economic systems of all developed states.

Point three In the present crisis, the state system of Russia demands as never before a precise process for making decisions and, more importantly, their execution. We desperately need combined, extremely well organised operation of legislative and executive powers. We need, firstly, a professional approach to problems of formulating the structure of power and government; secondly, the ability of all main participants in the hierarchy of state power to find a common language, to work together on the solution of concrete problems, to reach daily compromises for the sake of the common cause, in the interests of our society, our people. We are far from being in full possession of these attributes. The mean professionalism of executive power does not allow it to strive for compromise with parliament. If we do not learn this, other political powers and other politicians will quickly take our place. Every part of the state mechanism must possess its own personality, with its own values and characteristics.

Point four Legislative activity should be subordinate to completing the task of economic and financial stabilisation. Here, it is particularly important to take into account the striving of our fellow citizens to overcome corruption and organised crime. The restoration of control over the state sector of the economy, energy and transport, the implementation (with necessary corrections) of the programme for the revival of the Russian village, which today has completely failed, the accelerated development of free enterprise in the provinces, and an injection of dynamism into foreign policy clearly directed towards the determination and defence of Russian national and state priorities.

In economic policy, we need to create those conditions that will increase the interest of business and society as a whole in the preservation of the health of the nation, especially mothers and children. The interests of people and families must be kept in mind when devising social and economic plans. Foreign economic links need to be actively used in the implementation of state regulation in such a way that our strategic raw materials are not exported through various channels at ridiculously low prices by semi-criminal elements. In this sphere, there is great disorder, complete lack of control and the subjectivism of the talentless nouveaux riches, whose evil will was carried away on the crest of a wave of dirty spume, and provided power which they had never dreamed of. Power such as this is used pointlessly, to the enormous detriment of the state and its citizens.

At the same time, we must consider the provisions of our tax system in greater depth. Businesses have to pay so many different taxes that they lose all interest in efficient operation. In July we decided that, as from January 1993, value added tax will be reduced to 20 per cent. However, this is only the first stage. Taxes need to be reduced even further and it must not be forgotten that we will not move one step further towards surmounting the crisis if the legislative acts of the Supreme Soviet and Congress cannot rely on a clear, working mechanism of execution. This is exactly the same if the resolution of conflicts will be slowed down by ill thought out and chaotic legislative activity.

The core of the development and ensuing realisation of this policy should be not only the programmatic statements of the President, but also the proposals of specialists; people's deputies, entrepreneurs, economic leaders and experts. In this way, we should take upon ourselves that responsibility which is linked to the legislative formulation of initiatives in the reshaping of reforms.

We are still slow to implement the provisions of the Constitution concerning the realisation of the rights of the subjects of the Russian Federation. The crux of the matter is the devolution of power in Russia, endowing the Russian state with a genuinely federal character. What have we failed to do in this respect?

- The financial and economic autonomy of the republics, regions, autonomies, the whole system of representative bodies of power, have not been secured.
- Property has not been divided and municipal authority has not been formed to cope with the tasks devolved to local government.
- The principles for the development of municipal budgets have not yet been worked out.
- The law 'On local government in the RSFSR' gave urban authorities limited competency in the management of local affairs and the development of the local economy, building and local taxes.
- The resolution of the Supreme Soviet on procedures for the implementation of the law 'On local government in the RSFSR', including outlines of salary scales for managers and administrators of local soviets, has not been fulfilled.

The Supreme Soviet of the Russian Federation has already adopted many important laws, creating a solid legislative base for the decisive advance towards the market economy and strengthening the capabilities of democracy. Obviously, these laws have not been perfect, they sometimes lacked the necessary expertise, and this has been revealed when the laws have been implemented. Additions and clarifications are necessary, based on still more thorough expert work. For this, it is essential for us to have feedback, allowing us constantly to verify the effectiveness of our laws in practice. This work has been very much hindered by the chaotic and unsystematic passing of decrees by the executive, often exceeding the bounds of its authority and contradicting each other.

The Supreme Soviet ought to initiate a programme of far-reaching measures for the training and retraining of our scientists and specialists, above all for the needs of the legislature and the executive in Russia. The ideal combination of democratically elected political forces with specialists and professionals is one of the most indispensable conditions for the stable and confident advance on the road to reform, the preservation of stability in society and the extension of the democratic process. We need lawyers and sociologists, economists and experts in various spheres of industry, bankers and managing directors of industrial enterprises.

In this work, we must learn to distinguish between the long-term tasks of the Federation and the short-term, immediate tasks of overcoming the crisis, stabilising the conditions within the country and consolidating all our resources. These certainly cause anxiety about the fate of our great motherland.

CONCLUSION

The separation of powers leads to the creation of a strong system of power; parliament and its apparatus, the President and his apparatus, and the government and its apparatus. The current state of Russia has sharply heightened society's interest in the power structures, in the concept of the separation of powers and its application in civilised countries, which demonstrates that the separation of powers creates stability in democratic society, strengthens the structure of the state and its central authorities, and increases the rights of the common citizen.

The very process of the separation of powers and strengthening of power structures through election from below enhances the authority of the Constitution and the government itself, and requires professionalism from politicians, state officials and salaried workers. Their responsibility attracts businessmen, economists, managers, politicians, to compete for a career in politics. Mechanisms for the review of deputies, their defence and responsibility before electors, are important. The supremacy of the Constitution and law must apply equally to legislative and executive authorities, where the interests of the individual prevail over the interests of authority and the system. Judicial bodies have the task of implementing the Constitution and the laws of the country in daily life.

Russian statehood needs to create a stable means of realising presidential, parliamentary and government decisions, removing the contradictions between traditional and new structures of power in the Federation and territorial administrative structures.

Russia has advanced far towards democracy, away from the time when all organisations obeyed the Communist Party implicitly, but the country is still faced with comprehending democracy and all its intricate mechanisms, creating a balance of the powers governing the state.

Time and effort establishes and breaks the balance of powers. Strong parliamentary power can weaken executive and judicial power. There are many ways in which this can happen. Strong presidential power can trample down parliament and concentrate executive power in its own hands. Mechanisms of support or restraint come into force, worked out through history, such as control of the budget, the judiciary, delegation of authority, mechanisms for the review of deputies, commissions on ethics.

The country is changing as regards the problem of personnel; more democracy means more elections. Locally, much greater preference is given to natives of the place or those who have long been in permanent residence. This allows the firm establishment of all branches of power and the building up of the 'smaller motherland', relying on local patriotism to make her rich. They form a team of comrades-in-arms, like-minded people. The system of Stalinist 'cuckoos', or stooges, who were moved from area to area is becoming a thing of the past. Temporary work in parliament must become a good parliamentary school for the training of local cadres, and not the opposite.

The practice of the separation of powers provides a fruitful way of overcoming natural conflicts between legislative and executive power. It is easy to enter into conflict and antagonism, achieving positive cooperation is not simple. We need the professionalism and culture of institutes of power, a Constitution and independent courts, public prosecutor and the Bar. These reference points are the way to strengthen democratic power, just as unity and the separation of powers are guidelines of a superior kind.

In conditions of the separation of powers, it is important for us to recognise the political differentiation within Russia: what is happening on the right wing of society, on the left wing, at the centre, how this manifests itself in Congresses, in parliament, at demonstrations in the country, in the press. Differentiation cannot be predicted: there are no powerful parties to be seen on the horizon. Parliament needs the equal professional development of the centre and of a constructive opposition. Both right and left must be balanced.

In the republics and the administrative-territorial formations of Russia, the prerequisites for a democratic division of power are developing and there is also a need to search for a basis for the transition from the remnants of the totalitarian system of administration towards a democratic one. In the consciousness of the present generation, the Marxist-Leninist conception of unity of power and the seventy–year rule of Communist Party First Secretaries in administrative-territorial formations has taken root and significantly strengthened anti-democratic feeling, more so than in the centre, where the faster developing intelligentsia is shaking the foundations of totalitarianism.

The hopes of parliament rest particularly in the search for a power structure in the regions: from free zones to other forms of government. There, in the provinces, the fate of Russia will be decided. But today, in the face of national catastrophe, the country is swiftly sinking below earlier standards. Revival and strengthening of the country begins in the regions, where people will see, here and there, that life has improved, people begin to feel themselves to be master and put their own affairs in order. And then, we shall realise what democracy can give us if the people have confidence in it, if its conditions provide for structures of horizontal and vertical separation of powers, approved by world experience of administration.

The Russian parliament sees sound political sense in the theory of the separation of powers, a theory which has been proven by many centuries of practice. Hence, our task is to rely on the sound judicial sense of parliamentary legislation to put into practice whatever leads to the strengthening of presidential, parliamentary and governmental power, to establish the conditions for the working of independent courts and the press. The theory of the separation of powers is acceptable to the Russian Federation. The implementation of mechanisms for the coordination of power is the only path towards the creation of a great Russia.

During its thousand-year history, our country more than once overcame divisive and troubled times, was ruled by Tsars and emperors, states of emergency and provisional governments, and suffered under the world's strongest state party and came to economic crisis and a crisis of power. This is why it is extremely important now to move from the limited class approach to a study of social strata, layers and groups, in order to make a more detailed appraisal of forces based on sound sense, on business, on productive entrepreneurialism. Here, in the provinces and in the towns, there is a large number of people with national and patriotic views, the healthy forces of the army, youth and women's movements, the intelligentsia and the workers in towns and villages, the Union of Industrialists and Entrepreneurs. The crisis of statehood encourages Russia to adopt the theory of the separation of powers.

INDEX

262